Ari Rabin-Havt and Media Matters for America

Lies, Incorporated

Ari Rabin-Havt is host of *The Agenda,* a national radio show airing Monday through Friday on SiriusXM. His writing has been featured in *USA Today, The New Republic, The Nation, The New York Observer, Salon,* and *The American Prospect,* and he has appeared on MSNBC, CNBC, Al Jazeera, and HuffPost Live.

Along with David Brock, he coauthored *The Fox Effect: How Roger Ailes Turned a Network into a Propaganda Machine* and *The Benghazi Hoax.* He previously served as executive vice president of Media Matters for America and as an adviser to Senate Democratic Leader Harry Reid and former vice president Al Gore.

Media Matters for America is a Web-based, not-for-profit, progressive research and information center dedicated to comprehensively monitoring, analyzing, and correcting conservative misinformation in the U.S. media.

Lies, Incorporated

Lies, Incorporated

The World of Post-Truth Politics

**Ari Rabin-Havt and
Media Matters for America**

ANCHOR BOOKS
A Division of Penguin Random House LLC
New York

AN ANCHOR BOOKS ORIGINAL, APRIL 2016

Copyright © 2016 by Ari Rabin-Havt and Media Matters for America

All rights reserved. Published in the United States by Anchor Books, a division of
Penguin Random House LLC, New York, and distributed in Canada by Random House
of Canada, a division of Penguin Random House Canada Limited, Toronto.

Anchor Books and colophon are registered trademarks of
Penguin Random House LLC.

Reinhart-Rogoff chart on page 79 created by Jared Bernstein for jaredbernsteinblog.com.
Reprinted by permission of Jared Bernstein.

The Cataloging-in-Publication Data is on file at the Library of Congress.

Anchor Paperback ISBN: 978-0-307-27959-0
eBook ISBN: 978-1-101-97227-4

www.anchorbooks.com

Printed in the United States of America
10 9 8 7 6 5 4 3 2 1

Contents

Lie \ˈlī\
1: to make an untrue statement with intent to deceive
2: to create a false or misleading impression

Merriam-Webster's Dictionary

Politicians lie. This behavior is not the monopoly of any political party or ideology. They lie about their personal lives, their aberrant behavior, and their records. This book is not about those lies.

The types of lies this book is concerned with are the ones many politicians fully believe to be true—ones that have been passed to them by a staffer, a constituent, or a lobbyist. Those lies, sometimes repeated without intent, are designed to distort the policy-making process. Dig deep enough and you find an industry dedicated to the creation of lies and a group of people who profit from them.

They are Lies, Incorporated.

Preface:
Liar

Richard Berman is a liar.

He is a man who manipulates the truth on behalf of corporate clients and earns his living profiting from the invention and trafficking of lies. The fast-food industry, tobacco companies, and high-fructose corn syrup producers have all called upon him to do what few others would: shamelessly spread falsehoods, smear the reputations of well-regarded nonprofit groups, and purchase phony research.

For decades, when industries decided their last resort was the nastiest of PR campaigns, they have summoned him. Berman, who relishes the title of "Dr. Evil,"[1] is not just an operator for sale to the highest bidder. He is the purest representation of a growing force in American politics that creates and disseminates lies designed to disrupt the public policy process for monetary and ideological gain.

With a shield of anonymity provided by the tax code, Berman's donors use him to engage in a form of asymmetric public policy warfare.[2] For example, when agricultural interests sought to retaliate against the Humane Society for their advocacy work against factory farms, Berman launched a series of attacks against the organization. The companies funding this effort would never want their names associated with such a campaign. Attacking a popular organization like the Humane Society would damage their brands. Instead, Berman created a tax-exempt organization, HumaneWatch.org, to which they could anonymously donate and from which he would be paid a fee to manage.

In addition to running its website, which promotes daily smears of the Humane Society and spreads false information about their work, Berman has produced ads targeting the group. One particularly misleading commercial aired during the 2013 Academy Awards compared the Humane Society to the notorious Ponzi scheme operated by Bernie Madoff. The ad charged "HSUS gives less than one percent of its massive donations to local pet shelters but has socked away $17 million in its own pension fund."[3] This attack was misleading at best. Every year the organization cares for hundreds of thousands of animals through a variety of its programs[4]; in 2014, programmatic expenses made up 80 percent of the year's overall revenue and support.[5]

Berman is something of a caricature of the unprincipled lobbyist, the apotheosis of all that is wrong with Washington. It's a notoriety he enjoys. Whether appearing as a guest on *The Colbert Report* or defending his exploits on *The Rachel Maddow Show,* Berman oddly seems to relish being berated for making outrageous claims on behalf of his undisclosed clients,[6] [7] such as pregnant women should not worry about mercury levels in fish.

When Richard Berman appeared with Fox Business's host Stuart Varney in July 2013 to discuss low-wage worker strikes taking place in cities across the country and their potential for negatively impacting workers, he was identified as being from the innocuous-sounding EPI—Employment Policies Institute. "At fifteen dollars an hour, many, I won't say a majority, but many fast-food restaurants are out of business," he told Varney.[8] EPI's funding from the fast-food industry or its connections to Berman's consulting business was never disclosed.

The New York Times called Berman's work on behalf of the fast-food industry "a critical element in the lobbying campaign against the increase in the minimum wage," noting that industry insiders "often cite the [EPI's] reports, creating the Washington echo chamber effect that is so coveted by industry lobbyists."[9] This is a form of media manipulation mastered by Berman: a 2013 IRS filing from the Employment Policies Institute reports the organization's "media outreach" resulted in "over 830" stories on radio, TV, in print, and online in that year alone.[10]

The brilliance of Berman's strategy of creating front organizations is that reporters are often duped into quoting him (or his staff) not as an industry-funded lobbyist, but as the conservative, yet financially disinterested, head of a nonprofit.

When *The Wall Street Journal* covered an EPI-funded study on the impact of increasing the minimum wage, it referred to the organization as a "right-leaning" think tank and quoted the study's author as saying, "There's never a good time to raise the minimum wage."[11] Yet the paper did not disclose that the Employment Policies Institute receives its funding from the fast-food industry, nor did it justify the vast overstatement of calling the group a "think tank."

For one, the Employment Policies Institute has zero full-time employees. On its 2013 IRS Form 990, the group reported that $1.044 million of its $2.131 million budget was paid directly to Richard Berman's firm for management, advertising, research, and accounting. Meanwhile, the organization's lack of staff was evidenced by the fact that their total payroll for the year was $46,417, all of which save $3,500 was listed as a fund-raising expense. Furthermore, $20,175 of this total was paid to Richard

Berman personally.[12] Meanwhile, EPI's staff list on the same form includes just eight positions: six people each holding the title of "Director," all paid $500 for less than fifteen minutes of work per week; one "Secretary/Treasurer," who was paid $500 for less than twenty minutes of work per week; and Richard Berman, the "President / Executive Director," who, as previously mentioned, was paid $20,175 for less than nine hours of work per week. Of the total $46,417 in payroll expenses, just $3,500 was spent on management and general expenses (the amount paid to the Directors and Secretary/Treasurer).[13] The Employment Policies Institute exists as nothing more than a vessel to funnel money to Berman's firm, revealing his greatest achievement: the way he so effectively blurs the lines between political operatives, corporate lobbyists, and the think tank world, sowing confusion on behalf of his clients.

Richard Berman keeps his clients and their goals well hidden.[14] He has front groups layered upon front groups layered upon front groups—many, if not all, sharing the same office space. Berman heads up the larger organizations, which then develop smaller projects, which then create more small projects. The only way to truly get to the bottom of who leads and funds these organizations is to sift through hundreds of pages of IRS filings, and even then the information is murky at best.

Here are some of Berman's groups:

Berman and Company
President: Richard Berman[15]

Center for Organizational Research and Education (CORE)
President and Executive Director: Richard Berman[16]
CORE Projects:[17]
    Environmental Policy Alliance (EPA)

EPA Projects:[18]
    Big Green Radicals[19]
    EPA Facts[20]
    Green Decoys[21]
    LEED Exposed[22]

Center for Consumer Freedom (CCF)
    CCF Projects:
        HumaneWatch.org[23]
            HumaneWatch.org Projects:
                Maternity Pens[24]
        PETA Kills Animals[25]
        Prop 65 Scam[26]
    Center for Accountability in Science[27]
    Activist Facts[28]
    CREW Exposed[29]
    Humane Society for Shelter Pets[30]

Employment Policies Institute (EPI)
President and Executive Director: Richard Berman[31]
EPI Projects:[32]
    MinimumWage.com[33]
    TippedWage.com[34]
    Bad Idea New Jersey[35]
    Bad Idea California[36]
    Interstate Policy Alliance[37]
    Econ4U.org[38]
    Rethink Reform[39]
    Defeat the Debt[40]

American Beverage Institute (ABI)
President, General Counsel, and Director: Richard Berman[41]
ABI Projects:[42]

InterlockFacts.com[43]

NoDrinkTax.com[44]

ResponsibleLimits.com[45]

NegligentDriving.com[46]

The New Prohibition[47]

Center for Union Facts (CUF)[48]

President and Executive Director: Richard Berman[49]

CUF Projects:

Teachers Union Exposed[50]

DC Teachers Union Exposed[51]

AFTFacts.com[52]

EmployeeRightsAct.com[53]

WorkerCenters.com[54]

ProtectingBadTeachers.com[55]

SEIUExposed.com[56]

LaborPains.org (blog)[57]

Enterprise Freedom Action Committee[58]

President and Executive Director: Richard Berman[59]

For each of these groups, the goal is often not simply to advocate for their point of view. As Berman explained during a surreptitiously recorded speech to a room of industry executives gathered at the Western Energy Alliance conference in June 2014, he works to confuse the public so they "don't know who to believe," putting them and the policy makers they represent in a position of ideological "paralysis."[60]

After graduating from William & Mary Law School, Berman began his career as a labor lawyer, working on behalf of Bethlehem Steel. He then joined the U.S. Chamber of Commerce in the early 1970s, before moving into the restaurant industry, working for the Steak and Ale chain. He later did a stint as executive vice president of the Pillsbury Restaurant Group, which at the time owned Burger King, before founding his public affairs firm.

One of Berman's early clients was tobacco giant Philip Morris, which contributed $600,000 toward the creation of a front group known as the Guest Choice Network[61] to fight the growing effort to ban smoking in restaurants.[62] In the 1990s, restaurants were already taking steps to ban smoking on their premises. As the CEO of one company wrote Berman, "I have found that the majority of our guests (in some cases as high as 80%) do not want smoking in the dining rooms."[63]

Guest Choice Network, which Berman ultimately renamed the Center for Consumer Freedom, sought to fight this trend by "creating a proactive aggressive mentality by [restaurant] operators" in opposition to "government smoking bans."[64] Berman laid out his strategy in a letter to Barbara Trach, a senior program manager for public affairs at Philip Morris, noting that working to "appear driven by restaurant interests" and obfuscating the tobacco company's role would allow for "more flexibility and creativity."[65]

In 1991, Berman founded the American Beverage Institute. On behalf of restaurant chains, the group set out to fight against laws that aimed to reduce drinking and driving. As part of this mission, Berman targeted Mothers Against Drunk Driving, a wildly popular organization that has successfully fought to lower the legal alcohol limit.[66]

Berman has spent his career fighting for corporations at the expense of individuals but still told *The New York Times* that he "get[s] upset when people say we are putting out junk science and twisted economics."[67] In fact, that is exactly what his organizations do, as evidenced by emails unearthed as part of a lawsuit between sugar companies and makers of high-fructose corn syrup.

David Martosko, then a staffer at Berman's Center for Consumer Freedom, volunteered to "bury the data" for the high-fructose corn syrup makers if a study Berman and Company proposed did not deliver the funders' desired results.[68] This is not the behavior of an organization out to discover the truth—it is the work of a corporate front group more concerned with advancing its financial interests and a predetermined agenda.

Perhaps the most scathing critique of Berman's behavior came from his son David Berman, the former lead singer of the indie rock band Silver Jews. His father's identity was a secret, he wrote, "worse than suicide, worse than crack addiction."

David Berman went on: "You might be surprised to know he is famous, for terrible reasons. My father is a despicable man. My father is a sort of human molester. An exploiter. A scoundrel. A world historical motherfucking son of a bitch." David did ask his father to stop but "he refused. He has just gotten worse. More evil. More powerful."[69]

Unfortunately, if his son had succeeded and Berman closed up shop, there would be a long line of firms ready to take his place. In the decades since he began his practice, many others have adopted his tactics. Now there is no major public policy debate in Washington, D.C., that is not influenced by false data manufactured and spread by paid political operatives.

If there is a need for research to be manufactured, a fact massaged, or lies promulgated, Berman is the man to call. In a town full of people willing to sell their souls to corporations, he is the public policy process's proudest and most joyful mercenary. In his speech to energy executives, Berman was transparent about his philosophy: "I've had clients say to me, 'Well you know, I don't really want to attack, that's not who we are.' I say, 'Well, you know, you can either win ugly or lose pretty.'"[70] This is the clearest expression of both the mind-set and the strategy of Lies, Incorporated.

Lies, Incorporated

Introduction:
Lies, Incorporated

By any measure, the National Rifle Association is one of the most politically powerful groups in the United States. In 2013, the organization spent $3.4 million lobbying, hiring nine outside firms to assist in their efforts.[1] This followed a 2012 cycle during which the NRA spent nearly $26 million on election-related activities. They made direct contributions to the campaigns of 249 members of the House of Representatives and 11 Senators. Eighty-eight percent of these funds were given to Republican candidates. In addition to these donations, the NRA spent $18 million on negative advertising, primarily attacking President Obama and other Democrats. That year, the organization's total budget topped $250 million.

But standing in the Rose Garden in April 2013, the president, after losing a critical vote on gun-safety legislation in the Senate proposed in the wake of the Sandy Hook massacre, did not only blame the NRA's money and lobbying muscle for the bill's defeat. He told the assembled media "the gun lobby and its allies willfully lied about the bill."[2]

The president was right. The NRA's falsehoods were a critical component of the effort that undid the attempt to pass gun-safety legislation. This is because lies, along with money and lobbying, constitute three essential elements that distort our policy-making process. Like a barstool of corruption, each of its three legs offers support to groups that fight on behalf of financial or ideological interests. While most conversations about the ills of Washington tend to focus on the other two legs of the stool, the corrosive impact of the third—lies—is often ignored.

Stories about political corruption in Washington often hinge on the simplest explanations and most easily available data: lobbying disclosures, campaign contributions, and independent expenditure reports. This creates a tendency to simplify problems in our political system, whittling down failures of our democracy to unchecked political contributions, bloated lobbying budgets, Super PACs, and other forms of direct and indirect graft. Each of these factors obviously pollutes our political process. Yet focusing solely on them obscures a fundamental truth: our democracy has been hacked, manipulated by political practitioners who recognize that as long as there is no truth, there can be no progress.

Lies have a uniquely corrosive impact on the creation of public policy. At the most basic level, they destroy public trust in our political systems, causing the American people to lose faith in their government. Lies also distract from real debate, bogging down lawmakers and regulators, sometimes for years as settled science is argued over. Finally, lies create balkanization in our political culture, making ideological consensus impossible.

Over the past several decades, corporate and ideological interests have become better at manipulating the press to serve their policy goals. This often means muddying the facts in order to create a political climate where truth no longer exists—or where there are two opposing truths.

These erroneous factual disagreements, taken to their absurd conclusions, corrode public discourse. David Frum, a former speechwriter for George W. Bush, wrote about how conservative extremism limited the right's ability to win the debate over President Obama's health care bill: "How do you negotiate with somebody who wants to murder your grandmother? Or—more exactly—with somebody whom your voters have been persuaded to believe wants to murder their grandmother?"[3]

In *The Fox Effect,* David Brock and I detailed how Fox News, under the leadership of Roger Ailes, served as a conduit for conservative lies and propaganda, manipulating the political process on behalf of the Republican Party and right-wing organizations. From outrageous attacks on Barack Obama to falsehoods about every new policy his administration proposed, the breadth of the lies the network spread was astonishing. Yet, as we researched and wrote *The Fox Effect,* the question consistently arose: Where did these falsehoods originate?

Lies such as the existence of "death panels" in President Obama's health care bill, the notion that in-person "voter fraud" exists and has a significant impact on elections, and the dozens of varieties of climate denial that Fox News broadcasts are not the network's creation. Lies do not simply appear and take hold. They must be developed, introduced, and nurtured into the public discourse. While Fox News is dangerous because it is the first major television news network in our country to exclusively serve the aims of one political party, it only fertilizes and distributes the lies—it doesn't create them.

All my research pointed in a single direction: a growing industry that exists to create and disseminate fictitious public policy "facts" on behalf of business and ideological interests willing to pay for them.

These lies are part of a coordinated, strategic assault designed to hide the truth, confuse the public, and create controversy where none previously existed, with the goal of halting progress. They undermine our most basic democratic ideals by preventing people in government from effectively acting in the interest of the electorate. In recognition of the combination of deception and the for-profit motive, I termed this industry made of lobbyists, PR companies, media lackeys, unethical "experts," and unscrupulous think tanks "Lies, Incorporated."

Lies, Incorporated is not a singular company or firm. It has no office, no boardroom, and no reception area. Thousands staff it, yet they are among the most loath to acknowledge its very existence. A few of its practitioners collectively earn millions of dollars a year, and their efforts help generate billions of dollars in corporate profits.

You'll find many of the members of this group in the offices that line K Street in Washington's northwest quadrant, home to numerous public affairs firms that operate in the nation's capital. Yet Lies, Incorporated is not simply shorthand for Washington, D.C.'s influence industry. It is a strategic infrastructure, supported by many who make their living manipulating public policy. Though the practice has become so common in certain sectors of the public affairs field that it is often difficult to separate the honest advocates from the deceitful con artists.

The practitioners who use this strategy do so knowing a well-placed lie is the most effective obstacle to political action. It can be as powerful as an army of lobbyists or millions of dollars in campaign contributions—as the president saw when he tried to pass gun legislation.

The goal of this stratagem is simple: to halt progress on issues that their clients oppose either for financial or ideological reasons. Richard Berman explained what he considers success during a 2014 speech to energy industry executives. His mission was not to win a public policy debate but instead to "tie." According to the notorious influence peddler, a "tie basically ensures the status quo."[4]

The business of inventing and disseminating lies with the goal of freezing the public policy process has only grown during the Obama presidency. Many on K Street believed the new administration arrived in Washington with a mandate for change. The new occupant of the White House would challenge a myriad of entrenched interest groups: from energy companies who feared fossil fuel regulations, to financial interests who hoped to avoid further regulation of Wall Street, to elements of the health care industry that want to prevent government involvement in their business.

Each time Obama proposed a policy challenging these interests, even in the tiniest way, he faced a litany of lies and distortions from an opposition using a set of methodologies out of the same playbook: paid experts produced fake research that was converted into talking points and memes, then repeated on television by paid shills and spread through social media and, when necessary, hammered into the public consciousness through paid advertising campaigns.

What we see today is a highly organized industry built around the creation and dissemination of falsehoods supported by a media environment that aids and abets its work. Facts are conjured in purportedly academic studies that have only the thinnest veneer of legitimacy. In 2014, one corporate lobbyist explained to *The New York Times,* "Once you have the study, you can point to it to prove your case—even if you paid to get it written."[5]

Thus the explanation of why an industry whose function is to create lies that distort the public policy process was born: if the facts don't support your argument, make up your own facts. Because in our nation's capital, winning at all costs on behalf of a paying client or ideological interest matters more than truth or a government that works on behalf of the American people.

Leg One: Money in Politics

To understand the impact of lies, it is vital to also explore how the other two legs of the stool of corruption—money and lobbying—are critical tools for those who seek to manipulate public policy. The problems created by the money that infects our politics have been well explored over the past few decades. This reality is made abundantly clear every four years by the increasing amounts of cash that flood our nation's campaigns.

Modern campaign finance legislation dates back to the Progressive Era. In 1907, Theodore Roosevelt signed the Tillman Act into law, banning corporations from making political contributions. A series of other reforms designed to weaken the influence of the wealthy, corporations, and unions came into being over the next sixty years.

Our current campaign finance system has its origins in a series of reforms passed by Congress in the 1970s, followed by court and regulatory decisions that scaled back those efforts and created problematic loopholes.

In 1971, Congress passed the Federal Election Campaign Act (FECA), requiring reporting and disclosure of political contributions. Following the Watergate scandal, Congress added teeth to campaign finance regulations with the establishment of the Federal Election Commission.[6] The 1974 amendments to FECA added limits to contributions, self-financing by candidates, and even spending caps for campaigns.[7] These laws also created the now rarely used public financing option for presidential candidates.

In the 1976 case *Buckley v. Valeo,* the Supreme Court overturned limits on candidate spending and independent expenditures, while keeping in place the law's $1,000 contribution limit. The greatest impact of the case was enshrining the constitutional principle that money is speech. The court, in an unsigned opinion joined by all its members, ruled that money was a form of speech because even "the distribution of the humblest handbill" required financial support. Citing the need for television advertising in modern campaigns, the court went on to state, "The electorate's increasing dependence on television, radio, and other mass media for news and information has made these expensive modes of communication indispensable instruments of effective political speech."[8] This decision created an incredibly high constitutional barrier for reform, hamstringing those seeking to limit the role of money in politics.

In 2002, Senators John McCain (R-AZ) and Russ Feingold (D-WI) successfully passed a campaign finance measure updating FECA, limiting so-called soft money and issue-advocacy spending. Prior to the passage of the Bipartisan Campaign Finance Reform Act, political parties could raise unlimited amounts of money for non-election-related purposes. This "soft money" was supposed to be used for voter registration and other party-building activities, but over the years edged closer to direct electioneering. The McCain-Feingold law restricted uses of "soft money" and also limited the ability of outside groups to use candidates' names in advertisements airing within thirty and sixty days of an election.[9] [10]

Following the law's passage, a series of Supreme Court cases and Federal Election Committee decisions eroded the impact of the legislation. The most prominent case was 2010's *Citizens United v. Federal Election Commission,* which held that the federal government could not restrict independent political spending by nonprofit corporations.[11] Additionally, in 2007, *FEC v. Wisconsin Right to Life* rendered restrictions on issue advertising meaningless[12]; while that same year *Davis v. FEC* overturned the "millionaires amendment" that in theory would raise contribution limits for a candidate who was facing a self-financed opponent.[13]

These cases undermined many of the principles of campaign finance reform, opening the floodgates to Super PACs, organizations that could raise unlimited contributions and target single races with millions of dollars in advertising. One wealthy individual can now spend an entire fortune to defeat any elected official, and, by laundering money through several groups, do so in a way that could be nearly anonymous.

Leg Two: Lobbying

While the billions spent on elections create the appearance of, if not actual, corruption, corporations seeking to influence the legislative process devote significantly more of their resources to lobbying. Lee Drutman of the New America Foundation conducted a comprehensive study of lobbying in Washington. Among his findings were that "from 1998 to 2012, corporations spent on average 12.7 times as much on lobbying as they did on PAC contributions." According to Drutman, this ratio has been "highly consistent for a decade and a half."[14]

The desire of interest groups to influence legislation and policy making in the nation's capital city is as old as the republic itself. The first lobbyist of note during the infancy of our republic was William Hull. Hull, a decorated soldier who rose to the rank of lieutenant colonel during the Revolutionary War, went to the capital in Philadelphia in 1792 after being hired by Virginia veterans to lobby for increased pay for their wartime service. Hull ended up writing veterans groups from other states, encouraging them to send their own "agent or agents" to advocate for the same goal.[15] Thomas Jefferson later appointed him the first governor of the Michigan Territory. After surrendering Detroit during the War of 1812, Hull was court-martialed for neglect of duty, cowardice, and treason. While acquitted of treason, he was convicted of the subsequent crimes and sentenced to death, only to be pardoned by President James Madison.[16]

A few years after Hull's activities in the nation's capital, lobbying was already a significant industry. West Virginia senator Robert Byrd noted in his history of the Senate, which he delivered in a series of floor speeches from 1980 to '89, that "in 1795, a Philadelphia newspaper described the way lobbyists waited outside Congress Hall to 'give a hint to a Member, tease or advise as may best suit.'"[17]

One of the first major lobbying scandals occurred in the 1850s when a lobbyist for gun maker Samuel Colt, seeking to "to extend his patent for seven years," distributed pistols to members of Congress and in one case a member's eleven- or twelve-year-old son.[18]

In 1869, a White House correspondent painted a vivid portrait of lobbyists in the nation's capital, writing, "Winding in and out through the long, devious basement passage, crawling through the corridors, trailing its slimy length from gallery to committee room, at last it lies stretched at full length on the floor of Congress—this dazzling reptile, this huge, scaly serpent of the lobby."[19]

The most recent lobbying scandal to seep into the mainstream consciousness involved Jack Abramoff, a Washington fixture who sold his influence with little regard for ethics or legality. Abramoff was ultimately convicted of defrauding Native American tribes of millions of dollars.[20]

Thousands of emails, unearthed as part of the Abramoff investigation, revealed the depth of Washington's addiction to influence. Ralph Reed, the political mastermind behind the Christian Coalition and a friend of Abramoff's from their time in the College Republicans, sent the lobbyist an email expressing his desire to convert his influence and power into profit.

"Hey, now that I'm done with the electoral politics, I need to start humping in corporate accounts!" Reed wrote his former comrade after the 1998 election cycle. "I'm counting on you to help me with some contacts."[21] Perhaps no better phrase defines the current culture of Washington: "Now that I am done" with the cause to which I have dedicated decades of my life, I can prostitute myself to the highest bidder.

More than a decade after this email came to light as part of a Senate Committee on Indian Affairs investigation, Reed has not suffered as a result of his association with Abramoff or his apparent willingness to cast aside deeply held religious beliefs to start "humping" corporations, specifically on behalf of gaming interests. Reed currently runs the Faith and Freedom Coalition, whose conference is still well attended by Republican Party leaders and thousands of activists.[22]

The 1970s marked a significant shift in corporate behavior, best represented by the way in which businesses interacted with organized labor. In 1965, 42 percent of companies "immediately complied" when their workers filed petitions to form a union with the National Labor Relations Board. That dropped to 16 percent by 1973.[23] Throughout the intervening years, the regulatory threat faced by corporations increased dramatically. In the period between the formation of the Equal Employment Opportunity Commission in 1964 and the Nuclear Regulatory Commission in 1975, fifteen new government agencies, including the Environmental Protection Agency (1970), the Consumer Product Safety

Commission (1972), and the Occupational Health and Safety Administration (1973), were created.[24]

These regulations resulted from the success of liberal campaigners and journalists such as Ralph Nader and Rachel Carson, who helped convince the American public of the need for increased government participation in nearly every facet of business. Their victories provoked an inevitable backlash that helped fuel Lies, Incorporated.

In 1971, future Supreme Court justice Lewis Powell wrote a memo to Eugene B. Sydnor, Jr., chairman of the Education Committee of the U.S. Chamber of Commerce, recommending a shift in strategy by the business community to a more aggressive posture, opposing government regulation, consumer advocates, and unions.

Powell bemoaned the business community's lack of influence over the policy process, writing, "As every business executive knows, few elements of American society today have as little influence in government as the American businessman, the corporation, or even the millions of corporate stockholders."[25]

Powell proposed a national campaign by the Chamber that would be a battle for public opinion, in the halls of Congress and in courtrooms across America.[26] The strategy succeeded beyond even Powell's expectations, and corporate lobbyists have become the center of power in Washington, D.C., and belligerent opponents of progressive change.

In the years since Powell's directive, corporate lobbying has become a gigantic industry. According to Lee Drutman's study, every year corporations spend $2.6 billion lobbying Congress, while the entire budget of the legislative branch of government is just over $2 billion.[27]

There is an oft-peddled myth that there is a balance between white-hat and black-hat lobbyists. According to this Pollyannaish view of Washington, those working on behalf of the Sierra Club (white hats) are engaged in a fair fight against those who argue on behalf of the Chamber of Commerce (black hats). It is an arms race, with both sides competing equally.

This is not reflective of reality. Drutman, in his study for the New America Foundation, discovered that in 2012 businesses spent thirty-four dollars lobbying for every dollar spent by "diffuse interest groups and Unions combined."[28] This inequitable treatment puts progressives and those not regularly allied with corporate interests at an incredible disadvantage. It is also the reason Lies, Incorporated's tactics are primarily utilized by right-wing and business interests. Far from being an issue of morality, the left is simply insufficiently funded to compete using the same playbook.

The right wing and its corporate backers are keenly aware of the lack of progressive power in the policy-making process. Drutman, as part of the research for his book, asked corporate lobbyists to identify their opponents in major policy fights. Unions and progressive organizations are not even a blip on the radar. Instead, the opposition of corporate lobbyists was ranked as follows:

Members of Congress: 26%
Getting Visibility: 26%
Other Industry: 21%
Government Bureaucrats: 13%
No Opponent: 11%
Other Business: 2%
Diffuse Interest Groups or Unions: 0%[29]

That is how lopsided debate is in Washington. Corporations do not view noncorporate entities as an obstacle to achieving their legislative goals.

Just as Congress attempted to roll back campaign finance excesses through McCain-Feingold, it has attempted to deal with lobbyist power as well, most recently through the Honest Leadership and Open Government Act of 2007.[30] Additional reforms were enacted by executive order at the beginning of the Obama administration.[31] On paper, the executive order worked. Following the enactment of these new rules, the number of registered lobbyists in Washington, D.C., went down, although this does not tell the whole story. "Lobbying isn't dying; instead, it's simply going underground,"[32] wrote Lee Fang in *The Nation*.

Fang noted that the office responsible for administering lobbyist registrations, the Clerk of the House of Representatives, does not have the authority to investigate reporting errors or those who simply do not register. The U.S. Attorney's Office is responsible for investigation and prosecution, but without a whistle-blower, there is no way to truly know if someone is lobbying with having registered. This lack of investigative process means that no one has ever been indicted, much less convicted, for failing to register as a lobbyist.[33]

Part of the problem is the loose definition of what "lobbying" entails. Lobbyists are not simply those wandering the halls of Congress who have registered and publicly disclose their activities. Numerous unregistered lobbyists are part of the Washington influence machine, referring to their industry as "public affairs." Some of these paid advocates can even be found advocating for their clients' interests during appearances on cable news channels and on Sunday-morning political talk shows. During these media hits, their potential conflicts of interest are rarely acknowledged. Hence, the reported $2.6 billion spent annually on lobbying is only a fraction of what is spent influencing policy in Washington, D.C.

Some seemingly nonpartisan think tanks are part of this infrastructure as well. Public affairs firms encourage their clients to make significant contributions to these "independent" organizations, which then produce studies and reports that are distributed to the media and policy makers.

It's no surprise that Washington's "think tank" industry has boomed in the years since the Powell memo was written. In 1970, there were approximately 100 think tanks in Washington, D.C. By 1996, there were 306.[34] Most of these institutions do not consist of scholars developing solutions unmoored to ideology or funding. Instead, many are simply part of an ideological arsenal, used to manipulate public policy in favor of their corporate funders.

One particularly favored think tank of the lobbying community is the Bipartisan Policy Center (BPC). Founded in 2007 by former Senate leaders from both sides of the aisle—Tom Daschle, Bob Dole, George Mitchell, and Howard Baker—BPC provides a window into how these organizations can serve the interests of their corporate funders. In 2013 alone, BPC was "publicly criticized for taking: (1) money from Walmart to promote an industry-backed plan to handle workplace conditions in Bangladeshi garment factories; (2) oil and gas industry money to write a report promoting more drilling; and (3) Citigroup and American Banking Association money to create a 'Financial Regulatory Reform Initiative' to steer the implementation of Dodd-Frank in a way that would be favorable to industry."[35]

Each of the four founders of the BPC, all considered elder statesmen of the capital, have spent time in their post-Senate careers working at lobbying firms on behalf of corporate clients. No matter: the label "bipartisan," along with their personal stature and the lingering power of their former positions, is enough to make BPC reports carry weight, regardless of who funds them.

The manipulation of the public policy process combines political contributions and aggressive lobbying campaigns with grassroots support (real and invented) and, as we will explore, the invention and dissemination of lies. These forces fuel a political climate where the overwhelming majority of the American people feel the government does not serve their interests.

It should be appalling that, when all is said and done, during the political 2016 cycle it is estimated that more than $5 billion will be spent electing federal officials on top of the nearly ten thousand lobbyists (nearly twenty lobbyists for every member of Congress) registered in the nation's capital and thousands more unregistered fighting to put corporate interests over those of the American public.

These lobbyists will often work in coordination with large public constituencies, such as members of professional associations. Other times they are grassroots activists who share a common interest with a well-funded industry—the alignment between gun rights activists and small arms manufacturers, for example. When no grassroots support exists, or groups are too lazy to do the hard work of organizing, often the simplest answer is to invent it or engage in strategies to inflate public support for their position. Corporate special interest groups have used this tactic for more than a century.

In his book *The Politics of Upheaval: 1935–1936, The Age of Roosevelt, Volume III,* historian Arthur Schlesinger recounts an effort by utility companies to defeat the Public Utility Holding Company Act. He described how in 1935, during "the last two weeks of June," a flood of eight hundred thousand "letters and wires heaped up in congressional offices." This would have been an impressive display of public interest in the issue, except the messages were fake. After receiving hundreds of messages, Pennsylvania congressman Denis Driscoll thought they seemed irregular.

He replied to several of his constituents only to be told they had not sent him the telegrams.[36]

These fake constituent contacts led to an investigation headed by then Senator and future Supreme Court justice Hugo Black. It found that Western Union had coordinated with Associated Gas and Electric to send the fake messages. Many of the names were taken "from the early pages of the city directory." Others were acquired by paying "a messenger boy named Elmer" three cents per signature secured for the project.[37]

These same tactics are still in use today. In March 2015, a group called American Commitment boasted it sent 1.6 million messages asking Congress to take action to overturn the Federal Communication Commision's net neutrality ruling. Lockheed Martin, which is responsible for the software that many representatives use to manage constituent contacts, sent a memo expressing "some concerns" that the messages were not authentic. Some members of Congress who responded to these communications received replies claiming the constituent in question "had never signed up to send emails criticizing net neutrality."[38]

Groups continue to engage in these duplicitous tactics because the price of getting caught is very low while the reward is high, as corporate interests are willing to pay handsomely for these efforts. Even in the age of big money, demonstrating tangible constituent support for an issue is still a necessary part of politics.

Sometimes ideological groups will simply sell their support to the highest bidder. This is best exemplified by a long-standing Washington dispute between Federal Express and UPS over the role of unions at each company.

In 2009, David Keene, then chairman of the influential American Conservative Union (ACU), which convenes the yearly conservative conclave known as CPAC, offered his organization's services to FedEx. For a $2–3 million price tag they would conduct "Congressional outreach," lead a "center-right coalition" on the company's behalf, and "produce op-eds by Keene," noting that he "writes a weekly column that appears in *The Hill.*"[39]

Two weeks after FedEx chose not to "contribute" to his organization, Keene and the ACU joined several other conservative organizations in accusing FedEx of "misleading the public and legislators." Maury Lane, FedEx director of corporate communications, told *Politico,* "Clearly, the ACU shopped their beliefs and UPS bought."[40]

Even though a prominent group had been caught red-handed selling its ideology, the collective reaction from Washington amounted to a shrug. The behavior was par for the course. Conservatives are not alone in their willingness to sell their influence in exchange for donations. Progressive groups have been caught with their hand in the corporate cookie jar as well.

Jarrett Barrios, head of the LGBT civil rights organization Gay and Lesbian Alliance Against Defamation (GLAAD), was caught trading his organization's public support in exchange for contributions from AT&T.

When the telecommunications giant attempted to purchase T-Mobile in 2011, Barrios wrote the FCC, offering GLAAD's enthusiastic support for the merger, citing its "longstanding commitment to all forms of social justice." Claiming one of the largest corporate mergers in history was an act of social justice was a bridge too far. It quickly became apparent that Barrios's statement had little to do with policy and instead was a quid pro quo exchange: AT&T wrote GLAAD a check for $50,000.[41]

After this story emerged, the gay blogosphere was relentless, and Barrios resigned from the organization after the board voted for his dismissal. Additionally, AT&T was removed from the organization's board. Ultimately, GLAAD retracted its former president's statements about the merger.[42]

In some ways, Jarrett Barrios was the victim of bad luck—hundreds of nonprofits in Washington, D.C., take policy positions outside their core set of issues based on contributions from donors. Corporate contributions like AT&T's are a necessary part of the funding model for many groups—remove those gifts and cutbacks are inevitable.

Despite several publicly embarrassing incidents, advocacy group endorsements are still an effective weapon for Lies, Incorporated, which frequently uses the power of manufactured grassroots support to foist its agenda on the American people.

Corruption has become so ingrained in the media and public culture of Washington that there is even a daily newsletter, "Politico Influence," highlighting personal moves, client signings, and triumphs of the influence industry.[43] This publication is evidence of a world where politics is a cynical, financially lucrative pursuit. One in which professionals don't care about the outcomes they procure on behalf of clients, even those that can adversely impact millions of people's lives. In the petri dish of money and corruption that Washington has become, it is no surprise that lying and inventing lies is now an accepted part of doing business.

Think of every topic debated in Washington over the course of the Obama administration: health care, climate, guns, gay rights, and the national debt. Each one of these issues was influenced by a well-funded group of people—some of whom were paid to manipulate the truth. In this book I will introduce you to the players who sow confusion, the lies they conjure, and the industries they represent. Members of Lies, Incorporated are motivated by profit and ideological gain without caring about the ramifications of their actions. In most cases they knowingly lie and when caught never retract or apologize for their deceit. The saddest part of the current culture of Washington is many of these liars are repeat offenders, allowed to maintain platforms despite their well-known dishonesty.

The world of post-truth politics is the pathetic result of a political culture where ideological victory, not progress, is the ultimate goal. Where what is good for my country plays second fiddle to what is good for the bottom line of my clients. If we are to fix our corrupt political system, then legislation is not enough. We need to change the ethos of Washington so that profiting from lies is no longer acceptable.

Chapter 1

The Birth of Lies, Incorporated: Tobacco

Lies, Incorporated was born during a meeting of the titans of the tobacco industry at the Plaza Hotel in New York City on December 15, 1953. In attendance were the presidents of American Tobacco, Benson & Hedges, Philip Morris, and U.S. Tobacco—the four largest tobacco companies at the time—as well as the CEOs of R.J. Reynolds and Brown & Williamson.[1]

Previously, the group had gathered only for social occasions, at charity events and various industry award ceremonies. This meeting had a far more serious agenda. Earlier that month, Dr. Ernst Wynder of the Sloan Kettering Institute for Cancer Research published the findings of a study linking cigarette tar to cancer in mice.[2] The research attracted intense media attention and put a spotlight on the health risks associated with tobacco. Widely read publications including *Life* magazine, *The New York Times,* and the *Reader's Digest* (in a piece titled "Cancer by the Carton") had already published major articles on the dangers of smoking.[3] The looming crisis had to be dealt with, and the leading tobacco barons joined forces to fight back.

At the Plaza Hotel meeting, the heads of the tobacco companies met with John Hill, founder of the legendary public relations firm Hill & Knowlton.[4] The company had built its reputation working for chemical companies, big oil, and other heavy industries.[5] Profit was not Hill's only motivation. He was a committed conservative, opposed to the idea of government regulations, even of carcinogens such as tobacco.[6]

As far back as 1912, Dr. Isaac Adler suggested a link between tobacco and lung cancer in the "world's first monograph on lung cancer," while indicating more research was needed, as his conclusions were "not yet ready for final judgment."[7] In 1939, Franz Hermann Müller of Cologne Hospital published a study in which he demonstrated "that people with lung cancer were far more likely than non-cancer controls to have smoked." This was confirmed in another, "more ambitious" study by "Eberhard Schairer and Eric Schöniger at the University of Jena" in 1943.[8] These results became more conclusive as additional scholarly research was published through the 1950s and '60s.

By the time Wynder's study was published, the medical field—and the tobacco industry—had access to research concluding that the use of tobacco products posed a significant health risk.[9] Hill believed the way to fight back was for the tobacco companies to join together, sponsor additional studies, and issue new "pro-cigarette" messaging using the word "research" to highlight the scientific nature of their counterarguments.[10] The tobacco companies were not equipped internally to take on this role. For years they had worked to steal one another's clients. Now they would need to defend the industry as a whole.

Following the meeting, Hill & Knowlton drafted a white paper that laid out a plan for the industry. "The grave nature of a number of recently highly publicized research reports on the effects of cigarette smoking . . . [has] confronted the industry with a serious problem of public relations," wrote the firm. "The situation is one of extreme delicacy. There is much at stake and the industry group, in moving into the field of public relations, needs to exercise great care not to add fuel to the flames."[11]

Using the resources of the companies represented at the meeting, Hill & Knowlton recommended establishing the austere-sounding Tobacco Industry Research Committee.[12] "The underlying purpose of any activity at this stage should be reassurance of the public through wider communication of facts to the public," wrote Hill & Knowlton in the white paper. "It is important that the public recognize the existence of weighty scientific views which hold there is no proof that cigarette smoking is a cause of lung cancer."[13]

This purported research committee, whose public role was providing independent data on the risks of smoking, was in fact a front for Hill & Knowlton. The tobacco companies supplied an initial budget of $1.2 million and its offices were located one floor below Hill & Knowlton's in the Empire State Building.[14][15]

The group announced its existence with "A Frank Statement to Cigarette Smokers." Run as a paid advertisement on January 4, 1954, in more than four hundred newspapers around the country, the statement claimed:

1. That medical research of recent years indicates many possible causes of lung cancer.
2. That there is no agreement among the authorities regarding what the cause is.
3. That there is no proof that cigarette smoking is one of the causes.
4. That statistics purporting to link cigarette smoking with the disease could apply with equal force to any one of many other aspects of modern life. Indeed the

validity of the statistics themselves is questioned by numerous scientists.

The ad went on to describe the activities of the group:

1. We are pledging aid and assistance to the research effort into all phases of tobacco use and health. This joint financial aid will of course be in addition to what is already being contributed by individual companies.
2. For this purpose we are establishing a joint industry group consisting initially of the undersigned. This group will be known as TOBACCO INDUSTRY RESEARCH COMMITTEE.
3. In charge of the research activities of the Committee will be a scientist of unimpeachable integrity and national repute. In addition there will be an Advisory Board of scientists disinterested in the cigarette industry. A group of distinguished men from medicine, science and education will be invited to serve on this Board. These scientists will advise the Committee on its research activities.[16]

According to Hill & Knowlton's "progress report," this ad reached more than 43 million Americans, costing a total of just over a quarter-million dollars.[17] This advertising onslaught accomplished its intended purpose of overshadowing research informing the public of the dangers of tobacco.

The Tobacco Industry Research Committee was created to cast doubt on scientific consensus that smoking cigarettes causes cancer, to convince the media that there were two sides to the story about the risks of tobacco and that each side should be considered with equal weight. Finally it sought to steer politicians away from damaging the economic interests of the tobacco companies.[18] Hill & Knowlton helped the industry carry out this mission.

Due to the success of Hill's strategy, the methods he pioneered would be employed by a variety of players in Lies, Incorporated over the decades to come, impacting the public debate on issues including climate change, health care, and gun control. If your goal is simply to keep the status quo in place, in this case keeping millions of people addicted to a dangerous product with no government intervention, then confusion is a useful tool. If the science is in doubt, why take action that would harm the economic well-being of farmers and thousands of others who work in the tobacco industry, as well as telling millions of Americans they should not engage in a favorite leisure activity? What made this strategy morally reprehensible was that the companies knew from the moment they launched their effort that cigarettes were killing millions of people. Their success at delaying action by the federal government and other health care authorities, caused by an unnecessary battle over science, undoubtedly cost millions more Americans their lives, in addition to hundreds of millions, if not billions of dollars, in health care costs.

The "Frank Statement" was the first step in a major public relations campaign whose goal was to undermine scientific research. It represented a major break from previous PR strategies. The tobacco industry's prior instinct had been to mitigate the health risks suggested by the research, rather than to attack science head-on.[19] Thus, each company had been competing against the others with claims that its cigarettes were the healthiest on the market. John Hill convinced them this was a counterproductive strategy.[20]

In May 1954, Hill & Knowlton presented the Tobacco Industry Research Committee with a booklet titled "A Scientific Perspective on the Cigarette Controversy." More than two hundred thousand copies were printed and sent to 176,000 doctors as well as to thousands of reporters around the country.[21]

Seeking more heft, Hill & Knowlton hired a scientific adviser to serve as a public face for its efforts. Dr. Clarence Cook Little, who previously served as a director of the American Cancer Society, took on the role with vigor.

Little had impeccable credentials. He was a research biologist and a former assistant dean of Harvard and president of the University of Maine and the University of Michigan. At the Tobacco Industry Research Committee, Little supervised the distribution of millions of dollars in grant money, maintaining for decades that "there [was] no demonstrated causal relationship between smoking or any disease," even after the science on the subject was indisputable.[22] He insisted lung cancer was a genetic condition, not one caused by smoking.

Early on, Little's role created controversy in the medical community. In *The Atlantic,* Dr. David D. Rutstein, head of the Preventive Medicine Department at the Harvard Medical School, wrote "An Open Letter to Dr. Clarence Cook Little" in October 1957. Citing eighteen studies in five countries, Rutstein accused Little of having "consistently ignored or brushed off all of the human evidence whenever a statement relating cigarette smoking and lung cancer has been released to the press by a research worker, by the British government through its Medical Research Council, or by the Surgeon General of the United States Public Health Service speaking for the United States government."[23]

He asked, "Is there really any justification for your continuing to demand the discovery of the 'cause' of lung cancer before we attempt to save human lives by recommending a decrease in cigarette smoking?"[24]

If by 1957 the medical community had already reached consensus on the fact that smoking cigarettes caused lung cancer, why would a scientist like Dr. Little resist? Little was a believer in eugenics, which, post–World War II, had fallen out of favor. For Little, this belief was grounded in the notion that genetics predetermined the maladies our bodies were susceptible to, including cancer.[25] The idea that cigarette smoke and not our DNA was the cause of cancer would undermine his belief structure.[26] He would not be the first to turn a blind eye to facts in order to preserve his belief system. The scientists who work at the behest of corporate interests as part of Lies, Incorporated are often driven by ideology, sometimes tangentially linked to the subject at hand, not simply by money.

Employing scientists like Dr. Little as part of their effort would become a critical strategy for Lies, Incorporated. As Harvard science historian and coauthor of the book *Merchants of Doubt* Naomi Oreskes explained to me, "The credibility of the disinformation campaign depends upon having at least some real scientist who can stand up in public and make it seem as if there is a real scientific debate."[27]

In addition to publishing its own tobacco "research," Hill & Knowlton ran an active campaign to alter news stories that were critical of the tobacco industry. The firm bragged about a story in "*Cosmopolitan* magazine that 'was already in type'" when their efforts "resulted in 'seven revisions and five qualifying additions.'"[28]

According to a congressional investigation into the tobacco industry, the firm found it "quicker and more effective simply to hire free-lance authors to write favorable articles" on behalf of the Tobacco Industry Research Committee. "Especially-written articles are being developed that can be used or adopted for use in various media receptive to or seeking material relating to the subject," wrote Hill & Knowlton in a 1954 "confidential report."[29]

Hill & Knowlton meticulously documented these successes in memos now publicly available in University of California, San Francisco's Truth Tobacco Industry Documents archive. Just one example is an April 1955 memo in which the firm took credit for information in an article " 'Phony Cigarette Scare' in the March 23 issue of PEOPLE TODAY; for 'A Psychologist on the Cigarette Scare' in the April issue of POPULAR MEDICINE and for a piece scheduled for the August Issue of ARGOSY MAGAZINE."[30]

According to a congressional report, the group also "infiltrate[d] anti-smoking organizations to obtain advance information."[31] This would be useful in discovering what information needed to be debunked and the direction in which the science was heading. The tobacco industry's goal was clear: it would sabotage public knowledge.

Even media outlets that were held in the highest esteem could not shake the influence of tobacco. For example, an internal memo prepared by Hill & Knowlton explained how the industry's false information ended up influencing legendary CBS broadcast journalist Edward R. Murrow:

A conference was held with Edward R. Murrow [and] Fred Friendly, his producer ... at the Tobacco Industry Research Committee offices in the Empire State Building.... The Murrow staff emphasized the intention to present a coldly objective program with every effort made to tell the story as it stands today, with special effort toward balanced perspective and concrete steps to show that the facts still are not established and must be sought by scientific means such as the research activities the Tobacco Industry Research Committee will support. Mr. Murrow was assured of the continued cooperation from the Tobacco Industry Research Committee to the extent possible under the scope of the TIRC program.[32]

Murrow was not the only journalist to be influenced by Hill & Knowlton's efforts. A 1959 memo from the public relations firm bragged "H&K found that the American Cancer Society was preparing a film series on cancer for NBC. One session would be on tobacco and lung cancer." The firm contacted the network, which "agreed that there was no conclusive evidence—the film was revised and was not anti-tobacco."[33]

It is easy to look back with perfect hindsight and ask how a newsman as serious and seemingly incorruptible as Murrow could be duped into providing a group of charlatans like those at the TIRC an equal voice to legitimate scientists on his program. Famous and trusted scientists such as Clarence Little supported the TIRC. Furthermore, in the pre-Vietnam era, the American people and media had a greater level of institutional trust. Tobacco companies were blue-chip corporations, not fly-by-night snake oil salesmen. Companies run by respected men were not suspects for engaging in malevolent behavior. Even as a journalist, Murrow had little reason not to view them as part of a balanced perspective.

The TIRC's activities continued unabated for more than a decade until 1964, when the scientific data against smoking became so compelling that the surgeon general issued the now-famous warning stamped on every pack of cigarettes sold in the United States, making clear the danger of the product.[34] The TIRC then became the Council for Tobacco Research, which continued operating until it was shuttered in 1998.[35]

Hill & Knowlton's efforts to cast doubt on the dangers of tobacco is one of the most successful public relations campaigns in history. A *Businessweek* article "on the state of public relations in the 1960[s]" identified H&K's tobacco work as "probably one of

PR's best finger-in-the-dike jobs," running their campaign "based on the premise that 'there is no conclusive proof that cigarettes cause cancer, but that the industry has an obligation to get the full facts.' "[36]

Even as late as 1990, tobacco companies were blowing through an annual budget of $20 million, continuing the fight against evidence that smoking is harmful in what *Public Relations Journal* called "one of the most dramatic examples ever of [a public relations firm] fighting to the bitter end."[37]

After tobacco, Hill & Knowlton utilized the same techniques to assist a variety of other clients. In the 1960s, the company launched the Asbestos Information Association on behalf of asbestos manufacturer Johns Manville, questioning whether the insulating material caused health problems.[38] Asbestos has now been connected to hundreds of thousands of cancer deaths.

In the 1970s, the firm worked to create doubt about whether chlorofluorocarbons were harming the ozone layer. The team they hired to cast doubt on the science showing that CFCs were tearing a hole in the sky was so successful, they won a Nobel Prize.[39] It took nearly a decade for public policy to catch up with the known facts.

The methods used by Hill & Knowlton have since migrated across the entire public relations industry and the political process. Why correct bad behavior when you can simply deny the facts? Just cast doubt upon science and smear the reputations of your critics. Millions died of cancer and emphysema because of the lies spread by a single public relations firm, but the client made money and that's what matters.

We are aware of the industry's behavior because as part of their 1998 settlement with the federal government, the big tobacco companies—Philip Morris, R.J. Reynolds, Brown & Williamson, and Lorillard Tobacco, as well as the Tobacco Institute and the

Council for Tobacco Research—were forced to make millions of previously secret documents public. They have now been archived, made searchable and placed online. What emerged was a complete history of the tobacco companies' efforts to influence policy debates over several decades.

Viewing the tobacco companies' playbook in full allows us to understand how Lies, Incorporated has repeatedly used the same strategies on issue after issue, from climate change, to health care, to gun control, and even to undermine the right to vote. And we know the tobacco industry's tactics are carried forth today by a new generation and a whole network of practitioners even more comfortable with lies and spin than John Hill.

Chapter 2

Tobacco's Sequel:
Climate Change

In 1998, the American Petroleum Institute, the principal trade association and lobbying group representing the fossil fuel industry, convened a series of meetings at its Washington, D.C., offices to discuss potential industry responses to the major climate treaty being negotiated to reduce global emissions of greenhouse gases. Among the attendees were representatives from some of the country's largest oil companies, including Exxon, Chevron, and Southern Company.[1]

The plan to wage war against the treaty—the Kyoto Protocol—was multifaceted.[2] To challenge the science used to justify the need for environmental protections, industry leaders sought to recruit scientists who could counter with industry-approved "science." Early recruits included the Science and Environment Policy Project, founded by Fred Singer, a prominent physicist who had worked on early American satellite programs. He also argued against the health impacts of secondhand smoke in the 1990s, and by 1998 was a leading climate denier. In an interview for the documentary film *Merchants of Doubt* (based on the book coauthored by science historians Naomi Oreskes and Erik M. Conway), Singer expressed that he "still believes the EPA has cooked the data on secondhand smoke." He also told the interviewer he was "annoyed by the fact this tobacco business comes up every time when I speak about global warming, which has nothing to do with tobacco."[3]

Another early recruit was Frederick Seitz, one of America's most prominent scientists and head of the National Academy of Sciences from 1962 to 1969. Seitz was also chairman of the George C. Marshall Institute, which had defended the science behind Ronald Reagan's space missile defense system known as Star Wars and had been involved with the tobacco industry.[4]

Like the tobacco companies who met in New York in 1953, Exxon knew very early on that the burning of fossil fuels was changing the planet's climate and would impact the lives of billions of people. An investigation by the Pulitzer Prize–winning environmental news website InsideClimate News found that Exxon senior scientist James Black told the company's management committee in July 1977 that "there is general scientific agreement that the most likely manner in which mankind is influencing the global climate is through carbon dioxide release from the burning of fossil fuels."[5]

A year later, Black updated his presentation, alerting the company that if the concentration of CO_2 in the atmosphere doubled, global temperatures would increase by 4 or 5 degrees Fahrenheit and possibly 18 degrees at the poles.[6] He continued: "Man has a time window of five to ten years before the need for hard decisions regarding changes in energy strategies might become critical."[7]

In July 2015, *The Guardian* published an email from Lenny Bernstein, Exxon's former "in-house climate expert," that revealed his former company "first got interested in climate change in 1981 because it was seeking to develop the Natuna gas field off Indonesia." By 1989, Exxon knew that global warming was caused by burning fossil fuels, and that the Natuna project "would be the largest point source of CO_2 in the world." Even with this information, in the 1990s Bernstein led the science and technology advisory committee of a group funded by the fossil fuel industry, the Global Climate Coalition, that according to *The Guardian,* "lobbied aggressively against the scientific consensus around the causes of climate change."[8] The admission that Exxon and Bernstein knew about climate change so early exposes the depth of their dishonesty.

Exxon received scientific data about the causes of climate change in 1977, 1978, and 1981 and had access to additional, factual information in subsequent years. Yet in 1997, Exxon CEO Lee Raymond gave a speech to the World Petroleum Congress in which he said the claim that carbon emissions caused climate change "defies common sense and lacks foundation in our current understanding of the climate system."[9] Exxon knew the truth, but spent decades funding research to create confusion and public uncertainty about the very existence of climate change.

Exxon wasn't alone in this behavior. The year after Raymond's speech, Exxon and other major fossil fuel companies funded a coordinated effort to deny the existence of climate change and opposed the Kyoto Protocol. Not only did the companies seek to recruit scientists to fight real science with industry-created "facts," they also planned to train the scientists "in public relations so they [could] help convince journalists, politicians and the public that the risk of global warming" was not enough of a certainty to regulate fossil fuels.[10] This was precisely the model tobacco companies employed half a century earlier.

With a budget of $600,000, not including ads, the group would lead an effort to convince the media that climate science was "uncertain."[11] Their goal was for this misinformation to infiltrate the consciousness of the public at large, which would then "raise questions with policymakers."[12]

Their benchmarks for success were clear. According to a follow-up memo summarizing the results of the meeting, "victory will be achieved when" the media recognizes the "uncertainties in climate science," "recognition of uncertainties becomes part of the 'conventional wisdom'" accepted by average citizens, and the views of those supporting the Kyoto Protocol "on the basis of extant science appear to be out of touch with reality."[13]

The lessons learned from the decades-long fight waged by Lies, Incorporated on behalf of tobacco companies were applied to the fight over climate change. The parallels between the two campaign efforts could not be more striking, which is not surprising, since several of the critical players were the same. Principal among them was Dr. Frederick Seitz, who handed out $45 million in grants from the tobacco industry.[14]

According to *Merchants of Doubt* author Naomi Oreskes, Seitz's grant program for the tobacco companies was designed to be a diversion. She noted in an interview that much of the work "wasn't phony science, it was real science that was distracting." For example, Seitz would "fund research on the relationship between asbestos and cancer. Fund research on the relationship between radon exposure and cancer. And so then the CEO of a tobacco company can get up in public and say there are a lot of different causes of lung cancer."[15]

Ultimately, Seitz wore out his welcome with the tobacco companies, and in 1989, a Philip Morris executive wrote in an internal company memo that "Dr. Seitz is quite elderly and not sufficiently rational to offer advice."[16]

Yet in 2001, the Heartland Institute, one of the principal think tanks funded by the fossil fuel industry to deny the existence of global warming, found him rational enough to author an article in

their magazine, *The Heartlander.* In it, Dr. Seitz claims "the scientific facts indicate that all the temperature changes observed in the
last 100 years were largely natural changes and were not caused by
carbon dioxide produced in human activities."[17]

Even a decade and a half ago, this statement was out of step
with the views of the vast majority of scientists. The findings of
thousands of studies, and the consensus of the global scientific
community, had already concluded that the Earth was warming
and the cause was likely the carbon dioxide we were dumping into
our atmosphere.[18]

Oreskes and her coauthor Erik Conway observed in their book
that ideology, not necessarily money, drew scientists like Seitz and
physicist Fred Singer to help the tobacco and fossil fuel industries. They "shared a kind of political ideology" that was "deeply,
deeply anticommunist" and believed that government intervention, i.e., regulation, was detrimental to the marketplace.

Acknowledging that there is a giant environmental problem
such as climate change, one that can only be solved through a
massive regulatory scheme that must be negotiated on a global
scale, invariably conflicts with conservative ideology. In contrast,
Seitz did argue in favor of Reagan's Star Wars program, which was
viewed skeptically by many in the scientific community. In that
case, Seitz's Marshall Institute advocated for a huge allocation of
government resources because it was a tool America needed to
win the Cold War.[19]

According to Oreskes, as the Cold War ended, Seitz, Singer, and
some of their colleagues begin "systematically attacking" other
issues that shared a common thread: "the need for government
action." This behavior suggests their advocacy was not based on
science or financial gain but instead on a "political debate about
the role of government."[20]

Seitz and Singer came to believe that regulation of all kinds would inevitably increase government involvement in people's lives, which would ultimately lead to the Soviet-style totalitarianism they had fought against.

These beliefs seem extreme, but they are not uncommon in the anti–climate movement. As British writer James Delingpole explained to the libertarian magazine *Reason,* he titled his book *Watermelons: The Green Movement's True Colors* because environmentalists are "green on the outside but red on the inside. After the Berlin Wall came down, the communist movement" was lost and "needed somewhere else to go, and global warming has become the great proxy issue. It enables them to achieve many of the same aims as before but under a cloak of green righteousness." Environmentalism's goal is "global takeover by fascism, communism, call it what you will; their aims are much the same. It is about control."[21]

This is the link between corporate public policy goals and conservative ideology, the fear of government regulation, and the use of labels such as "fascist" and "communist" to demonize opponents. It is easy to see climate deniers in the media and rationalize their beliefs as the product of being bought off. But ideology often plays just as strong a role in these efforts as monetary gain.

The overlap between climate change and the tobacco industry did not simply consist of a few shared scientists. As the tobacco companies defended themselves against regulations targeting secondhand smoke, they actively participated in concurrent efforts to deny climate change. Philip Morris, with the help of lobbying and public relations giants APCO and Burson-Marsteller, formed the Advancement of Sound Science Coalition, which would argue the tobacco and fossil fuel industry's message on secondhand smoke and climate change, respectively. The group's activities were so successful in the United States that they encouraged companies across the Atlantic to duplicate their work. This was spelled out for a European audience in a 1994 memo drafted by APCO, including instructions to frame the debate around "broader questions about government research and regulations."[22]

The memo suggested an argument that "economic growth cannot afford to be held hostage to paternalistic overregulation," while claiming that "improving indoor air quality is a laudable goal that will never be accomplished as long as tobacco smoke is the sole focus of regulators."[23] By framing their arguments this way, APCO not only challenged limits on cigarettes and other tobacco products but also on carbon dioxide emissions.

As with tobacco use, beyond a few scientists primarily funded by the industry, the overwhelming consensus in the scientific community is that the Earth is warming and humans are the primary cause, due to our reliance on burning fossil fuels that release carbon dioxide into the atmosphere. The science backing up this assertion is decades old and comprehensive.

The basic premise of global warming is easy to understand. When we burn fossil fuels—gasoline or coal, for example—they release carbon dioxide into the atmosphere. This gas traps heat from the sun, preventing it from leaving Earth and escaping out into space, which warms the planet. The resulting temperature fluctuation leads to rising sea levels, droughts, and floods.[24]

Since the industrial revolution, humans have become ever more reliant on the burning of fossil fuels, and as a result, an increased quantity of gas becomes trapped in our atmosphere.

In recent years, the science around climate change has become even more conclusive. A May 2013 study measuring the level of support among scientists for human-caused climate change looked at four thousand "peer-reviewed scientific journal" articles that took a position on global warming and found that 97 percent of them agreed that humans caused climate change.[25] It is odd that a theory is still considered controversial or at least up for debate in the media when the vast majority of science is in agreement.

A number of scientists who were originally global warming skeptics changed positions as they studied the issue, and the data became more conclusive. Best known among this group is University of California at Berkeley physicist Dr. Richard Muller. At one time Muller was a leading climate change skeptic, doubting the underlying data that suggested the Earth was warming.

Now he calls himself "a converted skeptic." Muller wrote in *The New York Times* in July 2012 that after studying the data he "concluded that global warming was real and that the prior estimates of the rate of warming were correct" and that "humans are almost entirely the cause" of this change in temperature.[26]

Ironically, Muller's research was funded in part with a $150,000 grant from the Koch brothers, who control the largest privately held corporation in the world and have spent a not-insignificant part of their fortunes casting doubt on the existence of climate change.[27] There is no evidence the results of Muller's work has influenced their opinion on the existence of climate change.

Invariably, action to stop our planet's warming would mean scaling back the use of carbon fuels either through cuts in consumption, primarily achieved through increased efficiency, or by shifting our sources of energy away from carbon-based fuels—or likely both. Either way, this threatens the bottom lines of the oil and coal companies that extract trillions of dollars in energy reserves from beneath the surface of the Earth. With that much money at stake, it was no surprise the industry looked to stave off what it viewed as an attack on its financial viability. While in previous decades environmentalists won major victories concerning pollution and wildlife protection, addressing climate change would require a wholesale shift in how we produce and use energy, the very basis of our economy.

One new element of the climate battle has been the increasingly partisan divide of science. Unlike the tobacco industry, fossil fuel companies can rely on a political climate that allows conservative free marketers to turn science into a left versus right battle. This continues the policy stalemate that only benefits those whose bottom line relies on *not* solving the climate crisis.

Between fossil fuel and conservative interest groups, billions have been spent to fund a network of groups that seems to exist solely to deny the existence of climate change. As early as 1991, industry groups led by the Edison Electric Institute, the National Coal Association, and the Western Fuels Association began an aggressive campaign of misinformation. The Climate Council and the Information Council on the Environment (also known as ICE) was, like the Tobacco Industry Research Committee, formed as a public relations effort designed to muddy the existing science.

This group of deniers, according to Ross Gelbspan, an acclaimed climate change author and former editor of *The Washington Post* and *The Boston Globe,* "launched a blatantly misleading campaign" that was explicitly designed, according to an internal memo, to "reposition global warming as theory rather than fact."[28]

In addition to acting as a public relations clearing house for climate change skeptics, ICE followed the playbook of the Tobacco Institute by taking out newspaper ads with headlines like "If the Earth is getting warmer, why is Minneapolis getting colder?"[29] This message was clearly designed to obfuscate the issue—seasonal fluctuations in particular areas mean nothing when, as the grim results keep reminding us, global temperatures continue to rise.

Over the course of two decades, the climate denial movement has grown from industry-generated groups to the entirety of the conservative movement. From the largest conservative think tanks such as the Heritage Foundation and the American Enterprise Institute, to smaller organizations like the Heartland Institute, to grassroots organizations such as FreedomWorks and Americans for Prosperity, which served as the principal organizers of the Tea Party movement, Lies, Incorporated's climate denier network is deep.

This network also includes members of Congress and free-lance hit men, such as Senator James Inhofe (R-OK) and his former staffer Marc Morano. The senator regularly uses his platform, formerly as ranking member, now chairman, of the Senate Committee on Environment and Public Works to deny the existence of climate change, even authoring a book titled *The Greatest Hoax: How the Global Warming Conspiracy Threatens Your Future.*[30]

While serving as communications director for Senator Inhofe, Morano acknowledges using "nastiness" as a political tactic and having had fun mocking and ridiculing climate scientists. Morano, who also worked with Rush Limbaugh, admits, "What I enjoy the most is going after the individuals, 'cause that is where something lives or dies."[31]

Free from the few constraints of Senator Inhofe's office, Morano now runs the website Climate Depot—called "the No. 1 online destination for the truth behind today's global warming hysteria" by the conservative *Townhall Magazine. Rolling Stone* best described his website and tactics by dubbing Morano the "Matt Drudge of Climate Denial."[32]

Morano's mission is to sell climate denial using techniques he learned as a door-to-door salesman. "Communications is about sales. Keep it simple, people will fill in the blank [with], I hate to say biases, but with their own perspective in many cases," he said in an interview for the film *Merchants of Doubt.* During this conversation Morano also bragged, "I'm not a scientist, although I do play one on TV occasionally. . . . Okay, hell, more than occasionally."[33]

Morano explained the advantage he has when debating scientists on television: "You go up against a scientist, most of them are going to be in their own policy wonk world or area of expertise . . . very arcane, very hard to understand, hard to explain, and very boorrring."[34]

Like Richard Berman and other members of Lies, Incorporated, Morano's goal is maintaining the status quo. He explicitly makes this point in *Merchants of Doubt,* noting, "Gridlock is the greatest friend a global warming skeptic has because that's all you really want." Morano punctuated that point by stating, "There is no legislation we are championing. We're the negative force. We're just trying to stop stuff."[35]

The Lies, Incorporated campaign to deny climate change is a sophisticated, multilayered operation. Some participants serve as disseminators of false science, others as media spokespeople, still others operate grassroots organizations designed to spread misinformation and rile up the conservative base. Their combined efforts form one of the largest attempts at mass deception in human history.

The simplest explanation for this ideological alliance is money. The pockets of the fossil fuel industry run deep. Exxon alone has contributed tens of millions of dollars to dozens of conservative organizations whose work obfuscates the truth about global warming. This funding was partially cut off in 2008, when a group of shareholders led by members of the Rockefeller family, the founders of Standard Oil, objected to the companies' expenditures that helped create a culture of denial around global warming. As a result, the company ceased funding the Heartland Institute and a number of far-right institutions but continues to act as an ATM for a number of organizations that deny the warming of the planet.[36]

In late 2008, Barack Obama's ascension to the presidency sparked a panic. The oil industry feared he would successfully pass legislation to limit the use of or increase taxes on fossil fuels. Indeed, the president had made climate change one of his central legislative priorities for Congress.

In the summer of 2009, a bill that would create a cap-and-trade system for carbon emissions made its way to the floor of the House of Representatives. Under this proposed regulatory framework, the amount of CO_2 that could be released into the atmosphere would be capped. Companies would buy permits from the federal government to emit gas and could trade those permits with other companies, thereby putting a monetary value on carbon in the atmosphere and disincentivizing its use.[37]

This was coal and oil companies' worst nightmare, and they went on the attack. Their advocacy groups came out in full force against the House bill. One of the largest of these organizations was the American Coalition for Clean Coal Electricity (ACCCE), created by the industry to promote the idea of "clean coal."[38] ACCCE had been ubiquitous at the Democratic and Republican conventions in 2008, with street teams giving away free T-shirts, billboards, and online advertising that could not be missed.

In 2009, ACCCE spent $1.558 million in disclosed lobbying expenditures.[39] However, its Form 990 revealed more than $28 million in total spending, including money dedicated to advertising and other efforts to shape public opinion, as well as fees to influence-peddlers whose work went undisclosed.[40]

ACCCE recognized that to convince Democrats to vote against the bill, they would need to mobilize traditionally progressive constituencies. As the House debated the climate bill, Democratic representatives Tom Perriello of Virginia and Kathy Dahlkemper and Chris Carney of Pennsylvania, whose districts are among the most evenly divided between Democrats and Republicans, began receiving letters expressing opposition to the legislation from local civil rights organizations, such as the Charlottesville chapter of the NAACP.[41]

One letter, claiming to be signed by William Ernst of the Charlottesville NAACP, appealed to Perriello in economic terms. "We ask you use your position to help protect minorities and other consumers in your district from higher electric bills," the letter read. "Please don't vote to force cost increases on us, especially in this volatile economy."[42] Perriello received similar letters from the American Association of University Women and the Jefferson Area Board for Aging.[43]

These letters were forgeries—created by a public affairs firm, Bonner & Associates, which had been subcontracted by the ACCCE. The firm ultimately claimed the fraudulent letters were the work of a rogue employee, who was terminated, and went back to business as usual.[44]

Several months later at a hearing investigating the incident, then–Massachusetts congressman Ed Markey harangued executives from both ACCCE and Bonner, telling them, "We learned that the coal coalition learned two days in advance of the historic vote on the House floor that a fraud had been perpetrated. . . . Though the coal coalition knew, it took precious little effort to make sure the members of Congress knew that this fraud had been perpetrated."[45]

Despite the fossil fuel companies' massive effort to block any climate legislation, in the summer of 2009 there was real momentum in Congress to pass a cap-and-trade bill. As the bill advanced in the legislative process, the campaign of lies ramped up as well.

Almost as soon as the bill was introduced in the House of Representatives, a new lie began to circulate. The Environmental Protection Agency estimated the cost of the bill to American taxpayers was $146 per year.[46] House Republicans told a different story. On his official government website, House Speaker John Boehner claimed, "with the Congress taking heat from the American people about imposing additional taxes—to the tune of $3,100 per American household—in the form of 'cap and trade,' the Administration appears ready to circumvent Congress by labeling carbon dioxide as a 'pollutant.' "[47]

Boehner's statistics were from a study by MIT professor John Reilly, who promptly cast doubt on the Republican's interpretation of his data.

In a letter to the Speaker, Reilly wrote:

> The press release claims our report estimates an average cost per family of a carbon cap and trade program that would meet targets now being discussed in Congress to be over $3,000, but that is nearly 10 times the correct estimate which is approximately $340.[48]

Citing Professor Reilly's letter, the Pulitzer Prize–winning website PolitiFact rated Boehner's $3,100 figure a "pants on fire" lie. According to PolitiFact, "Not only is it wrong, but he told the House Republicans it was wrong when they asked him."[49] Interviewed by the website, the MIT professor said of Boehner's claim, "It's wrong in so many ways it's hard to begin."[50]

Yet facts would not stand in the way of a convincing message, and Republicans were determined to push the lie into the public consciousness. Nearly twenty GOP members of Congress cited this phony and misleading statistic in just two days.[51]

But it wasn't only members of Congress. Conservative media continued to parrot the lie. In June, during a segment on Fox News's *Fox & Friends,* as cohost Gretchen Carlson announced to the audience "the goal of the bill is to reduce emissions by 2020, but some say it's just another way to get more money from taxpayers without them realizing it," the falsehood was displayed at the bottom of the screen: "COLD TO THE CLIMATE BILL: SOME SAY COULD COST $3,100 PER HOUSEHOLD."[52]

The phony $3,100 figure remained part of the public discourse throughout the months-long debate over President Obama's climate bill, despite having been debunked and contradicted by numerous other studies by both think tanks and the federal government.

The climate legislation successfully passed in the House, but it fell short of the sixty-vote threshold in the Senate.[53] The birth of the Tea Party in 2009 and the raucous town hall meetings members of Congress faced when they returned to their districts for August recess had turned the tide against the president's policies. The Tea Party was almost uniformly convinced that climate change was a hoax, something they heard repeatedly echoed by Fox News and other conservative outlets.

In the years Congress failed to act, the president moved ahead with a different regulatory approach to reduce carbon emissions using the EPA's authority, sidestepping a failed legislative process.[54] This only increased the animus among those with a vested interest in stopping all climate legislation.

At moments like this, when political leaders decide to push landmark bills to address major challenges, Washington becomes a well-organized factory of deceit—an assembly line moving its product from think tanks to PR firms and lobbying shops into the hands of lawmakers and the media. In the case of the climate bill, all of the pieces came together to prevent President Obama from passing significant legislative change, even with his party controlling both chambers of Congress. The end of the fight over President Obama's climate bill did not mean the end of the lies.

The winter of 2009 marked a major milestone, with world leaders joining together in Copenhagen to negotiate a new climate treaty. As the meeting was about to begin it was revealed that email servers at the previously obscure University of East Anglia in the United Kingdom were hacked by a still unknown party. The hackers' target was thousands of pieces of email correspondence sent back and forth between climate scientists as they conducted their work. Excerpts posted on the blogs of climate change skeptics purported to show that the scientists, on whose work much of the theory of climate change had been based, had manipulated data to make the case that the Earth was warming and humans were the cause.[55] This was not true, but the emails provided a potent weapon for climate deniers.

The controversy was given the name "Climategate" by British writer James Delingpole.[56] "If you own any shares in alternative energy companies I should start dumping them NOW," he wrote in *The Telegraph*. "The conspiracy behind the Anthropogenic Global Warming myth ... has been suddenly, brutally and quite deliciously exposed after a hacker broke into the computers at the University of East Anglia's Climate Research Unit (aka CRU) and released 61 megabytes of confidential files onto the internet."[57]

According to a second *Telegraph* writer, Christopher Booker, a week after the story was published, the phrase "appear[ed] across the internet more than nine million times."[58]

Prominent climate denier and meteorologist Anthony Watts bragged on his blog that a little under a week after the term was coined, search results for "climategate" had surpassed "global warming" on Google.[59] Those skeptical of climate change viewed the scandal as definitive proof of their wildest fantasy—that scientists around the world had concocted a global warming hoax.

The impact was swift.

A study conducted by Yale University found that public belief in climate change between 2008 and 2010 dropped from 71 to 57 percent; concurrently, the percentage of Americans who believed global warming was not occurring doubled from 10 to 20 percent.[60]

A paper published in part based on this data summarized, "Climategate had a significant effect on public beliefs in global warming and trust in scientists," observing that "the loss of trust in scientists, however, was primarily among individuals with a strongly individualistic worldview or politically conservative ideology."[61]

This result was reflective of the coverage the controversy received from conservative news outlets, most notably Fox News. The network's Washington managing editor Bill Sammon ordered reporters to mention the controversy any time they discussed climate change. "Given the controversy over the veracity of climate change data," he wrote in a leaked email, "we should refrain from asserting that the planet has warmed (or cooled) in any given period without IMMEDIATELY pointing out that such theories are based upon data that critics have called into question."[62]

The entire "Climategate" controversy was a lie, perpetuated by groups with a vested interest in halting debate on the subject of climate change. This was not a random document dump. The first round of more than a thousand emails released by the hackers spanned a fourteen-year period from 1996 through 2009. The person or persons who illegally accessed these emails had clearly filtered and curated the released content to highlight specific portions in order to make their case in the media. The emails featured by climate deniers tended to be phrases taken out of context and presented in ways designed to obfuscate their meanings.[63]

One grossly manipulated and widely quoted example came from Kevin Trenberth, a doctor of science from MIT who works at the National Center for Atmospheric Research. As part of an email to a colleague in which he briefly summarizes a long piece of research, Dr. Trenberth wrote: "We can't account for the lack of warming at the moment, and it is a travesty that we can't."[64]

Many skeptics pointed to this email as evidence that even climate scientists "can't account for the lack of warming," and therefore warming did not exist. Glenn Beck presented the email in the following way on his show:

> What are these guys saying behind closed doors about their so-called bulletproof consensus? Well, Kevin Trenberth, he is a climatologist for the National Center for Atmospheric Research, he wrote, quote, "The fact is we can't account for lack of warming at the moment, and it's a travesty that we can't." Incorrect data? Inadequate systems? Yeah. Travesty, pretty good word for it.[65]

Washington Post columnist George Will claimed during a broadcast on ABC's *This Week with George Stephanopoulos* that "one of the emails said it is a travesty—his word—it is a travesty that we cannot explain the fact that global warming has stopped."[66] The email said nothing of the sort, but no matter—those few words were all the evidence skeptics needed to support their lie that global warming was not settled science. However, in context the emails reached a far different conclusion.

Following the leak of the emails, Trenberth explained that the "travesty" was that "we don't have an observing system adequate to track [global warming]." He went on to note "there are all other kinds of signs aside from global mean temperatures, including melting of Arctic sea ice and rising sea levels and a lot of other indicators, that global warming is continuing."[67]

Trenberth lamented, "The unfortunate thing about this is that people can cherry-pick and take things out of context."[68]

The email that created the most controversy related to the work of then–University of Virginia professor Michael Mann. Mann was famous for the development of the "Hockey Stick" graph that was prominently featured in Al Gore's Academy Award–winning documentary, *An Inconvenient Truth*. The graph was also included in the Intergovernmental Panel on Climate Change's 2001 report. This is perhaps one of the most important international documents used to make policy on a global scale. It elevated Mann's stature and made him a target for climate deniers.

The graph was a simple visual explanation of global temperature readings over the past two thousand years. What it showed was that the Earth's temperatures had been relatively consistent since the time of Jesus Christ until the twentieth century, when the planet experienced a significant increase in temperature coinciding with a drastically increased level of carbon in the atmosphere. The shape of the graph therefore closely resembled that of an ice hockey stick.[69]

Mann partnered with the University of East Anglia professor Philip Jones to gather the data for one thousand years of this estimate. Much of the elapsed time took place prior to the existence of thermometers or accurate ways to measure temperature on a global scale. To fill in this data, Mann used numerous sources, including tree rings and core samples taken from coral reefs and ancient ice deposits. This left much of the data open to interpretation and gave critics significant room to attack. One of the Climategate emails read, "I've just completed Mike's Nature trick of adding in the real temps to each series for the last 20 years (i.e. from 1981 onwards) and [*sic*] from 1961 for Keith's to hide the decline."[70]

By the time of the Climategate controversy, climate deniers were already frequently attacking Mann's research. In advance of a congressional hearing at which Mann was testifying in 2003, Senator James Inhofe questioned climate change and the conclusions of Mann's research, citing a "most comprehensive study [that] shivers the timbers of the adrift Chicken Little crowd."[71] Inhofe was referencing a study by Harvard astrophysicists Willie Soon and Sallie Baliunas, published in the journal *Climate Research,* which purported to demonstrate that the planet's warming over the last century was eclipsed by a period of warming in the Middle Ages. If this were the case, it would certainly reshape Mann's hockey stick and also cast doubt that CO_2 was the cause of climate change.

The press release announcing the publication of the paper boldly declared, "Soon and his colleagues concluded that the 20th century is neither the warmest century over the last 1,000 years, nor is it the most extreme."[72]

The political impact of Soon and Baliunas's paper was immediately clear. A report from the Bush administration on the environment used the study to deny the existence of climate change. "The recent paper of Soon-Baliunas contradicts a dogmatic view held by many in the climate science community that the past century was the warmest in the past millennium and signals human induced 'global warming,'" wrote Philip Cooney, chief of staff of the White House Council on Environmental Quality during the George W. Bush administration and a former lobbyist for the American Petroleum Institute.[73]

But Soon and Baliunas's work was fatally flawed. Dr. Hans von Storch, editor in chief of *Climate Research,* the journal that published the study, wrote that "the conclusions are not supported by the evidence presented in the paper."[74]

After heavy scientific criticism, the *Climate Research* publisher, Dr. Otto Kinne, acknowledged the journal erred in publishing the study. "I have not stood behind the paper by Soon and Baliunas," he wrote in an email to *The New York Times.* "Indeed: the reviewers failed to detect methodological flaws."[75]

It was also revealed that the aforementioned climate-denying George C. Marshall Institute paid both Soon and Baliunas.[76] Additionally, Soon had received nearly $1 million in grants from the American Petroleum Institute, Exxon Mobil, the Charles Koch Foundation, and the Texaco Foundation, casting further doubt on the motivation behind the study.[77]

Soon denied any impropriety. "I have never been motivated by financial reward in any of my scientific research," he told Reuters. "I would have accepted money from Greenpeace if they had offered it to do my research."[78]

Along with questions about his funding, Soon's scientific credentials to study climate science are also doubtful. As Naomi Oreskes said in an interview in 2015, "What kind of a scientist is he? He is an engineer. Astrophysics is not climate science."[79]

Having lost the principal scientific evidence they were using to cast doubt on climate change, it was no surprise that climate change skeptics leapt at what they believed was a smoking gun in the Climategate emails: the revelation that Michael Mann was being untruthful about the data behind the Hockey Stick graph. Climate scientists themselves wrote he was employing a "trick" to report temperature data. But what did "trick" mean?

In 2009, Bob Ward, policy and communications director of the Grantham Research Institute on Climate Change and the Environment at the London School of Economics, explained to *The Guardian*, "It does look incriminating on the surface, but there are lots of single sentences that taken out of context can appear incriminating. . . . You can't tell what they are talking about. Scientists say 'trick' not just to mean deception. They mean it as a clever way of doing something—a shortcut can be a trick."[80]

Nevertheless, a flurry of hatred followed. Mann was called a "fucking terrorist," "killer," and "one-world-government socialist."[81] These barbs are unfortunately now fairly typical for scientists whose work on climate change enters popular culture and attracts attacks from deniers.

Two public universities that receive grants from the federal government employed Mann and took seriously the allegations that one of their professors manipulated data in order to deceive the public. Investigations were launched by Mann's employer, Penn State University, and the Inspector General of the National Science Foundation. The IG's office "exonerated him . . . of suppressing or falsifying data, deleting e-mails and misusing privileged information" and found "no 'evidence of research misconduct.'"[82] Penn State University's investigation agreed and found there was "no substance to the allegation against Dr. Michael E. Mann."[83]

These exonerations did not halt attacks on Mann, in particular from those with a political motivation. Virginia attorney general Ken Cuccinelli attempted to investigate the professor, demanding his former employers at the University of Virginia hand over the contents of his email account. UVA took a stand against the clearly political nature of the attorney general's investigation and refused to comply, successfully fighting in court to block Cuccinelli's efforts.[84] At the time, he was planning a run for governor and attempting to establish a national platform primarily by appealing to far-right interest groups. Ultimately, he was unsuccessful, losing his gubernatorial bid to Democrat Terry McAuliffe.

In a 2010 *Washington Post* op-ed, Mann described the impact of this campaign of intimidation on future scientists. "The attacks against the science must stop. They are not good-faith questioning of scientific research. They are anti-science," he wrote. "How can I assure young researchers in climate science that if they make a breakthrough in our understanding about how human activity is altering our climate that they, too, will not be dragged through a show trial at a congressional hearing?"[85]

Even after Mann's exoneration, conservative think tanks, primarily those that received significant funding from the fossil fuel industry, continued to attack him. Not only did they refuse to disavow the inaccurate attacks against the scientist or the phony "Climategate" controversy, but they gloated about it. The Cato Institute, Washington, D.C.'s premier libertarian think tank, touted its role in the controversy in a report headlined "Cato's Pat Michaels at Center of 'Climategate' Controversy That Rocks Climate Change Establishment."

The report opened: "Cato senior fellow in environmental studies Patrick J. Michaels barely has time to sleep. With more than 150 media appearances since the breaking of what has come to be called 'Climategate,' he has quickly become the most recognized face decrying the obstructionism of global warming alarmists."[86]

The Competitive Enterprise Institute (CEI) published a post by scholar Rand Simberg comparing Mann to disgraced former Penn State football coach Jerry Sandusky, who had molested numerous children while employed by Penn State, claiming the university's investigation of the scientist was a "cover-up and whitewash."[87] Eventually, CEI removed the sentence comparing the scientist to a child molester, but the fact the comparison was written at all is a mark of the depths to which this group of people would go in order to smear climate scientists. Mann ultimately sued both CEI and the *National Review*, which had quoted Simberg's piece, for defamation. As of this writing, the suit remains pending.

Lost in all this controversy was the science itself. Other researchers have reconfirmed the validity of the theory behind the Hockey Stick graph time and time again. While there have been debates about specific data points, the overall theory that temperatures remained fairly constant on earth over 1,900 years and then suddenly spiked as humans began to dump carbon into the atmosphere is accepted as true, with near scientific certainty.

Live Science reported in 2013 that the journal *Nature Geoscience* published a paper "co-authored by 78 experts from 60 scientific institutions from around the world" finding "yet another hockey stick. Their temperature reconstruction shows a slow slide into a future ice age ending abruptly with a sharp rise in temperatures in the 19th and 20th centuries. Recent global surface temperatures are probably the warmest in the past 1,400 years."[88]

Yet those who have made it their mission to cast doubt on climate science have succeeded in freezing the political process. Turning a scientific debate into a political one made it nearly impossible for policy makers to take the steps necessary to mitigate the impact of a warming planet. Like the tobacco companies, for decades the fossil fuel industry has known their product is harmful. They also know combating climate change would likely force them to shift their business model. Instead the industry chooses delay and deceit over change, because as long as they can maintain the status quo, they can keep earning immense profits from the burning of fossil fuels.

The failure of the 2009 and 2010 climate change bills in Congress marked Lies, Incorporated's first successful campaign of the Obama administration. The White House strategically turned to focus on health care, recognizing that the likelihood of passing major legislation on both issues simultaneously was impossible.

On health care, they would also face another well-orchestrated campaign of lies. The techniques pioneered by the tobacco industry and perfected by climate deniers would in fact be used to challenge every portion of the Obama White House agenda.

Chapter 3

Lie Panel:
Health Care

You could spot Betsy McCaughey from across a room by her trademark binder containing Obama's health care law that always seemed to be in her arms. It accompanied her as she strolled onto the set of Jon Stewart's *Daily Show* in August of 2009, and it was with her at the Conservative Political Action Conference in 2012, more than three years after the health care bill was signed into law. As she walked through the busy convention center, the thick binder did not weigh her down. What began as a shtick became, over time, her most recognizable trait.

McCaughey initially used the binder in an attempt to support the claim that President Obama's health care bill, if signed into law, would result in the untimely deaths of disabled children and the elderly. Her evidence was loosely based on a previously uncontroversial bit of policy in the health care reform bill.

Palliative care has long been a challenging element of our health care system. Not only do the costs of treatment skyrocket in the final weeks and months of life, but often patients' wishes about how to end their lives are unknown to their loved ones or, in the worst cases, ignored, leaving those who are in the process of dying suffering needless physical and emotional pain.

To contend with these complicated issues, President Obama's health care reform proposal included provisions to fund counseling that would help seniors make choices about end-of-life care. The provision was supported by AARP along with other senior and medical organizations.[1]

But to Betsy McCaughey, these provisions provided the perfect opportunity to scare a confused public and a riled-up conservative base over a Democratic president's proposal to expand health care in the United States.

Fred Thompson, the former U.S. senator who also played a district attorney on the popular television crime drama *Law & Order,* had abandoned his failed 2008 presidential campaign to host a syndicated radio show. On July 16, 2009, his guest Betsy McCaughey claimed that, under Obamacare, "every five years, people in Medicare have a required counseling session that will tell them how to end their life sooner, how to decline nutrition, how to decline being hydrated, how to go into hospice care. And by the way, the bill expressly says that if you get sick somewhere in that five-year period—if you get a cancer diagnosis, for example— you have to go through that session again." She concluded this was "all to do what's in society's best interest or your family's best interest, and cut your life short."[2] This deceitful argument became one of the most well-known and oft-repeated attacks against Obamacare: death panels.

According to McCaughey, this provision, buried deep in Obamacare, would force seniors to end their lives sooner than they intended. She was lying and continued to lie about the provision for the duration of the health care debate. This was no surprise; McCaughey had been lying about health care legislation for decades.

Twenty years earlier, Bill Clinton had arrived in Washington promising change. He pledged to radically reform a health care system that many believed to be broken. To develop the policy, President Clinton appointed his wife, Hillary Rodham Clinton, to lead a health care task force. Before this advisory council even released a draft version of their bill, conservatives went on the attack. Their allies included not only the insurance and pharmaceutical industries, but also tobacco companies whose products— the source of expensive health problems affecting millions of Americans—would be subject to a new tax to pay for the law.[3]

An early line of attack came from McCaughey, then a fellow at the conservative Manhattan Institute who held a Ph.D. from Columbia University. In a February 1994 article published by Andrew Sullivan in *The New Republic* titled "No Exit," McCaughey excoriated the Clinton health care bill.

"If these facts surprise you, it's because you haven't been given a straight story about the Clinton health bill," she wrote.

McCaughey went on to claim, "Price controls on doctors' fees and regulations tying doctors' hands will curb the care physicians can give patients. Price controls on new drugs will keep people over 65 from getting the medications that can help them." Furthermore "government controls on medical education will limit what future doctors know, costing lives and suffering no one can calculate."[4]

McCaughey recited a litany of dire claims about the effects of the bill, concluding, "The Clinton bill will prevent people from buying the medical care they need. ... Price controls on premiums will push most Americans into HMOs and pressure HMOs into sharply cutting access to specialists and effective, high-tech cures."[5]

Newt Gingrich called the article "the first decisive break point"[6] in the campaign to defeat the Clinton health care bill.

What made the piece so powerful was that while McCaughey was a fellow at a conservative think tank, it appeared in what was widely regarded as a "liberal" publication. Published today, "No Exit" would be pilloried—not just by watchdogs like Media Matters, but by an entire online ecosystem devoted to fact-checking and critiquing journalistic malpractice in real time. At the time, however, no such system existed, and McCaughey's argument was free to take on a life of its own.

In addition to Gingrich's praise for the article, numerous leading conservatives made it the cornerstone of their efforts to defeat the Clinton health care plan. Senate Republican Leader Bob Dole, in his response to President Clinton's 1994 State of the Union address, took his talking points from Betsy McCaughey's *New Republic* article: "More cost. Less choice. More taxes. Less quality. More government control. Less control for you and your family. That's what the president's government-run plan is likely to give you."[7]

Project for the Republican Future, Bill Kristol's effort to guide the Republican Party, issued a strategy memo with guidelines to defeat the bill and used language echoing McCaughey's fear tactics.[8] Conservative columnists around the country used her words as talking points for their ferocious takedowns of "Hillarycare."

The White House attempted to fight back against McCaughey, preparing a fact check of her piece, but none of their efforts had much impact. *New Republic* editor Andrew Sullivan chose not to run the White House's reply, instead turning to McCaughey, allowing her to publish a second piece attacking the White House and the health care plan.[9]

Nearly two decades after the article was written, James Fallows of *The Atlantic* called it the "most destructive effect on public discourse by a single person" in the 1990s. He named Dick Cheney the most destructive person of the 2000s.[10] Back in 1995, in an age before the instant fact-checking of the Internet had blossomed into maturity, Fallows debunked "No Exit" in *The Atlantic*—but not until long after Hillarycare was declared dead. The piece, titled "A Triumph of Misinformation," took McCaughey and *The New Republic* to task. Fallows wrote, "I was less impressed with her scholarly precision after I compared her article with the text of the Clinton bill." He continued, "Her shocked claim that coverage would be available only for 'necessary' and 'appropriate' treatment suggested that she had not looked at any of today's insurance policies. In claiming that the bill would make it impossible to go outside the health plan or pay doctors on one's own, she had apparently skipped past practically the first provision of the bill (Sec. 1003), which said, 'Nothing in this Act shall be construed as prohibiting the following: (1) An individual from purchasing any health care services.'"[11]

In 2006, thirteen years after the publication of "No Exit," Franklin Foer, the editor of *The New Republic,* apologized for the article. "Over the last 25 years, liberalism has lost both its good name and its sway over politics. But it is liberalism's loss of imagination that is most disheartening," he wrote. "Since President Clinton's health care plan unraveled in 1994—a debacle that this magazine, regrettably, abetted—liberals have grown chastened and confused, afraid to think big ideas."[12] A limited apology to be sure, but at a minimum an acknowledgment of the damage that Betsy McCaughey's article did to the health care debate in 1994.

As it turns out, McCaughey was receiving guidance from some of the most insidious and self-serving opponents of the health care plan: the tobacco companies. One document unearthed from the tobacco archive and made public as part of the industry's settlement with the federal government suggests that McCaughey was acting in concert with the industry when she wrote "No Exit." A memo written for tobacco executives[13] laid out a media plan for a coordinated conservative attack on the Clinton health care reform bill.

It contained a list of conservative organizations and activists and the actions they were taking on behalf of big tobacco: the American Enterprise Institute would develop "a series of monographs examining various aspects of the Clinton Plan, and how other alternatives would provide a preferable health care system for the American people."[14]

Grover Norquist's Americans for Tax Reform (ATR), described in the memo as "a staunch ally of [Philip Morris] for a number of years in many tax battles," had a role in defeating the Clinton health reform plan; according to the memo: "ATR has sponsored print ads against the use of excise taxes to fund health care as well as [video news releases] on the subject, most recently one detailing the impacts of prohibitive cigarette excises in Canada on the economy and on crime which had a profound influence on the eventual decision to rollback the tax."[15]

Groups as far ranging as the Business Roundtable, the Cato Institute, the Chamber of Commerce, Citizens for a Sound Economy (the Koch brothers' front organization that would eventually split into FreedomWorks and Americans for Prosperity), the Heartland Institute, the Heritage Foundation, and the National Association of Manufacturers each played a role in the fight.

In the seven-page memo, the potential work of the organizations is mostly abstract and clearly under construction. However, in the paragraph on the work of the conservative Manhattan Institute, it describes the project in a very concrete way: "Worked off-the-record with Manhattan [Institute fellow] and writer Betsy McCaughey as part of the input to the three-part expose in *The New Republic* on what the Clinton plan means to [the American people]."[16]

The tobacco industry claimed McCaughey as an ally, yet she

had been sold to the public by *The New Republic* as "a scrupulous, impartial, independent scholar who, after leafing through the endless pages of the Clinton health proposals, had been shocked by what she found," according to James Fallows of *The Atlantic*.[17]

Clearly, McCaughey possessed neither impartiality nor independence. When the documents tying her to Philip Morris surfaced in 2009, Manhattan Institute president Lawrence Mone aggressively responded, stating the premise that McCaughey was in bed with the tobacco industry was "false." He continued, "Betsy McCaughey wrote two articles for the *Wall Street Journal* on the Clinton Health Care plan and an additional article for the *New Republic* which was solicited by its publisher. At no time were her ideas influenced or controlled by anyone but the author herself."[18]

McCaughey's first fall from grace came just as meteorically as her rise. In 1994, she joined George Pataki, a New York Republican challenging incumbent governor Mario Cuomo, as his lieutenant governor. She was initially viewed as an incredible asset to his campaign. McCaughey loved data and charts but was also an engaging speaker.[19]

Soon after the election, her relationship with Pataki fell apart. A 2009 profile in *The New Republic* recalled that staffers in the governor's office called McCaughey "a disloyal, self-promoting, 'unstable,' 'paranoid' 'ditz,'" and Zenia Mucha, a Pataki spokesperson, pondered, "How do you describe someone who is too bizarre to describe?"[20]

The governor even pulled his lieutenant's security detail "following allegations that she had been using her troopers as errand boys." *The New Republic* also reported, "The state GOP chairman publicly attacked her; she got into a radio smack down with the state parks commissioner; and, for a time, party leaders refused to make her a delegate to the 1996 Republican National Convention."[21]

After Pataki dropped her from his reelection ticket, she switched parties and became a Democrat to run against her boss—refusing to resign while doing so. After an unsuccessful end to her scandal-plagued campaign, which provided months of tabloid fodder, McCaughey slipped back into oblivion, connecting with conservative think tanks and running an organization dedicated to reducing the rate of life-threatening medical errors in hospitals.[22]

This fall must have been particularly painful for the onetime rising star in GOP circles. One former staffer of McCaughey's from her time as lieutenant governor said, "A lot of politicians are out for the limelight, but Betsy's constant need twenty-four hours a day was something I'd never seen."[23]

Throughout the Bush administration, she maintained a low public profile, but the election of Barack Obama and his goal of bringing health care to uninsured Americans brought McCaughey back into the public view. The question is, why would the media again trust someone with such a tarnished reputation?

By 2009, Betsy McCaughey was a known liar. Her crude distortions of the Clinton health care plan and her behavior during the Pataki administration should have disqualified her from being granted a platform in the media. Even though some disputed its impact, no one—other than blind partisans—claimed McCaughey's work against the Clinton health care plan fifteen years earlier had been honest. Yet here she was, despite her penchant for being less than truthful, accepted again as a media star and a trusted commentator on health care issues, not only by the conservative media but by nonideological sources as well.

Ezra Klein of *The Washington Post* offered a succinct description of why a known liar like McCaughey was welcomed back into the media fold like a long-lost relative: she was useful. "She's useful to the *New York Post* and Fox News and Sarah Palin. . . . McCaughey isn't just a liar. She's an *exciting* liar." McCaughey doesn't simply tell phlegmatic lies about specific public policy. She instead specializes in "the big lie" designed to spark a visceral reaction.[24]

As in 1994, McCaughey's 2009 arguments gave conservatives a talking point aligned with what they believed was the hidden intent of Obamacare. She was quotable and exciting, making her a welcome guest on Fox News and across the conservative radio spectrum.

Unlike 1994, this time a network existed to debunk McCaughey's lies from the start, including: nonprofits like Media Matters and ThinkProgress; journalists such as Ezra Klein; and nonpartisan entities like FactCheck.org and PolitiFact. She became a useful bogeyman for MSNBC and other liberal outlets, garnering outrage from viewers and becoming a symbol of everything wrong with the conservative debate over health care.

As attention grabbing as the circus was for the left and the right, none of this was beneficial in terms of the public conversation around health care reform. Instead of discussing how to help the millions of uninsured or debating the merit or feasibility of different proposed solutions, endless months were devoted to an irrelevant debate over whether Barack Obama secretly wanted to kill grandmothers. Members of Congress were begging for a response—their constituents were calling in droves, fearful of death panels. Mainstream reporters, who lacked understanding of health care policy, were excited about the ratings potential of this manufactured drama, or were unwilling to truthfully confront the issue, flooded the White House and pro–health care policy groups with questions.

McCaughey had located the piece on the policy Jenga tower that she thought would cause the entire puzzle to collapse. By loudly and unapologetically lying to a friendly audience of partisans in the media, at think tanks, on Capitol Hill, and to the public at large, she could throw health care reform into chaos. Her "policy points" were perfectly designed for a pundit culture that debated facts in television segments that were too short to adequately discuss the complexities of the issues—and her binder supported her claims of disastrous provisions "hidden" in the legislation.

A week after McCaughey's 2009 appearance on Fred Thompson's radio show, she wrote a column in the *New York Post* expounding on her lie. Not only would President Obama's health care bill put your life and death decisions in the hands of government bureaucrats, but the public should also fear those the president would entrust to make that choice. "The health bills coming out of Congress would put the decisions about your care in the hands of presidential appointees," McCaughey wrote. "They'd decide what plans cover, how much leeway your doctor will have and what seniors get under Medicare."[25]

Her column did not go unnoticed. Then-representative Michele Bachmann (R-MN), a leader of the Tea Party in Congress and herself a fountain of conservative misinformation, took to the floor of the House of Representatives and cited from McCaughey's column: "We need to know what the people who advise the President of the United States think and believe about health care reform, Mr. Speaker," said the Minnesota representative. "Listening to the president's adviser's actual words I believe is very enlightening. This morning I read a column written by Betsy McCaughey, and I would like to quote from it extensively now."[26]

By the time her *New York Post* column was published and Bachmann gave her floor speech, McCaughey's very premise had already been debunked. In the days between her appearance on Fred Thompson's radio show and the *Post* column, the nonpartisan website PolitiFact issued its judgment on the right-wing canard: "McCaughey isn't just wrong, she's spreading a ridiculous falsehood." They rated her lie "pants on fire."[27]

Sarah Palin, by then the former governor of Alaska, heard Bachmann's floor speech and amplified McCaughey's lie. In an August 7 Facebook post titled "Statement on the Current Health Care Debate," she cited Bachmann's floor speech.

"And who will suffer the most when they ration care?" Palin rhetorically asked. "The sick, the elderly, and the disabled, of course. The America I know and love is not one in which my parents or my baby with Down Syndrome will have to *stand in front of Obama's 'death panel'* [emphasis added] so his bureaucrats can decide, based on a subjective judgment of their 'level of productivity in society,' whether they are worthy of health care. Such a system is downright evil."[28] In that post, the "death panel" meme was born.

Palin had struck an emotional chord that would be repeated as a key talking point as the right fought against Obamacare. At nearly every rally and town hall meeting that followed, participants waved signs demanding Congress not kill their grandmas or disabled children. The imagery of a panel deciding the life or death of individuals was too graphic, too scary, and all too real in the minds of conservatives. In a repeat of the 1990s health care debate, McCaughey had once again created a set of "facts" that would give the right a singular talking point to latch on to.

Palin's statement went viral, spreading through the media. The following Monday, Brian Kilmeade, host of Fox News's morning show *Fox & Friends,* asked, "Are seniors going to be in front of the death panel?" Answering his own question, he stated, "And then just as you think, 'Okay, that's ridiculous,' then you realize there's provisions in there that seniors in the last lap of their life will be sitting there going to a panel possibly discussing what the best thing for them is."[29]

The meme continued to spread through the Fox ecosystem. Hosts from around the network repeated the claim, without any regard for the facts or questioning whether this outrageous assertion was true.

It was not simply the network's "opinion hosts" reporting the death panel falsehood. "Former Republican vice presidential nominee Sarah Palin says President Obama is misleading the public about what she has called 'death panels' in health care reform," said Fox News anchor Bret Baier. "Palin contends advanced-care planning consultations, which are an element in the House reform legislation, would not be voluntary as the President says."[30]

Fact-checkers and the mainstream media repeatedly debunked the death panel claim in an attempt to remove it from the conversation. Forty news organizations, including the Associated Press, issued fact checks of Palin, showing she was wrong. But by then it was too late. According to conservatives, the outlets declaring death panels a myth were simply part of the liberal media attempting to shut down an effective argument against Obamacare.

Death panels resurrected the public profile of Betsy McCaughey, who once again rose to prominence. Even progressive venues felt the need to host her on their shows. So this once-disgraced public policy prevaricator hauled one of her thick binders filled with the pages of the Affordable Care Act out onto the stage during an appearance on *The Daily Show*, where she attempted to convince Jon Stewart that death panels did in fact exist. The appearance highlighted McCaughey's inability to admit error, even when confronted directly with contradictory evidence. Stewart read the section of the law word for word, noting there was no language creating mandatory death panels for grandparents and disabled children. McCaughey tried to claim that if families changed their minds about a living will, they would be "penalized."

Stewart retorted, "It would be really wrong if that was in any way what this said."[31]

McCaughey softened some of her more aggressive rhetoric in a conversation with CNN health care reporter Elizabeth Cohen. "I had a PDF of the bill up on my computer. I said, 'Show me where in the bill it says that this bill is going to have the government telling your doctor what to do,'" wrote Cohen. "And [McCaughey] directed me to language—it didn't actually say that. But she said that it was vague enough that it would allow for that to happen in the future."[32]

AARP minced no words in response to these lies. "Betsy McCaughey's recent commentary on health care reform in various media outlets is rife with gross—and even cruel—distortions," said AARP's New York State director Lois Aronstein.[33]

Nevertheless, by the end of the summer, a substantial portion of the public believed Betsy McCaughey's lies. CNN conducted a poll in September 2009 that found 41 percent of the public was now certain that Obamacare included death panels.[34]

Making matters even worse, once it became the overwhelming focus of conservative attacks and, thus, the focus of every debate over the legislation at large, the end-of-life counseling provision was stripped out of the bill. In the minds of political staff at the White House it was a necessary sacrifice to preserve the rest of the bill.

McCaughey's talent, displayed both during the Clinton years and during the death panel debate, was her unique ability to invent falsehoods that create an emotional resonance for those already ideologically aligned against progressive reform of the health care system. The specter of "death panels" probably convinced very few Americans who were on the fence to oppose Obamacare. Instead, they created a rallying cry around which conservatives could focus their emotional energy, raising the volume of debate so loud that it crowded out the country's ability to engage in a constructive conversation on health care.

David Frum pointed out the impact of McCaughey's lie, writing on his blog, "Conservative talkers on Fox and talk radio had whipped the Republican voting base into such a frenzy that dealmaking was rendered impossible."[35] Frum also wrote that he believed Republicans would suffer electorally in the future due to their failure to stop health care reform, a strategy based at least partly on a giant lie.[36]

Frum's analysis of the goal of McCaughey and other professional political liars was spot-on. They do not want to further debate between two opposing political philosophies, but instead to shut down conversation. This is at the core of Lies, Incorporated's strategies. A true debate over health care reform, unencumbered by the idea that progressives were plotting through legislation to kill the disabled and the elderly, could result in not only reform but the ability of the president to tout it as a bipartisan victory. While McCaughey ultimately did not succeed, as she did in the 1990s, in killing Barack Obama's health care reform bill, she certainly shifted the debate in ways that were fundamentally unhealthy to the country.

The death panel lie helped to rile up the conservative base in such a way that it became impossible for Democrats and Republicans to reach any sort of compromise on health care reform. It confirmed for conservatives their worst fears about Barack Obama and what his presidency would mean for their lives, leaving no space for a public discussion on how to fix America's health care system.

As for Betsy McCaughey's motivation? For the first time since the 1990s, she was once again a relevant figure, welcome on Fox News and right-wing radio and a hero at conservative conferences around the country.

In the next chapter we will see another methodology Lies,

Chapter 4

Growth in a Time of Lies:
Debt

Ⅰt was a basic graduate school assignment.

In 2012, Professor Michael Ash, a labor economist who worked with the Council of Economic Advisers during the Clinton administration, asked students in a graduate class at the University of Massachusetts to choose a widely known economics paper and replicate the results.

Doctoral student Thomas Herndon chose "Growth in a Time of Debt," a highly influential paper by economists Carmen Reinhart and Kenneth Rogoff. The study seemed fairly straightforward. Reinhart and Rogoff examined the correlation between the deficits of various countries and their growth rates. They then established that when debt eclipsed 90 percent of the gross domestic product, GDP growth was cut in half. "Our main findings," they wrote, "are: First, the relationship between government debt and real GDP growth is weak for debt/GDP ratios below a threshold of 90 percent of GDP. Above 90 percent, median growth rates fall by one percent, and average growth falls considerably more."[1]

The paper was published in *The American Economic Review* in a 2010 edition of the journal that was not subjected to peer review, and became central to the worldwide debate over the importance of reducing public debt. To deficit hawks, the study, widely referred to as "Reinhart-Rogoff," was a critical piece of evidence for an idea they had been postulating for a long time: that countries that fell too deep into a fiscal hole were harming their economies, impeding growth due to higher interest rates and the expenditures necessary to service their debts.[2]

Progressive economists, who during a time of recession favored increased deficits to stimulate the economy, claimed Reinhart-Rogoff only showed a correlation, not a causality, between these two statistics.[3] Normally, debates like this are confined to academic journals and conferences while being largely ignored by wider audiences in the media.

But Reinhart-Rogoff was different. In the aftermath of the financial crisis and the massive stimulus effort used to prop up banks and the economy, a public debate had been raging. On one side were policy makers who did not want to cut spending, and in fact desired more short-term stimulus to boost an already shaky job market. On the other side were those who believed the government needed to cut both public spending and reduce budget deficits. The latter group, deficit hawks, argued that the short-term pain produced by fiscal austerity, in the form of increased unemployment, was simply the medicine our economy needed to avoid long-term calamity. Reinhart-Rogoff was the ironclad proof demonstrating the harm that could befall the economy if action was not quickly taken to curb the deficit.

In 2010, as "Growth in a Time of Debt" rose to prominence, the U.S. political environment was being shaped by the rise of the Tea Party. Formed around the notion that Americans were "Taxed Enough Already," the group not only argued for a lower tax burden but also for a smaller government (an exemption made for the military) and a sharp cut in the deficit.[4] Many adherents to Tea Party ideology firmly believed that Republicans, swept into office in 2010, should accept nothing less than a budget completely in balance. "Growth in a Time of Debt" gave them new ammunition.

Reinhart and Rogoff's paper appeared just as Greece's financial crisis first became a major international story. Here was a European country on the brink of collapse because of unsustainable government spending and deficits. Of course, such arguments usually ignored the particular challenges faced by Greece: as a member of the eurozone, it could not control its own currency, putting it at the mercy of Germany and other European powers that were unwilling or faced strong political disincentives to bail them out.[5]

A run-up in the U.S. debt at the end of the Bush and beginning of the Obama administration was caused by two contributing factors: (1) the shrinkage in GDP caused by the recession and (2) increased government debt due to both lower tax revenues and extra spending designed to boost the economy and shore up struggling American families.

House Budget Committee chairman Paul Ryan relied on Reinhart-Rogoff in his Fiscal Year 2013 budget plan, proposed a few months before the 2012 presidential election. In a section titled "The Consequences of Inaction," he claimed, "The economic effects of a debt crisis on the United States would be far worse than what the nation experienced during the financial crisis of 2008."[6]

Ryan then proceeded to cite Reinhart-Rogoff's "commonsense conclusion" to claim reducing the debt would be more beneficial to the economy than continued stimulus spending.[7]

Ryan was not alone. A myriad of politicians and media figures

cited the Reinhart-Rogoff study, including Representative Dave
Camp (R-MI), who chaired the powerful Ways and Means Committee, along with influential Republican senators such as Rob
Portman of Ohio, who served as director of the office of management and budget under President George W. Bush, and South
Dakota's John Thune. The 90 percent figure quickly morphed
from an economic theory proposed by two prominent economists in a paper into economic "law."

Republicans were not the only public officials singing Reinhart-
Rogoff's praises. "It's an excellent study, although in some ways
what you've summarized understates the risks,"[8] said former
Obama administration treasury secretary Tim Geithner.

Oklahoma senator Tom Coburn (R) described a bipartisan
briefing, with no media present, given by the two economists. In
this room, Rogoff had advocated for immediate action to cut the
deficit, telling the assembled senators, "Not acting moves the risk
[of an economic collapse caused by a deficit crisis] closer." Democratic senator Kent Conrad then sternly echoed the study's results,
warning of the dangers of crossing the 90 percent threshold.[9]

Members of the press eagerly covered Reinhart and Rogoff's
work. A search of Nexis reveals their findings were cited thousands of times across the media. *The New York Times* called it "a
study that set the tone for austerity."[10] And Matt Yglesias, then at
Slate, called "Growth in a Time of Debt" "literally the most influential article cited in public and policy debates about the importance of debt stabilization."[11]

Political commentators from MSNBC's Joe Scarborough to
those writing for the *Washington Post* op-ed page also touted the
study. Coverage became so ubiquitous that when appearing on
Bloomberg TV conservative economic historian Niall Ferguson
even called the paper a "law of finance."[12] This call for austerity budgets in the United States was reflected in Europe as well,

where Reinhart-Rogoff was touted as evidence by influential deficit scolds.

"Growth in a Time of Debt" was not simply a theoretical academic paper. Its consequences were real and felt by people all around the world in the form of higher unemployment rates in countries whose policy makers used the study as a justification for the necessity of austerity measures.

At the moment the study was published, the world was reeling from the effects of the financial crisis. Unemployment in the United States, while falling, was still perilously high. In the past this would have evoked a Keynesian response from policy makers on both sides of the aisle—a joint effort to use government expenditures as a tool for boosting a sputtering economy. Those touting the recommendations of Reinhart and Rogoff were advocating for the opposite: clamping down on government expenditures as a way of reducing the deficit.

Liberal economist Dean Baker of the Center for Economic and Policy Research explained the impact of the Reinhart-Rogoff study, writing that "in Europe, R&R's work and its derivatives have been used to justify austerity policies that have pushed the unemployment rate over 10 percent for the euro zone as a whole and above 20 percent in Greece and Spain."[13]

In the United States, the impact of these government rollbacks could be seen in the run up to the 2012 election. Even as the private sector recovered and new jobs created surged past the one million mark, hundreds of thousands of government positions at the federal, state, and local levels had disappeared. This not only impacted those left unemployed but also reverberated throughout the economy. Austerity at the federal level, encouraged by Reinhart-Rogoff, was holding back economic recovery.

Two years after Reinhart-Rogoff had taken the world by storm, graduate student Thomas Herndon set out to complete his class assignment and replicate the findings of Reinhart and Rogoff's study. It should have been an easy task. The two economists had created a spreadsheet containing countries' debt-to-GDP ratios and the GDP. All of this data was, and is, in the public domain.

Nevertheless, Herndon was repeatedly frustrated by the assignment. He assembled his data set from publicly available sources but could not get his spreadsheet to match the conclusions presented by the economists. Herndon's initial assumption was that it was he who had made the error. These were well-regarded economics professors whose work had been cited thousands of times. Their paper was guiding global economic policy, and people at the highest levels of the most powerful governments in the world looked to them for advice. Herndon was an unheralded graduate student who had yet to complete his coursework.

Even his professors doubted his efforts. "I remember I had a meeting with my professor, Michael Ash, where he basically said, 'Come on, Tom, this isn't too hard—you just gotta go sort this out,'"[14] Herndon recalled.

Finally, he reached out to Reinhart and Rogoff and asked for a copy of the spreadsheets they had based their work on so he could complete his assignment. The professors wrote back, supplying him with the data. With the numbers now in hand, Herndon set out to discover where he had made an error when compiling the data, and to his shock, he found several extremely significant problems with Reinhart and Rogoff's work.

In a paper published in the *Cambridge Journal of Economics* with his professors Michael Ash and Robert Pollin, Herndon explained, "While using RR's working spreadsheet, we identified coding errors, selective exclusion of available data, and unconventional weighting of summary statistics."[15]

What Herndon found was that Reinhart and Rogoff had excluded data from certain countries following World War II, those whose debt had risen above 90 percent but still experienced periods of strong economic growth. The pair also had weighted the data in a way in which a single year of economic malaise in New Zealand in a period of high debt above the 90 percent threshold counted equally to a nineteen-year high-debt period of prosperity in England. Additionally an error on their spreadsheet caused them to omit data from Denmark, Canada, Belgium, Austria, and Australia.

Ash, Pollin, and Herndon recalculated Reinhart and Rogoff's results using their newly corrected equation. Rebuilt with the new data, it presented a sharply different picture. Former White House economist Jared Bernstein, now a fellow at the Center on Budget and Policy Priorities, prepared a chart showing how these changes affected Reinhart and Rogoff's work.[16]

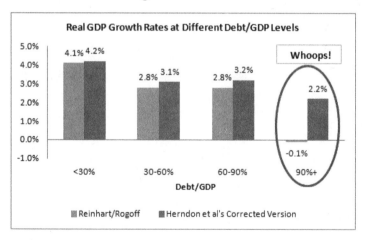

The data clearly demonstrates a significant difference. While many economists believe high levels of debt can constrain GDP, a debt-to-GDP ratio above 90 percent was simply not the catastrophe Reinhart and Rogoff described. While growth would drop to 2.2 percent, it certainly did not turn negative.

With the core of their research called into question, Reinhart and Rogoff responded in *The New York Times*. First, they acknowledged the error in their spreadsheet calculations "full stop," but went on to defend the overarching findings of their research. On other points, they strenuously objected to the UMass team's findings, in particular that they had "selectively omitted" data from New Zealand that caused their findings to skew toward their conclusion. They made the case that the data from New Zealand had only recently been tabulated, and it had not been "vetted" for accuracy. They also defended their weighting system that created a huge imbalance in the paper as "perfectly natural to us, and hardly unconventional."[17]

Reinhart and Rogoff, while acknowledging the spreadsheet mistake, refused to concede that the flaws in their results were significant and engaged in a very public battle with their critics, most notably Paul Krugman, whom they accused of "spectacularly uncivil behavior."[18]

Paul Krugman wrote a complete takedown of Reinhart-Rogoff in *The New York Review of Books,* noting that regardless of one's opinion about the impact of deficits in this study, reality—the actual results of the 2009 stimulus—had trumped these conclusions.

Krugman points out that the United States, Britain, and Japan were experiencing "large deficits and rapidly rising debt" while "their borrowing costs remained very low." Citing Belgian economist Paul De Grauwe, the Nobel Prize–winning economist noted that "the crucial difference ... seemed to be whether countries had their own currencies, and borrowed in those currencies." These nations "can't run out of money because they can print it if needed, and absent the risk of a cash squeeze, advanced nations are evidently able to carry quite high levels of debt without crisis.

"Three years after the turn to austerity, then, both the hopes and the fears of the austerians appear to have been misplaced." Krugman continues, "Austerity did not lead to a surge in confidence; deficits did not lead to crisis."[19]

Other economists began to review the work of Reinhart and Rogoff, developing their own critiques of the economic duo. Miles Kimball, an economist at the University of Michigan, and Yichuan Wang, his undergraduate student, re-crunched the numbers and determined they "could not find even a shred of evidence in the Reinhart and Rogoff data for a negative effect of government debt on growth." They concluded, "We find no persuasive evidence from Reinhart and Rogoff's data set to worry about anything but the higher future taxes or lower future spending needed to pay for that long-term debt.... Done carefully, debt is not damning. Debt is just debt."[20]

The impact of Reinhart-Rogoff on fiscal policy and media cannot be overstated. Bloomberg Business referred to the study as "the Excel error that changed history."[21] What is most appalling about this episode is that a study became accepted fact without any real academic vetting, only to be debunked by a graduate student.

When examining the issue of deficits and the reception of the Reinhart-Rogoff study, the question arises: Why, if the facts were so one-sided, if reality did not comport with the basic conclusions in the study, did this piece of economic misinformation infect the political process at such a staggering level? The answer lies in the coordinated effort to cut the debt and its principal benefactor, Peter Peterson. He supported not only the work of Reinhart and Rogoff but an entire movement focused on putting deficit reduction above all other policy goals.

Peter Peterson is one of the wealthiest men in America. He

made the bulk of his fortune as founder and eventual chairman of the private equity firm the Blackstone Group, from which he collected $1.9 billion when it went public in 2007. His father immigrated to America from Greece, speaking no English, and opened a diner in Nebraska. Peterson rose to prominence in the business world as CEO of Bell and Howell, a company that manufactured equipment for the film industry. In 1971, he entered politics, joining the Nixon administration as Assistant to the President for International Economic Affairs and executive director of the Council for International Economic Policy. The next year, Peterson was appointed secretary of commerce.

After leaving government, he became CEO of Lehman Brothers until he was forced out in the mid-1980s and went to make his fortune in private equity. For forty years he has maintained a singular focus on reducing the national debt and has spent a large part of his fortune, more than $500 million, to make that a reality. His primary financing vehicle to fund these efforts is a foundation that bears his name.

In a 2009 *Newsweek* column, Peterson explained the philosophy behind his largesse. "For years, I have been saying that the American government, and America itself, has to change its spending and borrowing policies: the tens of trillions of dollars in unfunded entitlements and promises, the dangerous dependence on foreign capital, our pitiful level of savings, the metastasizing health-care costs, our energy gluttony," wrote Peterson. "These structural deficits are unsustainable."[22]

This was a long journey for Peterson, one that began when he was buying a vacation home in the Hamptons in the early 1980s. The seller ran the Women's Economic Round Table. She said she would agree to his offer if he gave a speech to the organization on Ronald Reagan's budget. Peterson agreed, and in the course of researching for that speech he was "astonished" by what he found on government spending, in particular the dollars spent on programs such as Medicare and Social Security.[23]

Years ahead of his time—this was well before the national debt ballooned under Ronald Reagan—Peterson began to wave a flag of concern, in particular about the future of entitlement programs. "The Social Security system has become a high-risk gamble on economic progress and population growth—a bet by today's workers that their children and grandchildren will be rich and numerous enough to foot the bill for another round of generous retirement benefits," Peterson wrote in *The New York Review of Books* in 1982. "Should this hope go even mildly awry, today's workers will retire into a Social Security system running deficits larger than the total benefits it pays out today."[24]

Ultimately, Social Security was patched in the 1980s, thanks to the work of Ronald Reagan, House Speaker Tip O'Neill, and the Greenspan Commission, which developed a compromise to deal with this impending crisis.[25] For Peterson, though, the alarm bells never stopped sounding.

While deficit reduction is popular in theory, there is a limited constituency for the reforms necessary to make it possible. These reforms include tax increases and discretionary budget cuts, including defense and entitlement adjustments. Deficit-reduction efforts of the past decade have focused on slaying the sacred cows of both political parties. Democrats would be forced to accept cuts to Social Security and other cornerstones of the social safety net, while Republicans would need to compromise on increasing tax revenue. President Obama, in fact, was willing to propose this "grand bargain," but it was ultimately rejected by House Republicans. Many House Democrats would likely break from the president, not wanting to be on the record for both tax increases and safety-net cuts, leaving Republicans holding the bag for these unpopular votes. Even if then–house speaker John Boehner were willing to take such a step, it is unlikely that the rank-and-file members of his party would have been willing to march over that cliff with him.

Bill Clinton was able to champion deficit reduction, but it was achieved in a moment of high economic growth, with the stock market booming and the labor market at capacity, while inflation remained low. This economic tsunami of good fortune created an environment in which tax revenues increased, lowering the federal deficit.

Peter Peterson believes we are in a perpetual state of crisis with the deficit. Consequently, there is never a bad time to make cuts—even when that means starving an ailing economy during a famine. In fact, he saw the apex of the economic crisis that swept the globe as an opportunity, launching a foundation in 2008 as the start of a vigorous effort to lead a crusade against debt.[26]

In 2010, legislation was proposed to form a fiscal commission. While the bill failed in the Senate, President Obama proceeded to appoint the eighteen-member group without a legislative mandate in order to counter charges of fiscal irresponsibility in the run-up to the 2010 midterm elections. Both Senate Majority Leader Harry Reid and Speaker of the House Nancy Pelosi agreed to bring the commission's final product to the floor of their respective chambers.

The Simpson-Bowles commission began its work in April, with a deadline to report its results on December 1. The commission was doomed to fail from the start: the final report would require a supermajority of the commission for passage, which seemed impossible considering the bipartisan makeup of the body. This would require the agreement of labor leaders such as SEIU president Andy Stern, progressive members of Congress such as Jan Schakowsky, and conservatives such as Paul Ryan and Tom Coburn. Both progressives and conservatives put pressure on members of the body not to compromise their core values with the other side.

The chairmen of the commission, former Wyoming senator Alan Simpson and former Clinton White House chief of staff Erskine Bowles, released a draft proposal in November that failed to receive the requisite number of votes necessary for passage. Their document called for $4 trillion in deficit reduction through a combination of cuts to Social Security, some spending cuts, and changes to the tax code.

For conservatives, a single dollar of tax increases was too much. For the progressives on the commission, the plan to cut Social Security was unacceptable: it would employ a chained consumer price index, a new way of calculating cost-of-living increases not only for Social Security but also for veterans' benefits, which would invariably reduce vital payments to beneficiaries. The proposal would also raise the retirement age, which many pointed out amounted to an across-the-board benefit cut adversely affecting poorer workers, who tend to have careers in more physical environments. This makes later retirement a biological impossibility. The proposal was also unfair to certain minority populations who have shorter life spans on average than other Americans.

However, the failure of the commission to find a compromise inspired a new effort. Simpson and Bowles, with the financial backing of Peter Peterson, launched the Campaign to Fix the Debt, and began actively advocating for their doomed proposal.[27]

Peterson's obsession with debt represents a clear demonstration of how a single individual with a cause, a billion dollars, and smart strategy can manipulate the public policy process. By making strategic financial contributions to academics, think tank officials, and others, Peterson positioned his issue at the center of the Washington, D.C., political universe. In a town shaped by partisan warfare, one of the keys to his success is that he rises above the fray by contributing to both left- and right-wing think tanks focused on issues of fiscal responsibility. His annual fiscal summit, launched in 2010, brings together a who's who of bipartisan leaders from Bill Clinton to Chris Christie to Nancy Pelosi to Paul Ryan. This creates the perception that his positions carry broader public support than they do in reality.[28]

Beyond his annual conference and Fix the Debt, Peterson funds a network of nonprofits and political organizations, many with the same goal in mind—cutting back the size of the federal government.[29] These range from the bipartisan Committee for a Responsible Federal Budget, a more than forty-year-old think tank focused on deficit reduction and tax and entitlement reform,[30] to the nonpartisan Concord Coalition, which is "dedicated to educating the public about the causes and consequences of federal budget deficits, the long-term challenges facing America's unsustainable entitlement programs, and how to build a sound foundation for economic growth."[31]

At Columbia Teachers College, Peterson funded the creation of the curriculum "Understanding Fiscal Responsibility," which "focuses on the federal budget, national debt, and budget deficit in the United States in a way that enables students to analyze their significance and judge their consequences."[32] High school students will learn from this coursework that "the stakes are high, and they will see that the challenges we face are complex. The solutions will require not only a rugged tolerance for the ambiguities embedded in those challenges, but also a willingness to do the hard work of analyzing the trade-offs in less-than-perfect resolutions."[33]

Peterson worked with mtvU to create "a campaign for college students that raises awareness about the dangers of excessive personal and government debt, and promotes action to help stop the fiscal crisis in the U.S."[34]

There are dozens of other efforts, not to mention individual political activists and academics, financed at least in part by Peterson or his foundation to spread this same message.[35]

It was in this Peterson-influenced political environment, where concern about government deficits trumped other economic considerations, that Reinhart and Rogoff's article was published. Both academics are directly connected to the billionaire. Peterson personally cited their work when questioned by *The Washington Post* on the fact that the United States had both high deficits and low interest rates in contrast to the predictions he and other deficit hawks were touting. He told the paper, "No one, certainly not Pete Peterson, can make predictions about the market reaction. But you know [Kenneth] Rogoff and [Carmen] Reinhart—I've talked to them, and they say [debt crises] are sudden, they're sharp, they're very substantial. The risk is simply too big. At some point, if we lurch from crisis to crisis, then confidence will decline on our economy in general."[36]

Reinhart was appointed a senior fellow at the Peterson Institute for International Economics, funded and chaired by Peterson, in October 2010 and has spoken at Peterson's fiscal summit.[37] Reinhart's partner Rogoff was, and still is, a member of the Peterson Institute's advisory board.[38] Not to mention the duo's book, *A Decade of Debt,* was funded and published by the Peterson Institute.[39] With these connections, it is no surprise Peterson organs used their substantial media heft to push the study. Once its conclusions had been debunked, would the deficit hawks back off?

Those inclined to believe Reinhart and Rogoff's conclusions have continued to cling to the idea that cutting the deficit is a critical and immediate need, despite evidence to the contrary. Erskine Bowles, who joined Peterson's payroll at Fix the Debt, acknowledged the study's flaws but did not shy away or change his ideological stance.

"What [the discovery of errors in Reinhart and Rogoff's work] doesn't change," Bowles wrote, "is the common sense and my own personal experience in both the public and private sector that when any organization has too much debt that is an enormous risk factor and when your risks go up then people lending you money will want more money for their money."[40] However, the continued value investors place in U.S. debt, even after the last decade of increased borrowing, suggests Bowles is incorrect.

"Common sense and my own personal experience" is exactly the problem created by conducting research within an ideological bubble: Bowles is happy to accept the conclusions of Reinhart and Rogoff when they conform to his ideology. However, when the conclusions turned out to be wrong, they could be ignored.

Unlike the case of the tobacco scientists, Reinhart and Rogoff's research does not seem to involve an intentional attempt to deceive the public. Instead, a mistake was made that happened to confirm the ideological construction of those who made the error.

The faulty research was published and an industry of think tanks, policy campaigns, media figures, and politicians were eager to echo its findings. Through repetition, the false study was elevated from an academic article to economic law in the space of a few months. It was repeated over and over again, so even after the principal findings had been debunked, certain politicians continued citing its conclusions.

Former South Carolina governor Mark Sanford was on the campaign trail a few weeks after Herndon, Ash, and Pollin published their debunking article to wide public notice. Taking questions about the deficit from a local NAACP chapter, he cited Reinhart and Rogoff's conclusion, saying, "The math always works."[41]

Perhaps more noxious than the persistence of the study's

incorrect thesis in the media and public debates is that fiscal hawks have stubbornly refused to change their minds about the United States' need to make deep budget cuts. Even when presented with clear data, Peterson, his acolytes, and those on his payroll refuse to relent from their original position. It is one of the clearest demonstrations of the odious nature of lies in our political process. When academics produce a study whose conclusions match the ideology of their funder and others in the media, it is trumpeted and foisted on the public. When those results turn out to be false, the correct data is either ignored or the whole mess is swept under the rug, with the movement continuing as if nothing has occurred. When facts contradict an ideological group's accepted narrative, especially one that has received prominence in the media, it is far easier to ignore the truth than to confront the failure of your arguments. This motivated reasoning is why partisans on a variety of issues continue to fight for causes long after the underlying facts have been discredited.

This ideological dedication also causes those with deeply held beliefs to search for research to justify their positions. In worse cases, Lies, Incorporated will simply purchase convenient facts to make their case. They will cherry-pick data or cling to studies with dubious conclusions, which frequently, as we are about to see in the case of the anti-immigrant community, has led to ugly, false, and often racist misinformation shaping debate.

Chapter 5

On the Border of Truth: Immigration Reform

No debate over the past decade has promised more hope for progress and yet produced so many instances of legislative failure than efforts to pass comprehensive immigration reform. This issue unites traditionally progressive organizations like civil rights groups with traditionally conservative constituencies including the Chamber of Commerce and numerous other business interests. But a powerful and strident wing of the conservative movement opposes these strange bedfellows.

Opponents of immigration reform accuse its supporters, from across the political spectrum, of being disingenuous about why they want the United States to adopt a more open immigration policy. Democrats, they claim, support immigration reform because they seek to tap new pools of voters. Business interests, they believe, are looking for cheap labor so they can further drive down costs. And some insist that Hispanic and Latino civil rights organizations are looking to justify and excuse illegal behavior among their own ethnic group by giving "amnesty" to criminals who violated the law. Some even insist that Hispanic and Latino civil rights organizations are really pushing for reform in order to populate a fight for "Reconquista"—the imaginary effort to take back the American southwest for Mexico.[1]

For several decades, advocates have fought for reforms to our immigration system. Most of these proposals have contained a number of widely agreed-upon policies to toughen enforcement of current laws, such as increased budgets for border patrol and mandating an "e-verify" system to hold employers accountable when they hire those without authorization to work in the United States. The more controversial elements of these proposals are a variety of different measures to provide a path toward some sort of legal status for those already living and working in this country but without proper documentation.

Among those without documents are the individuals who were brought to America as very young children, have lived as Americans for most of their lives, and are often unaware of their undocumented status until they try to get a driver's license. Many of these "DREAMers," as they've come to be known, have no memory of the country in which they were born. Some speak only English. They want to go to college or join the U.S. military. For all intents and purposes, they are Americans.

In a political climate where comprehensive immigration was unlikely, this specific group became a priority for immigration advocates during President Obama's first term. The DREAM Act was written to help thousands of people—provided they met stringent criteria—along the path toward documentation, legal residency, and, possibly, citizenship. After Congress failed to pass this legislation, in June 2012 President Obama issued an executive action known as DACA—Deferred Action for Child-hood Arrivals—to give DREAMers some protection against deportation.[2]

Providing protection against deportation, even for a small num-

ber of the undocumented, was a slap in the face of those opposing any sort of pro-immigrant policy reform. Many opponents of
immigration reform advocate for the deportation of every person
in the United States without up-to-date paperwork. The number
of people in the United States without legal status has stayed at
about eleven million for the last several years.[3] The resources necessary to deport that many people make it a practical impossibility. Locating, verifying lack of paperwork for, legally prosecuting,
detaining—which means weeks of shelter, food, security, and
medical care—all eleven million people would be a huge under-
taking. Estimates place the cost of such an effort at $114 billion.[4]
That is why policy makers have proposed systems to address
undocumented immigrants' status, which often involves paying
fines and back taxes, undergoing a background check, proving no
crime greater than minor traffic violations has been committed,
and "going to the back" of the immigration line. By removing the
fear of deportation, we can maintain better records of who is in
the country, improve public safety services, create enforcement
mechanisms, and reset our broken immigration system.

President George W. Bush is reported to have always had a
personal interest in the plight of immigrants. He also recognized
that the growing Hispanic and Latino share of the electorate
demanded action on immigration reform. But this stance put him
in the minority of his party. Some elected officials recognized the
need to do something about immigration, but most Republicans in
Congress refused to support anything that "smacks of amnesty."[5]
Their base was ardently opposed to immigration reform, and the
legislation gained no momentum.

Following the 2012 election, advocates once again became
hopeful for movement on their issue. Obama's landslide win was
in part thanks to turnout from Hispanic and Latino supporters

who voted for Democrats in droves. In an election postmortem commissioned by Republican National Committee chairman Reince Priebus, the party conceded that immigration reform and courting the Hispanic vote were vital to their future.[6]

Republican senators Marco Rubio of Florida and Lindsey Graham of South Carolina joined the bipartisan Senate "Gang of Eight," which set out to craft a comprehensive immigration reform bill that could, and did, pass the Senate.[7] The House of Representatives was a different story. With gerrymandered districts that gave "Tea Party" conservatives an outsized influence, Speaker of the House John Boehner (R-OH) chose not to risk his power by bringing the Senate immigration bill to the floor for a vote. All acknowledged that with near unanimous support among the Democratic caucus, the bill would have passed, but Boehner could not risk the backlash from his members.[8]

Anti-immigration forces wanted to avoid at all cost the perception that they were opposing immigration reform based purely on xenophobia. Therefore, they needed to supply an acceptable justification to oppose this popular piece of legislation. It was during this period that conservative think tanks, most notably the Heritage Foundation, reinvigorated their campaign of lies and falsehoods about immigration.

Under the leadership of former senator Jim DeMint, the Heritage Foundation became more closely associated with the activist base of the conservative movement. *The New York Times* reported in February 2014, "Long known as an incubator for policy ideas and the embodiment of the party establishment, it has become more of a political organization feeding off the rising populism of the Tea Party movement."[9]

Heritage Action, its 501(c)(4) advocacy group, spent half a million dollars helping to lead attacks on Republican members of the House of Representatives in 2013 and 2014 for being insufficiently conservative, something that was previously unheard of in intra-party battles.[10]

Jumping full force into the immigration reform debate, two researchers at Heritage, Robert Rector and Jason Richwine, published a study on May 6, 2013, claiming that immigration reform, wrongly called amnesty in the report, would have a net cost to U.S. taxpayers of $6.3 trillion. The think tank claimed that the $9 trillion in expenditures of new government benefits for newly legalized immigrants would only be offset by $3 trillion in new tax benefits.[11] DeMint, as Heritage president, took to the cable networks to tout the results of this study.[12]

In an interview with Fox News host Martha MacCallum, he claimed, "We know over time that this [$6.3 trillion net cost] is going to increase more debt, increase taxes." According to DeMint and Heritage, achieving legal status would allow undocumented immigrants to both take the jobs of many Americans and depress salaries overall.[13]

The study's numerous flaws were immediately revealed, including a significant problem: the analysis began in November 2012, long before the bipartisan bill was introduced in April 2013. Robert Rector, whose official biography noted he was "dubbed the 'intellectual godfather' of welfare reform" has been a researcher at the Heritage Foundation for three decades.[14] When responding to critiques of the immigration bill, he acknowledged, "This analysis isn't of the whole immigration bill. . . . Other aspects of the bill are outside the scope of what I studied."[15]

One section of the Heritage report incorrectly described a "loophole" in current law that allows undocumented immigrants to receive permanent residency or citizenship, thereby granting them access to benefits such as Medicare, Medicaid, and Social Security simply if their citizen children ask for their parents to be made legal residents. Under the Fourteenth Amendment, children of undocumented immigrants born in the United States are automatically citizens—derisively called "anchor babies" by some. According to Heritage, when these Americans turn twenty-one, they can simply "demand" their parents receive citizenship.[16]

FactCheck.org refuted this distortion, citing Erin Oshiro, a senior staff attorney at the Immigration and Immigrant Rights Program at the Asian American Justice Center. The "loophole" does not exist as Heritage described. Far from a simple way to gain citizenship just by having a citizen child, undocumented parents face long processes to achieve legal status. Oshiro explained that in order for citizen children to sponsor their undocumented parents' legalization process, "the parents would have to return to their home country for at least 10 years before returning to the U.S. (something an immigrant living unlawfully in the U.S. for more than 21 years is unlikely to want to do)."[17]

Furthermore, the Heritage report estimated the costs of the bill over a fifty-year window, something regarded by many researchers as "highly speculative." "We have no idea what things will look like in fifty years," said Bob Williams of the nonpartisan Tax Policy Center. "In the long run, I don't think we know what the situation will be. [The $6.3 trillion figure in the Heritage report] is not a number that anyone should put a lot of faith in."[18]

With the party split on how to proceed on immigration reform, the report was not unquestionably accepted as it might have been on other issues. Conservatives had other research available that, unlike the Heritage report, did properly account for the economic growth driven by immigration. Douglas Holtz-Eakin—who served on George W. Bush's Council of Economic Advisers, was the director of the Congressional Budget Office for two years, headed up economic policy for Senator John McCain's 2008 campaign, and was even a senior fellow at the Peterson Institute[19]—

published a study in April 2013 indicating the clear economic *benefits* of passing immigration reform. As Holtz-Eakin explained: "A benchmark immigration reform would raise the pace of economic growth by nearly a percentage point over the near term, raise GDP per capita by over $1,500, and reduce the cumulative federal deficit by over $2.5 trillion."[20]

As the study's suspicious conclusions were analyzed, its authors also attracted attention, particularly Jason Richwine, a Harvard Ph.D. who earned his degree during a fellowship at the conservative American Enterprise Institute.[21]

On May 8, two days after the Richwine report was published, *The Washington Post* posted excerpts from Richwine's 2009 doctoral dissertation, titled "IQ and Immigration Policy," in which Richwine argued "the average IQ of immigrants in the United States is substantially lower than that of the white native population, and the difference is likely to persist over several generations." Richwine further asserted that the consequences of a large "low-IQ" population "are a lack of socioeconomic assimilation among low-IQ immigrant groups, more underclass behavior, less social trust, and an increase in the proportion of unskilled workers in the American labor market."[22]

Worse yet, Richwine argued that I.Q. levels are tied to genetic makeup, writing "the totality of the evidence suggests a genetic component to group differences in IQ" and further specifically targeted Latin American immigrants in his thesis: "No one knows whether Hispanics will ever reach IQ parity with whites, but the prediction that new Hispanic immigrants will have low-IQ children and grandchildren is difficult to argue against."[23]

The use of I.Q. as a measure with which to compare populations has been a controversial element of social science for decades. In the 1990s, political scientist Charles Murray, a fellow at the American Enterprise Institute, published *The Bell Curve,* a book arguing that "social inequality is caused by the genetic inferiority of the black and Latino communities, women and the poor."[24]

Daniel Strauss at *Talking Points Memo* described the book's reception: "Critics denounced it as racist, saying it essentially argued that African-Americans aren't as intelligent as white Americans because of genetic differences. In 1994 Bob Herbert, then a columnist at *The New York Times,* described the book as a 'scabrous piece of racial pornography masquerading as serious scholarship.'"[25]

Richwine, who personally thanked Murray for his guidance, writing, "I could not have asked for a better primary advisor,"[26] based his dissertation on similar arguments, but took them a step further to make "a strong case for IQ selection . . . since it is theoretically a win-win for the U.S. and potential immigrants." He even went so far as to offer messaging advice to make I.Q.-based selection more palatably and politically viable for those seeking to exclude immigrants based on their supposed genetic predisposition to a low I.Q.[27] To many, this was a step in the direction of eugenics and a bridge too far.

The condemnations were swift and came from all sides. Hours after *The Washington Post*'s expose, Heritage tried to distance itself from their researcher with a statement from a vice president, claiming Richwine's past work did "not reflect the positions of The Heritage Foundation or the conclusions of our study on the cost of amnesty to U.S. taxpayers, as race and ethnicity are not part of Heritage immigration policy recommendations."[28]

But Heritage's attempts to push Richwine aside were disingenuous at best. The idea that a think tank could hire a researcher almost immediately out of graduate school, with no knowledge of the subject of his doctoral dissertation, is absurd. Richwine wrote and published numerous reports, in addition to testimony and other writings, for Heritage during his time there.[29] Furthermore, Richwine had spoken openly about his beliefs even before completing his thesis—there was no attempt at hiding his belief in genetic superiority.

In 2008, while a fellow at American Enterprise Institute, Richwine appeared on a panel with Mark Krikorian, executive director of the anti-immigrant Center for Immigration Studies. During the discussion, Richwine openly promoted the ideas in his thesis—most prominently that some racial groups are intellectually inferior. "Races differ in all sorts of ways, and probably the most important way is in IQ," Richwine said. He continued by flatly stating that race and I.Q. must be a factor for public policy decisions: "These are real differences, and they're not going to go away tomorrow, and for that reason we have to address them in our immigration discussions and our debates."[30]

Richwine's beliefs about race and I.Q. highlight the strong undercurrent of racism that drives a significant part of the anti-immigrant political constituency in America. And Heritage's phony statistics on the cost of immigration reform were meant to create a false impression of the negative impact immigration legislation would have on the economy. Both Richwine's dissertation and the Heritage report he wrote are examples of how research can be manufactured to justify an ideological belief.

Behind much of this ideological battle is one man, neither a politician nor a political scientist, but an ophthalmologist from northern Michigan. Richwine is just one small part of a vast, interconnected, financially flush anti-immigrant movement that owes its existence to Dr. John Tanton.

Tanton is an unlikely leader of the anti-immigrant movement, but for thirty years he has been its godfather, founder, and fund-raiser, building an infrastructure that has been the source of nearly every lie told about immigrants in this country.

John Tanton's political activism was triggered by a desire to protect the environment. "A beekeeper and amateur naturalist of prodigious energy," he "had spent two decades planting trees, cleaning creeks and suing developers." Tanton believed that population growth was the culprit behind the environmental problems he was witnessing. The number of native-born Americans wasn't rising, so Tanton surmised that immigrants to the United States were responsible for the rapidly growing population.[31]

A leader at local chapters of Planned Parenthood and the Sierra Club in the 1960s and '70s, Tanton tried to get both groups to fight against immigration but failed. Tanton said he "finally concluded that if anything was going to happen, I would have to do it myself."[32]

From his home base in northern Michigan, he built a movement whose influence has been staggering. The groups he founded strike fear in the hearts of politicians, particularly Republicans, and maintain a vast and passionate grassroots network whose members are willing to call and write to politicians, show up at protests, and do the hard work of making change. To that effect, Tanton has built a movement that has, since Reagan's immigration reforms in the 1980s, had the ability to halt any political conversation about immigration in its tracks.

The Southern Poverty Law Center, a widely respected civil rights organization known for taking on neo-Nazis and other hate groups, compiled a list of the groups Tanton has influenced:

American Immigration Control Foundation (AICF),
　1983, funded
American Patrol/Voice of Citizens Together 1992, funded

> **California Coalition for Immigration Reform** (CCIR),
> 1994, funded
> **Californians for Population Stabilization** (CAPS),
> 1996, funded (founded separately in 1986)
> **Center for Immigration Studies** (CIS), 1985, founded
> and funded
> **Federation for American Immigration Reform** (FAIR),
> 1979, founded and funded
> **NumbersUSA** 1996, founded and funded
> **Population-Environment Balance** 1973, joined board
> in 1980
> **Pro English** 1994, founded and funded
> **ProjectUSA** 1999, funded
> **The Social Contract Press** 1990, founded and funded
> **U.S. English** 1983, founded and funded
> **U.S. Inc.** 1982, founded and funded[33]

Of these organizations, the three that have done the most to negatively shape attitudes toward immigrants in this country are the Federation for American Immigration Reform (FAIR), NumbersUSA, and the Center for Immigration Studies (CIS).

In many ways, Tanton's network has been more influential than better-known lobbying organizations like the National Rifle Association. It has ensured that no matter how close Congress comes to taking action on immigration, the legislative process ultimately is paralyzed by fear.

Senator Jeff Sessions (R-AL) credits Tanton's efforts with halting George W. Bush's immigration reform plans in 2007. On the Senate floor he stated NumbersUSA provided "the overwhelming grassroots response" that "was most evident when citizens called Capitol Hill in such volume that it shut down the Senate's telephone system."[34]

The Center for Immigration Studies, which produces highly biased "research," was a critical part of the coalition that defeated the DREAM Act.

But Tanton's groups also have the power to pass legislation, particularly in conservative states. This includes Arizona's controversial SB 1070 law that allows local law enforcement to demand immigration documentation from anyone whom they have a "reasonable suspicion" of being an undocumented immigrant.[35] SB 1070 was drafted by Kris Kobach, who worked for the Tanton-connected Immigration Reform Law Institute, which is the public-interest law affiliate of the Federation for American Immigration Reform, and who would go on to be elected secretary of state in Kansas.[36]

While many of the groups in Tanton's network were initially framed as middle of the road, they have long since shed that veneer. FAIR holds a conference at a hotel in the shadow of the Capitol, attracting a radio row with some of the most partisan and anti-immigrant hosts on the airwaves. Their message is not the call for inclusion expressed by the Republican National Committee's roadmap in 2012. Instead, the "Hold Their Feet to the Fire" event is a gathering of individuals who are extremely upset about the state of our country and focus their anger on its most recent arrivals.[37]

This is not unique to twenty-first-century politics. It is a strategy from an old playbook dating back to the Know-Nothing Party of the nineteenth century, whose platform was based on a suspicion and hatred of new immigrants. In fact, anti-immigrant sentiment is even older than the republic. In 1753, Benjamin Franklin wrote a letter decrying the dilution of our culture caused by German immigrants who, according to the founding father, were "generally of the most ignorant Stupid Sort of their own Nation, and as Ignorance is often attended with Credulity when Knavery would mislead it, and with Suspicion when Honesty would set it right; and as few of the English understand the German Language, and so cannot address them either from the Press or Pulpit, 'tis almost impossible to remove any prejudices they once entertain."[38]

Tanton pledged, when he began his work, that his views were not based on bigotry. However, private writings, donated to the University of Michigan, demonstrate his disturbing ideology. In the 1990s, Tanton encouraged employees of FAIR to subscribe to *American Renaissance,* which was published by the New Century Foundation, "a self-styled white supremacist think tank." According to the Anti-Defamation League: "The journal promotes pseudo-scientific studies that attempt to demonstrate the intellectual and cultural superiority of whites and publishes articles on the supposed decline of American society because of integrationist social policies."[39]

Tanton has accepted money from the Pioneer Fund, a foundation that donated money to white supremacists, and has clearly tolerated others within his movement who hold abhorrent views of racial minorities.[40] A Pioneer grantee from 1969 to 1976 was William B. Shockley, a Nobel Prize–winning physicist better known for his racist views on the genetic superiority of Caucasians.[41]

Tanton defended the Pioneer Fund's support of studies designed to demonstrate the genetic superiority of white people, writing, "It would take a bold person indeed to predict exactly where the question of the relative roles of nature vs. nurture will eventually settle out. Some of my opponents object to these studies, and have transferred their objections to me and immigration policy questions."[42]

In 2002, the Southern Poverty Law Center published an article on the opening of NumbersUSA's Capitol Hill office where "*The Citizens Informer,* a white supremacist tabloid put out by the Council of Conservative Citizens hate group, was available."[43] Dylann Roof, whose racism drove him to murder nine black congregants during a Bible study at an AME church in Charleston, South Carolina, in June 2015, was inspired in part by the writings of the CCC.[44]

Most damning was a series of strategy documents that came to be known as the WITAN[45] memos. Leaked in 1988, these memos were written for the anti-immigrant movement's retreats in which Tanton himself elaborates on the positions of the group. In one document, Tanton referred to Latino immigration to the United States as a "Latin onslaught," asking questions such as "Will Latin American migrants bring with them the tradition of the *mordida* (bribe), the lack of involvement in public affairs, etc.? What in fact are the characteristics of Latin American culture, versus that of the United States?"[46]

Additionally, Tanton questioned the economic value of immigration, "What are the consequences of having so many ill-educated people coming in to low paying jobs?" He also did not shy away from citing plainly racist tropes about immigrants' high birth rate, asking, "Can *homo contraceptivus* [*Whites*] compete with *homo progenitiva* [*Hispanics*] if borders aren't controlled? Or is advice to limit one's family simply advice to move over and let someone else with greater reproductive powers occupy the space?"[47]

In a 1993 letter to ecology professor Garrett Hardin, Tanton wrote, "I've come to the point of view that for European-American society and culture to persist requires a European-American majority, and a clear one at that."[48]

To the executive director of NumbersUSA, Roy Beck, Tanton wrote, "I have no doubt that individual minority persons can assimilate to the culture necessary to run an advanced society but if through mass migration, the culture of the homeland is transplanted from Latin America to California, then my guess is we will see the same degree of success with governmental and social institutions that we have seen in Latin America."[49]

In 1996, Tanton wrote to "eugenicist" Robert K. Graham, "Do we leave it to individuals to decide that they are the intelligent ones who should have more kids? And more troublesome, what about the less intelligent, who logically should have less? Who is going to break the bad news [to less intelligent individuals], and how will it be implemented?"[50]

This series of letters creates a clear track record elucidating Tanton's positions. While he might have begun as an environmentally minded progressive, by the 1980s he had become an anti-immigrant bigot, and through his support and founding of anti-immigrant groups, he was able to spread out and amplify his beliefs.

Along with their general bigotry, the lies created by these groups help to fuel the noxiousness of the immigration debate. Among their many tactics is scaring up fear and hatred of immigrants by exaggerating the frequency with which undocumented immigrants commit violent crimes.

In 2013, FAIR produced a chart claiming that while U.S. citizens could serve time in prison for crimes ranging from altering a Social Security card to tax evasion, undocumented immigrants would simply be "exonerated and legalized." The implication was that a special protection from prosecution existed for undocumented immigrants, and not for legal immigrants or even citizens. This was simply untrue. Immigration reform did not exempt immigrants from following the law or facing criminal prosecution.[51] However, the point of FAIR's chart was not accuracy. It was to paint a picture of a permissive attitude toward immigrants and their supposed crimes, while whites served time for lesser offenses.

Dan Stein, the president of FAIR, wrote an op-ed for FoxNews .com stoking racial resentment by claiming the Senate immigration reform bill "would give illegal immigrants tax amnesty." He explained, "The bill requires aliens to only pay taxes that the IRS has assessed at the time they apply for RPI [Registered Provisional Immigrant] status." Stein continued, "If the IRS had no knowledge that the individual had been working here, there would obviously be no tax liability assessed and the alien has nothing to satisfy for the purpose of getting RPI status."[52]

This was simply a misreading of the legislation. "The bill states that immigrants may not receive provisional status until any federal tax liability is satisfied in accordance with regulations to be established by the Secretary of the Treasury," Media Matters noted.[53] Immigrants could lie on their tax forms, but this, too, was already a crime and one that would affect the process of achieving legal status.

Stein had a history of false attacks on the Senate immigration bill. He had previously claimed, "Senate Judiciary Committee Chairman Patrick Leahy will not even allow hearings on a bill"[54]— when at the same time, one could have easily read in public news reports that "Senate Judiciary Committee Chairman Patrick Leahy has formally announced an April 17 hearing on comprehensive immigration reform legislation."[55]

Another of Stein's claims, that "Democrats will not agree to border security and other enforcement requirements as a prerequisite to amnesty,"[56] was easily refuted by the Associated Press. Undocumented immigrants "could begin to get green cards in 10 years but only if a new southern border security plan is in place, employers have adopted mandatory electronic verification of their workers' legal status and a new electronic exit system is operating at airports and seaports."[57]

Another lie put forward by the members of John Tanton's network is that allowing more legal immigration puts both job prospects and working conditions for African-Americans at risk.

Daniel Griswold of the Cato Institute told the House Judiciary Committee this was "an especially pernicious myth. . . . As with most other Americans, few African Americans compete directly with immigrant workers."[58]

Griswold went on to cite a 1997 report from the National Research Council that concluded:

> None of the available evidence . . . suggests that in the aggregate the economic opportunities of black Americans are substantially reduced by immigration. . . . Some black workers have lost their jobs to immigrants, especially when they live in a place with a large concentration of immigrants. But the vast majority do not live in such places, and their economic opportunities are determined by other things.[59]

These findings were reflected by numerous other studies conducted on the subject over the years. But this topic had been a personal obsession of Tanton, who also raised the issue in his WITAN memos. Just because the data proved otherwise did not mean the Tanton network would stop spreading these lies.

The purpose of these lies was clear: to muddy the waters, making it impossible for a complex piece of legislation with various moving parts to get through Congress. Additionally, they sought to provide palatable justification for clearly racist sentiments. This was the specific goal of the anti-immigrant movement. Like those opposed to confronting climate change, or passing gun safety legislation, they knew that if you can tell enough lies, you can halt progress.

The power of the Tanton network is that these lies would be amplified not only throughout the echo chamber created by the loosely affiliated organizations, but also by Fox News and the vast network of anti-immigrant radio hosts who frequented the FAIR conference.

Reporters who covered these issues without accepting anti-immigrant lies are simply biased, according to the members of the Tanton network. Thus, immigration policy in this country has stalled for at least the last decade with little hope of passage without a significant change in the makeup of Congress. Part of the brilliance of John Tanton, who is no longer an active public participant in the immigration debate, is that he organized these groups in such a way that they are no longer strategically or financially dependent on his leadership, but will continue to fight for the ideology he espoused.

Falsehoods spread during the immigration debate raised the emotional ire of an anti-immigrant constituency who would express that rage in emails and phone calls to Congress, not to mention water-cooler conversations with friends, so that these misrepresentations ultimately seeped into the political zeitgeist, where falsehoods are converted into one side's truth. This conversion has occurred on a number of issues. In the next chapter we will examine the lie that "more guns" means "less crime," something that has been consistently discredited by researchers yet is repeated ad nauseum by those who steadfastly fight against limitations on gun ownership.

Chapter 6

Two Dangerous Weapons:
Guns and Lies

At 9:35 a.m. on the morning of December 14, 2012, twenty-year-old Adam Lanza entered Sandy Hook Elementary School, armed with an AR-15 assault rifle and two pistols.[1]

Per procedure, the school's doors had automatically locked at 9:30. Lanza used the AR-15 to "literally (shoot) an entrance into the building," according to Connecticut governor Dan Malloy.[2] Wearing camouflage and a military vest, he proceeded into the school where more than seven hundred elementary students had just begun class for the day.

Hearing gunfire, "school psychologist Mary Sherlach and vice principal Natalie Hammond went out to investigate."[3] Lanza shot both women, wounding Hammond and killing Sherlach. He then quickly moved toward a kindergarten classroom. Once inside, he murdered all fourteen students and their substitute teacher. In the next room, teacher Victoria Soto moved her "students away from the door."[4] Lanza entered, shot Soto, and killed eight of her students.

Two and a half minutes after the first call to 911, first responders arrived at the building. Upon hearing the sirens, Lanza used one of the pistols to kill himself, putting an end to one of the most horrific mass shootings in American history.[5]

In the aftermath of this shocking carnage, it seemed as if more than a decade of reticence on the subject of gun control ended. Faced with the scale of this massacre, and the age of its victims, politicians (in particular Democrats) felt the country demanded they once again address the issue of gun violence.

Prior to the Sandy Hook Massacre, the White House had declined every opportunity to galvanize public support and tackle the gun issue. After the July 2012 mass shooting at a movie theater in Aurora, Colorado, Barack Obama consoled the victims' families not "as president" but "as a father and husband,"[6] absolving himself of responsibility to take action, much less legislate on the issue. A similar response came from the White House after the attempted assassination of Representative Gabby Giffords in 2011.[7]

During the 2008 presidential campaign cycle, conservatives generated fears that Democrats—and Barack Obama, in particular—would disarm the American people. The response to these two incidents demonstrated the fallacy of the conservative myth that President Obama was eager to dismantle the Second Amendment.

Other than a minor rule from the Bureau of Alcohol, Tobacco, and Firearms regarding the registration of the sale of certain long guns, no real limitations were ever proposed by the Obama White House. Just the opposite: during his first term, Barack Obama signed legislation to advance gun rights, allowing visitors to carry weapons inside national parks.[8]

Despite the lack of action on the part of Democrats, the myth that a liberal politician might seek to confiscate the weapons of lawful gun owners was a profitable tale for the NRA's financial backers in the firearms industry. Barack Obama's election and reelection, and the paranoia they stoked on the right, dramatically spiked gun sales during his presidency. "He is the best thing that ever happened to the firearm industry," stated Jim Barrett, "an industry analyst at C.L. King & Associates Inc."[9] That is one reason the NRA, on behalf of their funders in the gun industry, eagerly promoted the fantasy in 2008 and 2012 that Barack Obama's election would result in a massive effort to ban weapons.

But in the wake of Sandy Hook, fear of the NRA was overridden by a public outcry that was simply too loud to ignore. President Obama called on Vice President Joe Biden to head a task force proposing new gun safety legislation. The product of that committee's work was a moderate list of proposals, including improvements to the FBI's background check system. The most politically controversial element of this effort was the inclusion of an assault weapons ban, the last iteration of which had expired in 2004. Previous versions of this law even had the support of George W. Bush during his first presidential campaign.[10] While the media portrayed a country deeply divided on this issue, in January 2013, polling showed support for the policies set by the task force, including broad public approval of background checks: "89 percent of all respondents, and 75 percent of those identified as NRA members, support universal background checks for gun sales."[11]

Republican Patrick Toomey of Pennsylvania and Democrat Joe Manchin of West Virginia, both stalwart NRA supporters, joined together in the Senate to sponsor an amendment to the Safe Communities, Safe Schools Act of 2013, which was widely regarded as compromise legislation.[12] First, the amendment specifically banned a national gun registry in response to the gun lobby's early fear mongering that the bill's language surreptitiously mandated one. Second, the amendment clarified that giving or selling a gun to a family member did not require a background check; likewise, private gun sales between friends—provided the sale was not advertised—did not necessitate a background check, either.[13] Simply put, the amendment caused the expanded background check requirement to be applied just to gun shows.

However, the NRA and their allies used a powerful weapon to great effect: a lie. They claimed that the Manchin-Toomey amendment "criminalized certain private transfers of firearms"— essentially making it illegal for friends and family to gift or sell to one another.[14] The gun lobby also claimed that "virtually all" gun transactions would enter both parties into a national gun registry.[15] It was a loss of freedom considered by NRA activists to be a step toward the confiscation of firearms: if the government knew who had guns, then a tyrannical president and his justice department could simply go out and seize those weapons. This was paranoid to an absurd degree, but so is much of the rhetoric that dominates the gun rights movement.

Manchin and Toomey attempted to preempt the claims of a mandatory national gun registry they knew would come by including language that very specifically prohibited any sort of registry or list of American gun owners:

Section 102: "Congress supports and reaffirms the existing prohibition on a national firearms registry."

Section 103: "Nothing in this title, or any amendment made by this title, shall be construed to—(1) expand in any way the enforcement authority or jurisdiction of the Bureau of Alcohol, Tobacco, Firearms, and Explosives; or (2) all the establishment, directly or indirectly, of a Federal firearms registry."

Section 122 (C): "Prohibition of National Gun Registry. Section 923 of title 18, United States Code, is amended by adding at the end the following: The Attorney General may not consolidate or centralize the records of the (1) acquisition or disposition of firearms, or any portion thereof, maintained by (a) a person with a valid, current license under this chapter; (b) an unlicensed transferor under section 922 (t); or (2) possession or ownership of a firearm, maintained by any medical or health insurance entity."[16]

The text of the bill did not matter, and pro-gun supporters continually and baselessly claimed that the background checks in Manchin-Toomey would create a federal registration of firearms. The highly trafficked conservative website *The Daily Caller* wrote, "The so-called 'background check' bill is really about gun registration—ultimate and imminent registration of every gun and gun owner in America."[17]

Members of the Senate, in particular Republicans and conservative Democrats undecided on the bill, were flooded with thousands of calls and angry emails from constituents. The NRA spent half a million dollars on an ad telling Americans that Congress should "listen to America's police instead of listening to Obama."[18] The legislative text was no match for the messaging from the National Rifle Association, the rest of the gun lobby, and their allies in conservative media.

Ultimately, the bill was defeated. President Obama, speaking in the Rose Garden of the White House, expressed anger and frustration that was absent from earlier statements about gun violence: "The gun lobby and its allies willfully lied about the bill. . . . This pattern of spreading untruths about this legislation served a purpose, because those lies upset an intense minority of gun owners, and that in turn intimidated a lot of senators."[19]

The NRA and their allies on the right knew that a lie would help them maintain the status quo. They used the false threat of gun registration to stir the passion of their membership at a moment when their activism mattered most: a legislative battle.

Four days after the massacre at Sandy Hook Elementary School, the NRA issued a brief statement offering "meaningful contributions to help make sure this never happens again."[20] A week after the shooting, the NRA held a press conference in which Executive Vice President Wayne LaPierre blamed mass shootings on "gun-free zones," video games, music videos, and said what has been something of a trademark: "The only thing that stops a bad guy with a gun is a good guy with a gun."[21]

Since the NRA was avoiding the press, filling the media void was John Lott, the gun rights community's favorite economist. Lott carries an air of respectability, having taught at the University of Chicago, Yale, and the Wharton School of the University of Pennsylvania. He also worked for the American Enterprise Institute.[22] Seemingly, whenever there is a public outcry around a shooting, he can be found in the greenroom of a cable channel or eagerly chatting up reporters.

"It's not true" is a favorite refrain of Lott's when parrying with the press, and the phrase makes for good TV. He often uses it to pivot to his own invented facts, even when a great body of evidence exists that proves him wrong. In July 2012, following the mass shooting in Aurora, Colorado, he told Piers Morgan it was "not true" that "America has the worst incidents of gun murders of any of what they call the civilized world."[23] Lott's assertion contradicted numerous studies, including one from the Harvard School of Public Health, which found "the firearm homicide rate in the United States is 19.5 times higher than the average rate found in other high-income nations."[24] Not only did the United States have the worst record, it was many, many times higher than the accepted norm in other countries.

Julia Lurie, a reporter for *Mother Jones,* counted more than one hundred television appearances by Lott between 2013 and 2015, and a search of Nexis reveals hundreds of quotes and citations of his research in major publications.[25]

Lott does not confine his media blitzes to conservative outlets. The night of the Sandy Hook shooting, Lott appeared on Piers Morgan's CNN show. The host, a clear proponent of gun legislation, began the interview with an example of the steps taken to curb gun deaths that had been taken in other countries. In 1996, thirty-five people were killed in a massacre in Tasmania. "And the Australians, led by the prime minister, John Howard—he was right wing, friends of George W. Bush. He brought in pretty Draconian new laws after that." Morgan continued: "He banned semiautomatic and automatic rifles and shotguns. As a result, over the next decade, [the] firearm homicide rate fell by 59 percent. The firearm suicide rate fell by 65 percent."

Lott responded, "It's not true."[26] But it was true: deaths by firearms dropped drastically after Howard's efforts, and there was no corresponding increase in non-firearm deaths.[27]

In the face of data he could not adequately refute, Lott unleashed the argument that had made him famous: "All these attacks this year have occurred where guns are banned." According to Lott, "Look at the movie theater one, for example. There were seven movie theaters showing the 'Batman' movie within a twenty-minute drive of where the killer lived. Only one of those banned guns. He didn't go to the movie theater closest to his home. He didn't go to the movie theater with the largest screen. He went to the one movie theater that banned guns."[28]

Lott later exclaimed: "I'm upset because I worry that the gun control laws that you are pushing have killed people."[29] Hours after twenty children were murdered by a gunman at their elementary school, John Lott had the audacity to say it happened because of the school's ban on guns. He has been making these claims for years.

In an appearance on CNN in April 1999, a week after the Columbine High School shooting, Lott explained, "Take one law for example, the 1995 law that bans guns within one thousand feet of a school; what I fear happens in that case is it is the law-abiding citizens who obey the law. The criminals who are intent on harming our children don't. . . . If I put a sign up on my home that said, 'This Home Is a Gun-Free Zone,' would it make it more attractive or less attractive for a criminal to come in and try to attack myself or my family?"[30]

Arguing that "reducing the amount of weapons in our society doesn't decrease gun violence" is Lott's bread and butter, popularized in his 1998 book, *More Guns, Less Crime.* Instead, he claims, the opposite is true: that violent crime drops in states with laws that make it easier for citizens to carry concealed weapons. Therefore, legislation to limit the number of weapons in our country would increase the crime rate.

The book became a favorite among NRA members. This wonky academic went from an obscure professor to a bestselling author and in-demand conservative speaker. While there is no evidence of financial payments from the NRA or the gun industry to Lott, he has still benefited greatly from his pro-gun advocacy. Lott's place as a television pundit and bestselling author is directly linked to the views espoused in his book. Gun rights advocates repeat his claims in arguments at the kitchen table, in the workplace, and on the floor of Congress.

While Lott's book has become a sort of infallible bible for the gun rights community's talking points, his results and methodology have been in question for more than a decade. Yet the *Stanford*

Law Review conducted a rigorous examination of Lott's work and found that "the more guns, less crime hypothesis is without credible statistical support."[31]

When a group of researchers convened by the National Academy of Sciences examined Lott's thesis that the liberalization of concealed-carry laws leads to a decrease in violent crime, fifteen of the sixteen panel members found "no credible evidence" to support this theory.[32]

Even some of Lott's supporters have turned into skeptics. Criminologist Gary Kleck of Florida State University positively reviewed *More Guns, Less Crime* but now says the study "was garbage in and garbage out." After reexamining Lott's work, Kleck says, "Do I know anybody who specifically believes with more guns there are less crimes and they're a credible criminologist? No."[33]

Lott's fundamental data was called into question, but that did not stop those with a predisposition to oppose gun regulations from citing it as fact. And why shouldn't they? It confirmed their fundamental worldview. Even among those who have no idea who John Lott is, his theories remain fundamental to their advocacy against gun control.

More Guns, Less Crime was not Lott's only work to face skepticism from other academics. Most notable is a 1997 survey Lott conducted that found that when a gun is used for defense, 98 percent of the time the weapon is only brandished. When other academics asked to review Lott's data, he responded that it had vanished after a computer crash.[34] The survey involved more than 2,400 respondents, research that often would have cost thousands, if not tens of thousands of dollars, and yet there was no paper trail or other evidence of the survey.

James Lindgren, a law professor at Northwestern University, was suspicious of Lott's response: "I had never heard of a professor doing anything of that size with no funding, paid support, paid staff, phone reimbursements, or records (though there are probably precedents for such an unusual method)."[35]

The idea that his data would be stored on only a single computer, with no backups or hard copy from which it could be reassembled, was laughable on its face. Tim Lambert and a second scientist, sociologist Otis Dudley Duncan, found other reasons to call this data into question. According to the researchers:

1. Dr. Lott claimed his survey was conducted over a three month period in 1997. He also claimed that survey data shows that 98% of defensive gun uses involve merely brandishing weapon as early as Feb. 6, 1997, in his testimony to the Nebraska legislature.
2. Long before Dr. Lott ever mentioned that the 98% figure came from his survey, he had (erroneously) attributed it to various other surveys.

Lambert and Duncan also doubted that the researcher's results "could have been legitimately produced by a sample of the size Dr. Lott has mentioned."[36]

Furthermore, Duncan pointed out the unprofessional way in which the data was released—in Lott's book, with no supporting evidence or data—by writing: "Such piecemeal announcement of results from a major piece of research is, shall we say, unusual in scientific circles. (No, we shall not resort to such a euphemism. It is a clear breach of the ethics of scientific inquiry, one that comes up over and over again in regard to premature announcements of new medical 'discoveries,' and so on.)"[37]

Other researchers began asking Duncan and Lambert's question: Lott's data was allegedly gathered over three months in 1997, how then could he have cited it during a hearing in February 1997? Lott finally responded to criticism by conducting a second survey in 2002. Of the one thousand respondents, only seven people acknowledged using a firearm in self-defense, and of those seven, six people said they had only brandished the gun. The survey was not a statistically significant sample, but six out of seven people brandishing instead of using a gun meant Lott felt justified to assert that 90 percent of firearm defense is only brandishing the weapon.[38]

If Lott's errors were rare or sporadic, they could be discounted as the careless work of a potentially absentminded professor. However, because they are so egregious, lack any sort of data or paper trail showing his work, and invariably tilt in a single ideological direction, they must be considered intentionally deceptive.

It is not only progressives who question Lott's claims. In 2003, firebrand conservative columnist Michelle Malkin wrote at Townhall.com, "For those few of us in the mainstream media who openly support Second Amendment rights, research scholar John Lott has been—or rather, had been—an absolute godsend." Malkin then went on to provide an overview of the criticism of his data. When asked about the "coverage of the 1997 data dispute," Lott brushed it off, telling Malkin it was "a bunch to do about nothing."[39]

For his part, Lott responds by offering "statements from nine academics, four of whom I was coauthoring papers with at the time and who remember quite vividly, also losing the data that we had on various projects."[40] While these statements do speak to a hard-drive crash, they did not speak to the loss of the gun survey data. As to the rest of the questions about his reliability, Lott has lots of excuses: he has no financial records of the study because, unlike other academics, he doesn't stoop to asking for government grants; he doesn't have records of hiring people for the study because he is only required to keep IRS documents for three years; the bank doesn't have records because they keep them for only five years.[41]

Lott's response when he was forced to concede errors is suspect as well. Rather than issue a correction and admit fault that could call into question his fundamental assumptions, he simply swaps out or deletes numbers to achieve his intended results. When some of his data was questioned, Lott claimed to have noticed a coding error and posted new data tables online—new data that still proved his point. However, an analysis of the "corrected" data showed that Lott had left out a significant calculation whose omission kept the table the way Lott wanted.[42]

When confronted with unflattering details he doesn't like, Lott will simply try to erase them. This strategy is even employed by Lott when confronted with errors made in less serious venues. Media Matters researcher Chris Brown quoted Lott as claiming Barack Obama's administration "imposed much more extensive reporting requirements on sales of long guns" and pointed out the statement was obviously false because the administration had at that point imposed no such regulation. Lott changed his post to read, "'They *have also tried imposing* much more extensive reporting requirements on sales of long guns' and accused Media Matters of misquoting him [emphasis added]."[43]

Lott played victim, writing, "In fact, my quote is 'They have also tried imposing much more extensive reporting requirements on sales of long guns.' Besides, even if the point had been honestly misread, if someone has tried to check the link, the point would have been clear."[44] Unfortunately for Lott, the Internet has a memory that cannot simply be wiped clean like his hard drive: saved screenshots of his original postings show the error.

Lott's most embarrassing public episode was only tangentially related to his research. When questions about Lott's survey data first appeared online, a former student named Mary Rosh spoke up, attacking the professor's critics.

Rosh, it turned out, had an extensive history of writing pro-Lott posts on message boards and in other venues. The loyal fan wrote that Lott was "the best professor I ever had." And according to the former student, "Lott taught me more about analysis than any other professor that I had and I was not alone."

Rosh claimed she had taken a "PhD level empirical methods class [from Lott] when he taught at the Wharton School at the University of Pennsylvania back in the early 1990s."[45]

She would battle critics of Lott online; for example, she responded to Tim Lambert with: "Boy, you are a dishonest person." To someone else (who is unknown) she wrote: "YOU ARE AMAZINGLY DISHONEST. HAVE YOU ABSOLUTELY NO SHAME?"[46]

On Amazon.com, Rosh reviewed *More Guns, Less Crime,* telling readers, "Save your life—read this book." She went on to praise Lott's writing and ability to explain his subject in "an understandable commonsense way." Rosh continued, "If you want a book with the facts, a book that tells you the benefits and risks from protecting yourself and your family from crime, a book that will explain the facts in a straightforward and clear way, this is the book to get."[47]

The problem? Mary Rosh did not exist. The name itself was simply a mash-up of the first two letters of the names of John Lott's four sons. Libertarian researcher Julian Sanchez, who previously attracted the online ire of Mary Rosh, caught Lott, who acknowledged Rosh was simply a sock puppet of his own creation.[48]

In her post about Lott, Malkin rightly calls the Rosh incident "creepy" and goes on to say, "it shows his extensive willingness to deceive to protect and promote his work."[49] As with Malkin's other statements, Lott had bizarre excuses for the Mary Rosh incident: yes, I made up Mary Rosh and I picked a female name because women can't defend themselves; I didn't write that I was my own favorite professor, everyone in my family uses that pseudonym.[50]

So why, after repeated examples of brazen deception, is John Lott still regarded as a trusted source in the media? Primarily because he is willing to make arguments others are unwilling to. In the aftermath of a tragic shooting, the NRA is in a difficult position. Going on television in those moments is a dangerous proposition for the organization. Lott is willing to take those arrows. And unlike the NRA, or other lobby groups, he can sell himself as a disinterested academic, an econometrics professor who is simply reciting numbers on a page.

In the case of some hosts who disagree with him, like Piers Morgan, he makes an excellent foil. The "liberal" host gets to scream at his guest and call him a liar, but Lott is still presented to the audience as an expert in the topic while his history of lies and misstatements is glossed over.

Lott's appearance on Piers Morgan's show was not his only television appearance in the aftermath of the Sandy Hook shooting. On the Sunday following the massacre, he appeared on a CNN special and was allowed to continue speaking out against new gun safety legislation. "Every place in the world that we have crime data, both before and after a gun ban has gone into effect, every single place has seen an increase in murders after the ban has been put into place," he told the network. "And there's a simple reason for that and that is when you ban guns, it's basically the most law-abiding citizens who turn in their guns, not the criminals."[51]

That same day, Lott's influence over the conservative movement was demonstrated by ultra-conservative Texas representative Louie Gohmert. A darling of the Tea Party movement, one of the most outspoken conservative members of Congress, Gohmert appeared on *Fox News Sunday* to discuss the Sandy Hook shooting and its aftermath. Gohmert cited Lott to blame the lack of guns at mass shooting locations for increasing violence. "Once we have this actually open dialogue about the situation, Chris, you find out that—and John Lott has done some great investigation and study into this—every mass killing of more than three people in recent history has been in a place where guns were prohibited."[52]

Lott repeated this "logic" on yet another CNN show in the days after Sandy Hook. To a clearly skeptical Soledad O'Brien, Lott argued that "with only one exception" mass shootings have taken place where "guns are banned."[53]

CNN wasn't the only mainstream network to host the pro-gun advocate in the aftermath of Sandy Hook. National Public Radio, the Fox News Channel, and *Today* also turned to Lott during his post–Sandy Hook media tour.

Despite this constant refrain, the data Lott presented was simply wrong. According to a Mayors Against Illegal Guns study analyzing the locations of mass shootings in the United States between January 2009 and January 2013, "Nineteen of the 43 incidents (44%) took place in private residences. Of the 23 incidents in public spaces, at least 9 took place where concealed guns could be lawfully carried. All told, no more than 14 of the shootings (33%) took place in public spaces that were so-called 'gun-free zones.' "[54]

Lott's main point in the aftermath of these shootings was that concealed carry laws—more guns—would serve as a protection from crime. This assertion, too, has been disproven. The Johns Hopkins Center for Gun Policy and Research pointed to the many researchers who found "serious flaws" in Lott's work and further reported: "The most consistent finding across studies which correct for these flaws is that [Right to Carry] laws are associated with an increase in aggravated assaults."[55]

Contrary to Lott's suggestion that more guns equaled less crime, a fair-minded, unmanipulated look at the available data demonstrated the opposite of Lott's conclusions. The economist still presents his data as undeniable fact in interview after interview, and has never admitted to these flaws.

Lott's distorted data, because of his prestigious pedigree, ends up in the hands of respected reporters. For example, a little more than two weeks before the Sandy Hook shooting, *The Atlantic*'s Jeffrey Goldberg quoted Lott as saying "one way to make it riskier [to commit crimes] is to create the impression among the criminal population that the law-abiding citizen they want to target may have a gun."[56]

In most cases outright deception, publishing questionable data, and creating an alter ego to compliment yourself would mark the end of a career. But Lott has been excused for his errors, because the manipulated statistics he doggedly presents make a critical case for the conservative argument against gun safety regulations.

During an MSNBC appearance in May 2012, Lott claimed the "Stand Your Ground law isn't relevant to the George Zimmerman–Trayvon Martin case," ignoring the fact that the city manager in Sanford, Florida, cited the Stand Your Ground law as the reason he did not immediately arrest George Zimmerman.[57]

In the fall of 2013, the Senate Judiciary Committee called Lott to testify as a reputable authority on guns during a hearing titled " 'Stand Your Ground' Laws: Civil Rights and Public Safety Implications of the Expanded Use of Deadly Force."[58] Other invited witnesses included Lucia McBath, mother of slain teen Jordan Davis; and Sybrina Fulton, the mother of Trayvon Martin, whose killing drew attention to Stand Your Ground laws.[59]

In his testimony before the committee, Lott claimed that Stand Your Ground laws, which have been heavily criticized for their racial bias, actually were to the benefit of the black community. "Poor blacks who live in high-crime urban areas are not only the most likely victims of crime, they are also the ones who benefit the most from Stand Your Ground laws," he testified. "The laws make it easier for them to protect themselves when the police can't be there fast enough. Therefore, rules that make self-defense more difficult disproportionately impact blacks."[60]

This was an invention of conservatives like Lott. The numbers demonstrate a clear racial disparity in the enforcement of these laws. According to a National Urban League study, "homicides were 'justifiable' in 49 percent of cases in which a white man shot a black man compared to just 8 percent of cases in which the roles were reversed."[61] The public data behind this study can be examined and confirmed.

Lott appeared on an NRA News radio show a few days later to discuss how difficult it was to testify alongside a "prop" witness like Trayvon Martin's mother. He told host Cam Edwards, "Well, I thought [the hearing] was somewhat surreal. Look, we had two very sympathetic witnesses that were there. Trayvon Martin's mom and another mother who had lost her son in a shooting, both of them were black, and they were there to go and try to serve as props essentially for the case that there was racial bias in Stand Your Ground laws. As I say, it's very hard to say anything when you're having to deal with a mother who has lost her son, under any circumstances."[62]

In 2013, Lott founded the Crime Prevention Research Center (CPRC), an organization seemingly designed to house his research and promote his media appearances. The center's small board includes rocker Ted Nugent, who serves as secretary of the organization.[63] CPRC does not make its funders public, though its website claims it "does not accept donations from gun or ammunition makers or organizations such as the NRA or any other organizations involved in the gun control debate on either side of the issue."[64]

Of the thirty-two items posted in the "research" section of CPRC's website between December 2013 and August 2015, five are columns Lott wrote for FoxNews.com, and five are critiques of different efforts by Michael Bloomberg's organizations to combat gun violence. Other subjects researched include:

- Do Blacks trust the police more than whites or Hispanics do?
- UPDATED information on K-12 and University School Shootings Deaths: The number of deaths has been declining over time
- Discussion of Chicago's crime problems ignore what Rahm Emanuel has done to the police department
- The incredibly flawed FBI study on active shooters, CPRC original research[65]

As long as Lott continues to provide statistical credence to their ideology, the right will embrace him with open arms. For more than a decade, other respected researchers have found his work to be suspect, but that has not limited his media stardom, public speaking engagements, or book sales. His data helps to justify the legislative whims of a multibillion-dollar industry.

"More guns, less crime" has become not only a book, but also a mantra for the gun rights movement. In the aftermath of tragedy, it provides a talking point to those seeking to justify the right to carry firearms. If only those in the theater, elementary school, or other sites of a mass shooting had access to guns these tragedies wouldn't have occurred. There is no evidence in support of claims such as Aurora shooter James Holmes having chosen the specific theater in question because guns were banned. His diary shows evidence of him weighing the pros and cons of different targets. For example, he did not choose an airport because of security, and because if he did his actions might be considered terrorism, which "isn't the message" he intended to send.[66] Additionally, numerous studies, such as the one cited earlier from Mayors Against Illegal Guns, cast doubt on the theory that mass murderers choose the location of their kills by examining firearm policy.

Like many effective arguments from Lies, Incorporated, the principal use of John Lott's research is the maintenance of a status quo. If one side claims a reduction in access to firearms improves public safety and a second claims more weapons makes us safer, this deadlock still produces the desired outcome. By becoming the gun rights community's favorite academic, John Lott has developed a following in a community that uses his flawed research to justify this false worldview, helping to prevent any progress on the issue of gun safety.

In the next chapter we will see Lies, Incorporated use the creation of a mythology to disenfranchise voters they believe will oppose them at the ballot box. As with guns, a singular figure will rise to prominence in the conservative movement based on his ability to effectively distort the facts around a singular issue. And like with guns, unfortunately, Lies, Incorporated will succeed, with major consequences for our democracy.

Chapter 7

One Lie, One Vote:
Voter I.D. Laws

Concerns about in-person voter fraud have been repeated ad nauseam in conservative circles in the lead-up to nearly every election since 2000. In the mind of the right-wing base, undocumented immigrants, voters with fake I.D.s, nefarious party operatives, and the deceased plague our elections—all to ensure Democrats come out on top.

According to *The Washington Post,* just prior to Election Day in 2008, "McCain campaign manager Rick Davis said the reports about investigations of the community organizing group ACORN (the Association of Community Organizations for Reform Now) suggested 'rampant voter fraud as it relates to voter registration.'"[1]

"I'm always concerned about voter fraud, you know, being from Kenosha, and quite frankly having lived through seeing some of it happen," Republican National Committee chairman Reince Priebus told his hometown paper in 2012. "Certainly in Milwaukee we have seen some of it, and I think it's been documented."[2]

Dick Armey, former Republican House Majority Leader, brought similar arguments to the Lincoln Club of Orange County,

California, a conservative political group in one of the reddest areas of the country. Armey argued that voter fraud accounted for as much as 3 percent of the Democratic vote, a statistic no study has ever come close to demonstrating. "I'm tired of people being Republican all their lives and then changing parties when they die," he said to the delight of the assembled audience.[3]

During the Bush years, the Justice Department caved to intense Republican pressure and made a huge effort to crack down on voter fraud. Then–White House deputy chief of staff Karl Rove had a long history of using "voter fraud as a handy political weapon" in elections throughout his career.[4] Rove and other Republicans frequently alleged that Democratic voter fraud was rampant and had "corrupted the political process." Their accusations that U.S. attorneys were not investigating succeeded, resulting in the Justice Department targeting Democratic districts and spending tens of thousands of hours on what would prove to be fruitless inquiries.[5]

The result: virtually nothing. Five years of investigations resulted in charges being brought against just 120 individuals. Of those, 86 were ultimately convicted primarily of committing relatively petty crimes and errors. Most were simply unaware they were ineligible to vote.[6]

The problem with many voter fraud prosecutions is that they are costly and typically do not significantly benefit the integrity of our election system. Election law expert Richard L. Hasen, the Chancellor's Professor of Law and Political Science at the University of California, Irvine, said: "If they found a single case of a conspiracy to affect the outcome of a congressional election or a statewide election, that would be significant. But what we see is isolated, small-scale activities that often have not shown any kind of criminal intent."[7]

Some of the incidents of fraud were innocent mistakes that

changed lives. Usman Ali, a legal Pakistani immigrant who had lived in Florida for a decade, accidentally filled out a voter registration card while he was renewing his driver's license. He was convicted of fraud and deported.[8] Kimberly Prude spent more than a year in jail after casting a vote—mistakenly believing she was permitted to vote while on probation—and was convicted of voter fraud. At a hearing for Prude's case, appellate court judge Diane P. Wood commented, "I find this whole prosecution mysterious." She continued, "I don't know whether the Eastern District of Wisconsin goes after every felon who accidentally votes. It is not like she voted five times. She cast one vote."[9]

In a few cases, the Justice Department has convicted local officials in vote-buying scandals, but this is not the rampant Democratic voter fraud conservatives have used to stoke public fears about the validity of our electoral process.[10] The GOP screams voter fraud when they lose elections, often making claims such as that "dogs and dead people"[11] voted. What they're really saying is that too many people of color voted. Voter I.D. requirements tip the scales back in their favor.

The Bush administration was so intent on pursuing voter fraud, they targeted prosecutors who would not do their bidding. Before the renewed interest of the Justice Department, federal prosecutors were able to only pursue large-scale "schemes to corrupt elections," not instances of individual wrongdoing. Additionally, prosecutors "had to prove an intent to commit fraud, not just an improper action." These guidelines meant prosecutors were wary of targeting minor incidents of reported fraud—inaction that was used to justify voter fraud fearmongering. Following complaints made to the White House from local Republican elected officials, New Mexico U.S. attorney David Iglesias was dismissed in 2006 for not aggressively pursuing voter fraud cases.[12]

A 2008 investigation by the Justice Department's inspector

general found that "the evidence we uncovered in our investigation demonstrated that the real reason for Iglesias's removal were [*sic*] the complaints from New Mexico Republican politicians and party activists about how Iglesias handled voter fraud and public corruption cases in the state."[13]

Oddly, as a prosecutor, Iglesias had taken voter fraud extremely seriously, even forming a task force to handle and prosecute complaints. His work was so exceptional, he was invited to deliver a "voting integrity symposium" at the Justice Department in 2005. In its investigation, the Justice Department reviewed how Iglesias responded to complaints about voter fraud and saw that he had "received recognition from within the Department as an example of how to handle voter fraud investigations. In addition, the Chief of the Public Integrity Section's Election Crimes Branch, Craig Donsanto, told us that he thought Iglesias pursued voter fraud cases vigorously and fairly, and that he had no complaints about Iglesias's office's attention to those matters."[14]

Regardless, according to the inspector general's report, "New Mexico Republican officials were dissatisfied with Iglesias's task force approach and its prosecutorial decisions on individual voter fraud cases." As a result, "they began making repeated and vociferous complaints about Iglesias's handling of these cases, first directly to Iglesias, then to the Department, to New Mexico Republican members of Congress, and to the White House."[15]

This led to explicit calls for Iglesias's firing that "reached the highest levels of the White House, including Karl Rove." Ultimately, the president himself was informed of these complaints, and David Iglesias was removed from his position as U.S. attorney.[16]

Robert Kengle, a former deputy chief of the Justice Department's voting-rights section, told *The Washington Post:* "Very shortly after [Attorney General John Ashcroft] came in, he launched . . . a voting integrity initiative, which was supposed to be half civil rights and half voter fraud, but the focus very clearly was finding and prosecuting voter fraud."[17]

Perhaps this was because Ashcroft believed voter fraud contributed to his failure to capture a Senate seat in 2000. On Election Day, it was discovered that hundreds of voters could not vote because their names were not on the rolls, leading to a day-of court struggle. Some voting places stayed open forty-five minutes past official closing time to allow these people to cast a ballot. When the election was called, Republicans immediately blamed the loss on voter fraud.[18] However, the evidence did not weigh in Ashcroft's favor. The Brennan Center for Justice, a New York University Law School think tank devoted to issues of democracy, investigated the accusations. The inquiry revealed "only six substantiated cases of Missouri votes cast by ineligible voters . . . amounting to an overall rate of 0.0003%" voter fraud for that election.[19]

The failure of the Bush administration to find any significant voter fraud affecting electoral outcomes did not dampen the conservative movement's desire to pursue these investigations.

After taking office as Iowa's secretary of state in 2011, Republican Matt Schultz vowed to crack down on voter fraud and spent $250,000 investigating cases throughout the state. *The Des Moines Register* reported in 2014 the effort "found evidence of 117 illegally cast votes, led to charges against 27 suspected fraudulent voters and has resulted in six criminal convictions."[20] In a state where more than one million ballots are cast, just six people were convicted of voter fraud—a revelation that cost taxpayers over $40,000 per conviction.

Five of the six instances were resolved with guilty pleas by

December 2013. Those five included a man who had stolen his brother's identity to get a driver's license and registered to vote during that process, two felons who had mistakenly been told their voting rights had been restored, one noncitizen felon who didn't understand the voting restrictions applied to him, and a mother who filled in her daughter's absentee ballot while she was away at school, not realizing she had already voted. Recognizing her error, she turned herself in, and paid a fine of $147.75.[21]

Voter fraud is so rare that Senator Cory Booker (D-NJ) claimed on ABC's *This Week* that "you're more likely to get struck by lightning in Texas than to find any kind of voter fraud." PolitiFact checked the veracity of his statement, rating it True. The odds of getting struck by lightning in Texas are one in 1.35 million. The likelihood of in-person voter fraud in Texas? One in 18 million.[22]

The minuscule numbers of voter fraud in Iowa and Texas are not unique. A study of the 2004 election in Wisconsin "found just seven cases of fraud out of 3 million votes cast during the 2004 election—and none of these seven cases were the kind of in-person voter fraud that is prevented by a voter ID law."[23] And this in the state where the RNC chairman insisted fraud had been documented as a real problem.[24]

For years, Republicans have made accusations of dead Democrats showing up at the polls, rising from the graveyard on Election Day. These zombie voter fraud stories are perpetual myth spread by the right. South Carolina attorney general Alan Wilson explicitly claimed: "We know for a fact that there are deceased people whose identities are being used in elections in South Carolina."[25] Another South Carolina official, DMV director Kevin Shwedo, claimed: "Well over 900 individuals appear to have voted after they died."[26]

The state's election commission investigated these reports and found that "of the initial batch of six names of allegedly dead voters on the DMV's list, one had cast an absentee ballot before dying; another was the result of a poll worker mistakenly marking the voter as his deceased father; two were clerical errors resulting from stray marks on voter registration lists detected by a scanner; and two others resulted from poll managers incorrectly marking the name of the voter in question instead of the voter above or below on the list." Another two hundred cases of zombie voting were investigated by the agency, which "found zero cases of illegal activity."[27]

Unsatisfied with this result, the South Carolina attorney general's office ordered the "State Law Enforcement Division" to launch its own investigation. The results, only obtained through an open records request by the *Free Times,* revealed the state had "found nothing nefarious."[28]

An Ohio investigation following the 2012 election found a "minuscule amount" of voter fraud. Out of 5.6 million votes cast, there were 135 cases of possible election violations. Of the results, Ohio secretary of state Jon Husted said, "This report demonstrates that voter fraud does exist; but it is not an epidemic."[29]

These dead-end investigations have been replicated by Republicans in state after state and have never uncovered a shred of evidence that voter fraud is the epidemic conservatives claim it to be. If these investigations were simply a waste of taxpayer money and government resources, it would be problematic but not a tragedy. But beyond decreasing confidence in our electoral process, these stories of voter fraud have been used for much more nefarious ends: encouraging the passage of policies that result in voter suppression.

For decades, some conservatives expressed the belief that a greater franchise harms Republican candidates. In 1980, Paul Weyrich, an influential conservative strategist who helped found the Heritage Foundation and other conservative institutions, including the American Legislative Exchange Council (ALEC), laid out the conservative doctrine on voting, telling a Dallas audience, "I don't want everybody to vote." He went on to claim that conservative "leverage in the elections, quite candidly, goes up as the voting populace goes down."[30] In other words, the more people who vote, the worse the outcome will be for conservatives. Even in 1980, before the country experienced the demographic shifts that have shaped today's electorate, conservative electoral victory depended on higher voter turnout among traditional Republican constituencies than among liberal groups including women, minorities, and young people.

Conservatives, then, faced a challenge. There would be no way the public, even the right-wing electorate, would accept a direct effort to disenfranchise minority voters. Furthermore, the courts made it clear that those actions would be deemed explicitly unconstitutional.

Phony accusations of voter fraud are the principal justification behind a variety of voter suppression bills introduced in state legislatures around the country. Though the inevitable result of these laws is the disenfranchisement of minority populations, legislators can deny that is the primary motivation and claim it is coincidental that the laws disproportionately affect minority voters. In state after state, voter I.D. requirements have been signed into law. Early voting hours have been scaled back. Voters have been "purged" from the roles, supposedly to remove convicted felons and others ineligible to cast ballots, but often at the expense of minority voters who happened to share personal details with those who were supposedly ineligible.

These changes were all made in the name of cleaning up an electoral process supposedly rampant with fraud. But in most cases, they just cost taxpayer money while adding confusion and disarray to the process. Behind the lies, scare tactics, investigations, secretaries of state, and ever more voter suppression is one man. No longer kept alive by Karl Rove, the myth of voter fraud is now sustained by Hans von Spakovsky.

Von Spakovsky is a Republican lawyer who rose to prominence during the George W. Bush administration. He has since become a well-known advocate for voter I.D. laws. Whenever a new law restricting the right to vote is introduced or accusations of voter fraud hurled, von Spakovsky invariably lurks in a corner.

In his book *The Voting Wars,* Richard L. Hasen credits von Spakovsky with the public prominence of the myth of voter fraud. "Before 2000, there were some rumblings about Democratic voter fraud, but it really wasn't part of the main discourse," wrote Hasen. "But thanks to von Spakovsky and the flame-fanning of a few others, the myth that Democratic voter fraud is common, and that it helps Democrats win elections, has become part of the Republican orthodoxy."[31]

Von Spakovsky's political career grew alongside his voting rights activism. He volunteered as a poll watcher in 1992 and claims he saw illegal activity during that first election. By 1997, he was working against the National Voter Registration Act, was appointed to an Atlanta-area election board, and wrote articles advocating for voter rolls to be regularly purged. In 1999, von Spakovsky was chairman of the Fulton County Republican Party, which includes the city of Atlanta, and sat on the board of the Voting Integrity Project (VIP). While von Spakovsky was on the board, VIP gave an award to the tech company whose process of scrubbing the voter rolls led to the disenfranchisement of thousands of Florida voters in 2000.[32]

After a volunteer stint in Florida on the Bush recount team, he joined the Justice Department and was quickly promoted to counsel for the assistant attorney general of the Civil Rights Division.[33] Von Spakovsky was part of John Ashcroft's effort to take a more aggressive approach to dealing with the problem of voter fraud.[34]

At the Justice Department, von Spakovsky had many opportunities to suppress votes. In 2003, he approved changes to voting districts that his colleagues believed had been designed to disenfranchise minority voters.[35] House Majority Leader Tom DeLay had taken the unusual step of pushing Texas to issue a redistricting plan outside the scheduled change window created by the census. Angry about the new map, which gerrymandered predominately Hispanic neighborhoods to reduce the number of Democratic districts and shore up Republican seats, many Texas Democrats "took off for Oklahoma" in order to prevent a vote. After much interstate travel, the Texas legislature approved the new map. However, the Supreme Court ruled against the redistricting in 2006.[36]

In 2005, von Spakovsky again went against his colleagues by endorsing a new Georgia law requiring an I.D. to vote. Since some people would have to purchase an I.D., other lawyers at the Justice Department thought the law instituted a poll tax—which is illegal under the Voting Rights Act.[37] Approval of the law caused public dissent on von Spakovsky's team: "Staff members complain that higher-ranking Justice officials ignored serious problems with data supplied by the state in approving the plan, which would have required voters to carry photo identification," wrote *The Washington Post,* noting that "a team of voting-section employees [had] concluded that the Georgia plan would hurt black voters." According to the paper, "higher-ranking officials disagreed, and approved the plan later that day," claiming "that as many as 200,000 of those without ID cards were felons and illegal immigrants and that they would not be eligible to vote anyway."[38]

During his time at the Justice Department, von Spakovsky was accused of politicizing the Election Integrity Commission (EIC)—a body created by the Help America Vote Act passed in the wake of the hanging chad chaos of the 2000 election. He tried to have the group's chairman, Republican Paul DeGregorio, removed for being insufficiently partisan, among other accusations of impropriety.[39]

When an EIC study suggested that voter I.D. laws might lead to disenfranchisement, von Spakovsky asked Lies, Incorporated economist and *More Guns, Less Crime* author John Lott to recalibrate the data. "This study is now being trumpeted as proof that voter ID hurts turnout, and if it is a flawed study, someone with your kind of reputation needs to point that out," von Spakovsky wrote to Lott. "If you are interested in doing this, Caroline Hunter, one of the new commissioners at the EAC, would be happy to provide you with whatever information you might need."[40]

In December 2005, George W. Bush placed von Spakovsky on the Federal Election Commission via recess appointment. The appointment, however, did not allow him to avoid a Senate confirmation hearing to permanently secure his position as commissioner. In fact, the question of his appointment garnered most of the attention surrounding the hearing.[41]

The congressional delegation from Georgia wrote a letter to the Senate Rules and Administration Committee, charged with managing confirmation process, to protest von Spakovsky's nomination. Six members of Congress, including civil rights legend John Lewis, wrote: "The track record on voting suppression of one of the nominees, Mr. Hans von Spakovksy, could potentially turn back the clock on fifty years of progress. Unfortunately, we are well-acquainted with Mr. von Spakovsky's legacy in our home state of Georgia. . . . We believe that his actions in Georgia and at the federal level raise serious concerns about his ability and willingness to administer the nation's election laws fairly."[42]

Additionally, six attorneys who had worked with von Spakovsky in the Civil Rights Division wrote a letter to Senators Dianne Feinstein and Bob Bennett, the chairwoman and the ranking member, respectively, of the Senate Rules and Administration Committee. According to his former colleagues, "Mr. von Spakovsky played a major role in the implementation of practices which injected partisan political factors into decision-making on enforcement matters and into the hiring process, and included repeated efforts to intimidate career staff."[43]

The group further accused von Spakovsky of using his position to interfere in partisan election disputes, always to the benefit of the Republican Party. Just before the 2004 election, he "drafted legal briefs in lawsuits between the Republican and Democratic parties in three battleground states, Ohio, Michigan and Florida, just before the election, all in favor of the Republican Party's position, and included a position that the Civil Rights Division had never taken before with regards to statutes it enforces."[44]

After several months on the FEC in a recess appointment capacity, von Spakovsky withdrew his nomination in May 2008, recognizing that the Senate would never confirm him.[45] He joined the Heritage Foundation that year and began using the conservative think tank as a platform to continue his war on voting, appearing as a frequent guest on conservative radio shows and Fox News.

This media presence has had a significant impact on public awareness of voter fraud. David Wilson and Paul Brewer, professors at the University of Delaware, published a study in October 2013 measuring not only the perception of voter fraud and I.D. measures but also the respondents' media consumption habits. What they discovered was far from surprising. "Fox News viewers"—the very ones most exposed to the arguments of von Spakovsky—"are particularly likely to support voter ID laws," and "perceptions of voting fraud as 'common' are associated with support for voter ID laws." Additionally, while Fox News had an effect on respondents' support of voter I.D. laws, no other media outlet had an effect on viewers' position on the laws.[46]

Von Spakovsky's media exposure translated into legislative success. Thirty-six states now have voter I.D. laws on the books;[47] this number has steadily increased since 2000.[48]

Other states, such as Wisconsin and Pennsylvania, have seen their voter I.D. laws struck down by courts. Before defending its law in court, the state of Pennsylvania was forced to undermine the very reason for its existence. The state signed a document acknowledging there "have been no investigations or prosecutions of in-person voter fraud in Pennsylvania" and agreeing to "not offer any evidence in this action that in-person voter fraud has in fact occurred in Pennsylvania and elsewhere." Additionally, the state would not claim "that in-person voter fraud is likely to occur in November 2012 in the absence of the Photo ID law."[49]

While the law would have no impact preventing voter fraud, it would have disenfranchised voters like Viviette Applewhite. A ninety-three-year-old widow who had voted in nearly every election since 1960 and marched with Dr. Martin Luther King, Jr., Ms. Applewhite had no driver's license. Her I.D. had been stolen, and she had been unable to obtain a new one because in her tenth decade of life she could not locate her birth certificate.[50] Applewhite was not alone. The state reported that 758,000 Pennsylvania residents, more than 9 percent of the state's voters, did not have a driver's license.[51] It's astonishing that tens, perhaps hundreds of thousands of voters in one state could be deprived of a constitutional right in order to stop a crime that was an extreme rarity at best.

If one were to believe that the voter I.D. proponents were acting in good faith, then the best that could be said for them is that their cure is a thousand times worse than the disease.

But there is a simpler explanation for these lawmakers' fanatical devotion to voter I.D. laws. In a moment of candor, Pennsylvania House Majority Leader Mike Turzai acknowledged the political motivation behind the law during a 2012 Republican State Committee meeting: "We are focused on making sure that we meet our obligations that we've talked about for years," he said. "Pro-Second Amendment? The Castle Doctrine, it's done. First pro-life legislation—abortion facility regulations—in 22 years, done. Voter ID, *which is gonna allow Governor Romney to win the state of Pennsylvania,* done [emphasis added]."[52] The state passed a voter I.D. law in 2012 with one motivation: to restrict the votes of minority groups likely to vote for President Obama, allowing Mitt Romney to win the state.

To be fair, elections *have* been stolen in the United States, through a variety of means: local election officials stuffing the ballot box, disenfranchising large swaths of the population, mailers with the wrong Election Day and polling location, and the outright purchasing of votes by political machines and criminal organizations. None of these methods of election theft would be prevented by the passage of voter I.D. laws. Stealing an election through the use of false I.D.s would require a massive conspiracy with hundreds, if not thousands, of people voting through fraudulent means. At best, such a plot would be hugely inefficient and easy for any law enforcement agency to uncover.

Yet Hans von Spakovsky and his associates, "experts" with a history of partisan lies, continue to weave yarns about this myth that provide ammunition to politicians needing excuses for their senseless and partisan laws.

Along with former *Wall Street Journal* columnist John Fund, von Spakovsky authored a 2012 book titled *Who's Counting? How Fraudsters and Bureaucrats Put Your Vote at Risk,* which made dozens of outlandish and demonstrably false statements about the existence of voter fraud in America.

The authors claimed that Al Franken's narrow victory over Norm Coleman in 2008 was the result of voter fraud. This election was one of the closest in recent memory, with recounts and court challenges that dragged on for months. Franken was not sworn in as United States senator until July of 2009. Von Spakovsky and Fund noted the importance of the race: "Franken's seating gave the Democrats the critical 60 votes they needed to overcome Republican filibusters, and proved vital to the passage of ObamaCare."[53] By arguing that fraudulent voters helped Franken win his seat, the authors implied that his vote was invalid, and therefore everything that passed because of his vote was also invalid.

This claim was based on "evidence" from a conservative watchdog group, the Minnesota Majority, which found there was "compelling evidence that at least 1,099 ineligible felons voted illegally in the Franken v. Coleman contest." This, they pointed out, was "more than three times the victory margin Franken eventually achieved through litigation."[54]

Hennepin County attorney Mike Freeman responded to the book's allegations, saying, "After the most closely scrutinized election in Minnesota history in 2008, there were zero cases of fraud," pointing out that, "even the Republicans' lawyers acknowledged that there was no systematic effort to defraud the election."[55]

Furthermore, he noted, "The Minnesota Majority presented us with 1,500 cases that they felt there were problems with voting. Our own election bureau gave us 100. At the end of the day, we charged 38 cases. And all but one of them are felons voting who were still under the penalty [of not legally applying to regain individual voting rights]. There was no fraud."[56]

This did not stop von Spakovsky and Fund from further inventing charges of fraud. During the canvass and recount of absentee ballots, the authors claim, "the Franken legal team ginned up an additional 1,350 absentees from Franken-leaning Democratic counties."[57]

"Finding" additional ballots, or ballot stuffing, would be a serious offense (one, as noted earlier, that would not be solved by implementing stricter voter I.D. laws), but that is not what the authors claim. There is no evidence that Al Franken's campaign team fraudulently created ballots or that those 1,500 votes were invalid.

The Franken race was not the only election von Spakovsky and Fund claim was won through voter fraud. They claim that Loretta Sanchez's victory, by a margin of "979 votes," over Bob Dornan in 1996 "may have been stolen by noncitizen voting." According to von Spakovsky and Fund, a congressional investigation found 624 "invalid votes by noncitizens" in addition to "124 improper absentee ballots." Furthermore, in the case of another 196 cases, there was "circumstantial" evidence that ballots had been cast by noncitizens—a total of 944 fraudulent ballots cast. Although this was still not enough votes to give Bob Dornan the margin of victory, they argue "the possibility is strong that undetected illegal votes changed the outcome of the election."[58]

Yet von Spakovsky and Fund's tally of fraudulent votes is suspect. Not in the least because the Orange County Registrar of Voters determined Sanchez won by 984 votes, not the 979 claimed by von Spakovsky and Fund.[59] What would be a minor error in other instances, not being able to accurately report years-old, publicly available data in your argument about voter fraud where every vote counts is much more problematic.

Additionally, according to the Brennan Center for Justice, of the 624-noncitizen votes, "only 71 voters matched name, date of birth, and signature; other matches were less reliable." Furthermore, an organization that registers newly naturalized citizens to vote was responsible for many of the 624 supposedly ineligible votes, and at least 372 of those individuals took the oath of citizenship before the election.[60]

Ultimately, the state of California spent fourteen months and $1.4 million investigating instances of fraud in the Loretta Sanchez election. The investigation that involved federal, state, and county agencies resulted in not a single prosecution. The few who were identified as being "illegal, non-citizen voters," the Republican secretary of state did not prosecute after "deciding they had registered in error and not from criminal intent."[61]

Like his peers in Lies, Incorporated, von Spakovsky has a history of being unable to produce the hard data that backs up his assertions. Richard L. Hasen discussed von Spakovsky's methods during the keynote speech at a national conference on election law and politics.[62] In 2008, Hasen read and was suspicious of a column by von Spakovsky. The Fox News op-ed read, in part: "One doesn't have to look far to find instances of fraudulent ballots cast in actual elections by 'voters' who are figments of active imaginations. In 1984 a district attorney in Brooklyn, New York, a Democrat, released the findings of a grand jury report that reported extensive registration and impersonation fraud between 1968 and '82."[63]

Curious about the example and interested in using it for his own research, Hansen searched for the grand jury report. Neither he nor two other experts he reached out to could find it. He and von Spakovsky had written to each other before, so he emailed to ask for the report. Two requests directly to von Spakovsky and one email to the head of the Heritage Foundation, where von Spakovsky worked, all went unanswered.[64]

Not until an article about the missing grand jury report and subsequent unanswered emails appeared on the Talking Points Memo website did Hasen make progress.[65] A law librarian at U.C. Irvine contacted the Brooklyn District Attorney's office and was able to get a copy of the report. After reading it, Hasen was unclear why the report had been so difficult to obtain from von Spakovsky, because "the report contains the only apparently successful effort in the last 40 years of which I'm aware to actually affect election results through impersonation fraud." He went on to note, "Perhaps the reason is that the way in which the fraud was done almost certainly could not happen today."[66]

Hasen pointed out that the report does show that unsavory things happened, particularly at the Brooklyn Board of Elections, and that some election officials were involved in "impersonation fraud" that likely kept people from voting. However, it does not indicate that "extensive impersonation fraud" took place on the part of voters. Nothing in the report supports the claim that "extensive registration and impersonation fraud" took place: no examples of voter fraud "where people were showing up at the polls in some kind of conspiracy, claimed [sic] to be someone else, and tricking election officials." This grand jury report that, according to von Spakovsky, proved how pervasive voter fraud is, did not demonstrate anything of the kind.[67]

Jane Mayer, award-winning reporter for *The New Yorker,* asked von Spakovsky why he didn't turn over the document to Hasen. He replied, "What am I—his research assistant?" Mayer also raised Hasen's point that when election officials are part of the fraud, a voter I.D. law would not help prevent it, to which von

Spakovsky replied: "That's not what the grand jury said. They recommended voter I.D.s."[68]

Mayer's review of the grand jury report contradicts von Spakovksy's assertion: "The report recommends nine specific procedural changes to help prevent corrupt behavior by election officials, but says of voter identification only that it should be studied as one of several 'possible remedies.'"[69]

The affair over the grand jury report clearly shows that von Spakovsky is not above lying about the evidence he uses for his claims, does not have enough confidence in his claims to share his evidence with other scholars, and is so secure in his position as a conservative expert that he is comfortable lying to a renowned reporter about the contents of a document she had obviously read for herself.

Hans von Spakovsky not only operates as a single entity pushing the myth of voter fraud, he has actively coordinated with several groups working to disenfranchise minorities. One such group is True the Vote, a grassroots organization of Tea Party activists that has challenged voter registrations around the country, often using erroneous and unchecked data. The disenfranchised voters most often fit neatly into minority voting blocks. True the Vote also helps voter integrity organizations around the country challenge "suspicious" registrations by providing software for volunteers to use for examining voter registrations—one of the criteria the software flags is those households where six or more registered voters live. Once those households are flagged (many of them homes of extended families, students, and poor people), the volunteer can challenge those voters' ability to vote.[70]

True the Vote's activities have included challenging college students for failing to include their dorm room number on registration cards; they have also claimed that occupied homes were vacant lots. Tom Burke, a board of elections chairman from Ohio who had to deal with challenges from the group, was quoted by ABC News as saying he believes their anti-fraud campaigns are simply "a smoke screen for their real effort, and that is to intimidate and prevent Democrats, and especially African-American Democrats, from voting."[71]

Like von Spakovsky, True the Vote has spread mythical stories of voter fraud, claiming, for example, that buses off-loaded ineligible voters in San Diego and Wisconsin. The buses are allegedly coming from other countries, Native American reservations, Chicago, or Detroit. It's a popular and oft-repeated lie, even though no evidence has ever emerged of these voter fraud mobiles. Reid Magney of the Wisconsin Government Accountability Board told *The New York Times,* "It's so stealthy that no one is ever able to get a picture and no one is able to get a license plate."[72]

It should come as no surprise that von Spakovsky has been "very, very helpful" to True the Vote's efforts and has served on their advisory council. The admiration is mutual. Von Spakovsky told Jane Mayer he believes the group is "doing a great job."[73]

In addition to True the Vote, von Spakovsky has worked closely with and has spoken at conferences hosted by the American Legislative Exchange Council. At these events, conservative members of state legislatures write and vote on draft legislation to introduce in their chambers back home. One of the organization's biggest pushes since 2009 has been the voter I.D. bill advocated by von Spakovsky.[74] Thirty-seven states introduced voter I.D. bills in 2011 alone based on model legislation drafted and approved by the organization. According to a report in the *San Francisco Chronicle,* "More than half of the 62 separate bills introduced in the 2011 and 2012 state legislative sessions were sponsored by members or conference attendees of ALEC."[75]

Perhaps von Spakovsky's worst lie is that these voter I.D. laws are without impact. "Numerous academic studies have also shown that voter ID does not depress the turnout of minority, poor, and elderly voters," he wrote in *USA Today*. "Georgia and Indiana saw no decrease in the turnout of such voters in elections after their voter ID laws went into effect."[76]

Evidence from around the country tells a different tale. In Indiana, "a dozen nuns and an unknown number of students were turned away" and more than thirty Indiana voters were turned away in another county in the first application of the state's voter I.D. law. As Justice David Souter pointed out in his dissent of the Supreme Court decision on Indiana's voter I.D. law, an "'estimated 43,000 individuals' (about 1% of the State's voting-age population) lack[ed] a qualifying ID" and therefore could not vote.[77]

The Fifth Circuit Court of Appeals struck down a voter I.D. law in Texas after hearing expert testimony outlining how the law affected minorities.[78] Harvard professor Stephen Ansolabehere "conducted a study of ID possession rates among Texas voters by matching voter databases to databases of people who hold various forms of acceptable ID." He then testified that "minority voters are significantly less likely to possess the requisite ID and they will be affected more than other voters." Specifically, blacks are twice as likely to lack proper I.D., Hispanics are 40–50 percent more likely to lack proper I.D., while only 4 percent of whites would lack an I.D.[79]

Von Spakovsky's lying is pervasive and transparent. His lies have a clearly political bent, and he has built a career in conservative media and as a fellow at the Heritage Foundation that is based not on solid research, but on his quest to disenfranchise Democratic voters.

His role in Lies, Incorporated is providing fuzzy data to legitimize a position that in the absence of his research would be obviously discriminatory. Von Spakovsky is actively putting into use the "coded" language Lee Atwater suggested in 1981. Atwater, the former chairman of the Republican National Committee who helped elect Ronald Reagan and George H. W. Bush, once explained the delicate balance the Republican Party must play when using racially tinged issues to win elections without appearing outwardly racist—by "getting abstract" when talking about race:

> You start out in 1954 by saying, "Nigger, nigger, nigger." By 1968 you can't say "nigger"—that hurts you, backfires. So you stay stuff like forced busing, states' rights, and all that stuff. And you're getting so abstract now that you're talking about cutting taxes, and all these things you're talking about are totally economic things and a byproduct of them is, blacks get hurt worse than whites. And subconsciously maybe that is part of it. If it is getting that abstract, and that coded, then we're doing away with the racial problem one way or the other.[80]

Hans von Spakovsky and others on the right provide the lies to justify voter I.D. regulation while keeping the policy discussion abstract enough to hide the fact that these laws are motivated by race. His role in Lies, Incorporated is to make an otherwise politically untenable and noxious position entirely acceptable.

The debate over abortion has been shaped in similar ways. Unable to overturn *Roe v. Wade,* activists, aided in some cases by doctors, have manufactured a series of lies that have led to laws designed to limit the availability of abortion.

Chapter 8

Shut That Whole Lie Down: Abortion

I f it's a legitimate rape, the female body has ways to try to shut that whole thing down."[1]

That is how Republican Senate candidate Todd Akin answered a question as to why there was no need for a rape exemption in the harsh antiabortion laws he supported as a member of Congress.

His statement was unequivocally false and prompted immediate outrage from women's rights groups and Democrats around the country.[2] A three-year-long study published in the *American Journal of Obstetrics & Gynecology* in 1996 estimated that each year in the United States, 32,101 pregnancies are the result of rape.[3] One of the study's researchers and director of the National Crime Victims Research and Treatment Center at the Medical University of South Carolina told *The Washington Post* that when adjusted for population, today's rate of pregnancies resulting from rape is closer to 50,000 a year.[4] Another study estimates that the rate of pregnancies resulting from rape is higher than the rate of pregnancies resulting from consensual sex, because when sex is consensual, women are able to use birth control.[5]

Akin was pilloried across the media landscape—it was August 2012, and the country was gearing up for the final rush toward Election Day. His comments made him so toxic that John Cornyn, chairman of the National Republican Senatorial Committee— the organization explicitly tasked with winning the Senate for the GOP, which would require winning Missouri's seat—saw fit to throw his candidate under the bus at the height of the campaign season with an unusually aggressive statement: "Akin's statements were wrong, offensive, and indefensible." Cornyn and several other Republican leaders publicly suggested Akin "spend some time" thinking about what is best for him and the country—a very thinly veiled request for him to drop out of the race.[6]

Conservative Super PACs felt the need to distance themselves from the Todd Akin race, pulling their ads and critical backing.[7] With Democrats united behind incumbent senator Claire McCaskill, the Senate race was essentially surrendered.

However damaging the comment was to Todd Akin's career, his belief that a woman could not conceive as a result of rape is widespread in the antiabortion movement, which for decades has made similar statements in publications, from the pulpit, and at protests in front of abortion clinics. Preachers, political leaders, and trusted authorities on the right repeat this claim.[8] To them, the shock was not at the substance of Akin's remarks, but that political allies were now fleeing their cause.

While much of the country reacted to Akin's comments with horror and derision, many in the Christian right could not figure out why Akin's statements were incorrect or even controversial. *Growing Pains* star Kirk Cameron, who had transitioned from 1980s child sitcom star to evangelical spokesperson, came to Akin's defense on CNN: "I get the sense there that this is a guy who is defending life and he wants to go to all lengths he can to protect the life of the unborn."[9]

Bryan Fischer of the American Family Association said that "real, genuine rape, a case of forcible rape," would "make it impossible for her or difficult in that particular circumstance to conceive a child."[10]

The conservative Christian Family Research Council defended Akin in a press release from their PAC: "This is another case of 'gotcha politics' against a conservative leader."[11]

Matt Lewis of *The Daily Caller* went so far as to attempt to provide some background on what Akin meant. Lewis asked, "Was he implying that exceptions to abortion law leads women to retroactively *claim* that consensual sex was a rape—in order to procure abortions for convenience?" Lewis went on to say there might be a scientific basis for Akin's comment: "I've heard speculation that women are perhaps more likely to conceive with a partner they deem successful or handsome—or that they are in love with," he claimed. "Others believe that female orgasm actually increases the odds of conception. This may or may not be junk science. But it would at least provide context."[12]

Any number of conservative politicians could have been caught in the same conundrum that Akin faced. The myth that women who are raped cannot get pregnant was passed down from conservative to conservative. Conjecture became theory, and theory was, over several decades, converted into fact. Within the pro-life movement, the lie that rape could not result in conception became true.

This provably incorrect lie about conception not resulting from rape provides evidence for two components of the right's efforts to stop abortion. First, it allows pro-lifers to argue that rape exceptions are unnecessary because it happens so rarely. Second, it implies that rapes rarely occur at all. Many on the right argue that rape accusations are really just women who changed their minds about the man, want to get the man in trouble, or are looking for a free abortion to take care of their irresponsible decision. If a woman claims she was raped and turns out to be pregnant, these lies help "prove" her wrong.

In the days following the public firestorm around Todd Akin's remark, Garance Franke-Ruta of *The Atlantic* attempted to trace the myth back to its origin.

One perpetrator of the lie was John C. Willke, a physician and former president of the National Right to Life Committee. In a 1999 issue of the magazine *Life Issues Connector,* Willke stated: "What is certainly one of the most important reasons why a rape victim rarely gets pregnant, and that's physical trauma. . . . To get and stay pregnant a woman's body must produce a very sophisticated mix of hormones. Hormone production is controlled by a part of the brain that is easily influenced by emotions. There's no greater emotional trauma that can be experienced by a woman than an assault rape."[13]

In 1995, North Carolina state representative Henry Aldridge alleged: "The facts show that people who are raped—who are truly raped—the juices don't flow, the body functions don't work and they don't get pregnant. Medical authorities agree that this is a rarity, if ever."[14]

In 1980, former president of Arkansas Right to Life and future George W. Bush federal judicial appointee James Leon Holmes wrote in a letter: "Concern for rape victims is a red herring because conceptions from rape occur with approximately the same frequency as snowfall in Miami."[15]

One of the earliest and most prominent citations of this myth appears in a 1972 essay written by ob-gyn Fred Mecklenburg. His essay, "The Indications for Induced Abortion: A Physician's Perspective," was published in a book titled *Abortion and Social Justice.* Writing for nineteen pages with seventy-six footnotes, Mecklenburg argued against "hardship" exceptions, primarily for rape, incest, and the health of the mother, in the bans on abortion that were the norm in America at that time. He opened his essay by saying that these exceptions "are calculated to win over a sympathetic concerned public to the acceptance of abortion as a simple expedient solution to grave 'medical' problems."[16]

Mecklenburg further wrote, "Medical research indicates that a woman exposed to emotional trauma (such as rape) will not ovulate even if she is scheduled to." As evidence, Mecklenburg cited a supposed experiment conducted by Nazi doctors during World War II in which women were sent into the gas chambers and then brought back out unharmed. They found the result of this traumatic experience was that "an extremely high percentage of these women did not ovulate."[17]

Mecklenburg acknowledged early in the essay that pregnancies could result from rape but argued they were "extremely rare." In addition to the trauma itself preventing pregnancy, he also suggested rapists were infertile "because of other aberrant sexual behavior, such as frequent masturbation."[18]

Mecklenburg, like Akin forty years later, also argued about the definition of legitimate rape. "Just when does an act of intercourse become rape?" the doctor wrote in his essay. "How does one define or prove rape when the allegation is made many weeks or months later? In all too many cases, the rape victim is in fact not a victim at all, but very much a rational participant."[19]

He argued that when rape becomes a justification for legalized abortion, reports of sexual assault increase. As evidence, he cited Colorado law, which in 1967 made rape an extenuating circumstance that allowed for victims to have an abortion. According to Mecklenburg, the fact that no rapists were charged or convicted of a crime during the period before the law was changed "casts some real doubt on the reality of the alleged rapes."[20] Mecklenburg failed to account for other reasons one might not be charged or convicted of rape in 1960s America, such as cultural and legal biases that discouraged women from even reporting sexual assaults. It was not uncommon for rape victims' own sexual histories to be used as evidence against them. A shift began in the 1970s with an anti-rape movement pushing for changes, including the creation of rape shield laws, designed to protect victims from invasive cross-examinations by defense attorneys.[21]

Mecklenburg's medical career did not suffer for his contribution to this pervasive lie. He served as chairman of the ob-gyn department at Inova Fairfax Hospital,[22] which is ranked number 30 on *U.S. News*'s 2015–16 list of best hospitals for gynecology.[23] Thousands of women utilize the services of this hospital, likely unaware that it employs a doctor who in the past has used questionable logic to deny women health care.

Mecklenburg, it turns out, was mistaken in his citation of Nazi medicine. A footnote in the book indicated he learned of the Nazi study from a lecture given by Georgetown professor Andre Hellegers in 1967. According to bioethicist Arthur Caplan and two physicians, Sabine Hildebrandt and William Seidelman, it was likely that Hellegers was citing research actually conducted by Professor Hermann Stieve of the University of Berlin during World War II. Stieve was "internationally recognized" for his research in which he "exploited female prisoners for research on the effect of stress on the female genital tract," however it doesn't appear his work included "a study of rape and its impact on pregnancy." As his research was directly relevant to the work and writings of both Hellegers and Mecklenburg, the bioethicists think it likely they were aware of the nature of Stieve's work.[24]

Whether or not Stieve can be accurately called a Nazi is under debate, but he did certainly work with and benefit from Nazi practices. Emily Bazelon reported for *Slate* that Stieve did his anatomical research on bodies acquired from Plötzensee Prison, outside Berlin. In return for the favor of disposing of the bodies for the prison, Stieve was given access to the prisoners before their executions—allowing him to track the menstrual cycles of women before they died. He concluded that chronic stress affected ovulation and that women sometimes had "shock bleeds."[25] There is no reference to an experiment in which women were put into gas chambers to test their ovulation.

Stieve's conclusions—which only prove that life in prison awaiting execution affects ovulation—have been used as medical evidence in numerous claims that rape cannot cause pregnancy.

There is a clear path of misinformation: Stieve and his experiments during World War II were misquoted by Hellegers at Georgetown in the late 1960s; Hellegers, in turn, was cited by Mecklenburg in the 1970s; and Mecklenburg's article has been a reference point for the wider pro-life movement as they spread this destructive myth—ultimately resulting in Todd Akin's statement and subsequent fall from grace. Falsehoods that were seeded during the Third Reich ended up costing Todd Akin a seat in the United States Senate in the twenty-first century.

Akin's story is also demonstrative of how difficult a lie is to extract once it enters the mainstream consciousness, not just from the mainstream but from the individual perpetrators themselves. Nearly two years after his loss, the former member of Congress published a book in which he claimed he was punished precisely because he apologized: "By asking the public at large for forgiveness, I was validating the willful misinterpretation of what I had said."

Akin then wrote, "My comment about a woman's body shutting the pregnancy down was directed to the impact of stress on fertilization. This is something fertility doctors debate and discuss." He continues, "Doubt me? Google 'stress and infertility,' and you will find a library of research on the subject."[26]

Following the 2012 election, Republicans were so disheartened by Akin-like gaffes that they decided to train their candidates on how to better address issues impacting women without turning off wide swaths of voters.[27]

So why did Akin keep clinging to a point that would further isolate him to the fringe of the Republican Party, after a broad and public shaming over this lie? Because living in the post-truth world means never having to acknowledge facts. Conceding may actually cause harm, because that act is the equivalent of justifying the other side's position and alienating your core supporters—as Akin clearly felt had happened when he apologized in 2012. The practitioners of Lies, Incorporated understand this dynamic and exploit it as a critical part of the strategies they employ.

To this day, some activists in the pro-life community insist on the veracity of Akin's "legitimate rape" statement. In March 2013, more than six months after Akin's comments cost Republicans a seat in the Senate, prominent California Republican Celeste Greig mirrored Akin's claim. The Bay Area News Group quoted the party leader as saying Akin probably regretted his "insensitive" statement before ironically stating herself that pregnancies rarely result from rape "because it's an act of violence, because the body is traumatized."[28]

While Akin's statements were egregious, a far more cynical approach has emerged in the antiabortion movement: an effort to manufacture lies in order to limit women's reproductive health care options. The movement uses falsehoods to create regulations designed as a barrier to stop women from pursuing safe and legal medical procedures.

Like other issues that rely on lies, the antiabortion movement manufactures confusion and phony science in order to pursue their ideological goals. Even if they fail at the state house or at the courthouse, they stand outside clinics and harass women directly or use confusing and phony marketing tactics to draw women away from the care they deserve. There is, in fact, no other issue where proponents have so completely shrouded their ideology in falsehoods.

Antiabortion activists have sought to end abortion through a death-by-a-thousand-cuts strategy, pushing legislation designed to make getting an abortion all but impossible. The laws they advocate for include imposing mandatory waiting periods, requiring doctors to have admitting privileges at local hospitals, and mandating that doctors give women false information about the effects of abortion. Because of these so-called TRAP (Targeted Regulations of Abortion Providers) laws and the repeated harassment of doctors performing abortions, several areas of the country are left with limited access to providers. Laws currently being contested in federal court, if upheld, could shut down even more clinics serving women, limiting their health care options. The principal effect of these policies is to deny poor women, particularly those from rural areas, the ability to get abortions.

The antiabortion movement has been fairly upfront about its intentions. At the 2012 Values Voter Summit, an annual conclave of the religious right, Michael New, a scholar at the antiabortion Charlotte Lozier Institute, exhorted the crowd: "The best thing you can do when you get home is support a variety of state pro-life bills, and essentially, if your state has them, they can be strengthened." He continued, "You can defund abortion by stopping Medicaid funding or by defunding Planned Parenthood. You can strengthen parental-involvement laws, by requiring both parents to be involved. You can strengthen informed-consent laws:

Require the woman to see an ultrasound, or require two trips to the clinic. That raises the costs; that stops the abortion from happening. You can lengthen the waiting period. Don't be like the other states that do 24, 48, 72 hours. Do it for nine months—that'll stop abortions in your state. I guarantee it."[29]

Between 2010 and 2014, more than two hundred new laws restricting abortion were passed. Many of these bills were based on legislation initially drafted by Americans United for Life, whose president, Charmaine Yoest, was quoted in the *National Catholic Register* as stating, "We don't make frontal attacks." Their plan is detailed in a seven-hundred-page playbook distributed to lawmakers by the organization, outlining potential laws that would limit access to abortion.[30]

A filibuster in the spring of 2013 by Texas State senator Wendy Davis galvanized public attention on the debate around one of these laws. While she succeeded in temporarily blocking an antiabortion bill, Governor Rick Perry called the chamber back into session to pass one of the most restrictive antiabortion measures in the country, reflecting the goals spelled out by Michael New and Americans United for Life. Under the law, abortion would be banned in the state after twenty weeks. Clinics performing abortions must be certified as surgical centers, and doctors are required to possess admitting privileges at nearby hospitals.[31]

On the surface, the regulations on clinics and doctors may seem reasonable. However much they appear to be geared toward protecting women, they are in fact based on a number of blatant lies that, like the falsehood told by Todd Akin, had been passed through the pro-life movement to generations of activists.

Antiabortion activists manipulate medical data to force the information to conform to their worldview. For example, the website AbortionFacts.com presents "overwhelming" evidence that abortion is more dangerous than carrying a child to term: "some maternal deaths in full-term pregnancies are actually caused by earlier abortions"; and in the year after an abortion, women are at high risk of dying in a multitude of ways: "60% more likely to die from natural causes," "fourteen times more likely to die from homicide," "seven times more likely to die from suicide," and "four times more likely to die of injuries related to accidents."[32]

The site also includes warnings of the problems abortion causes future children: abortion can cause "both premature births and low birth weights" in later children; "malformations, both major and minor, of later children are increased by abortion"; and, "some women are unable to conceive after having abortions."[33] The website takes information from a variety of far-right, evangelical, and nonmedical sources.[34]

Contrary to this "evidence" and other messaging of the pro-life movement, abortion is one of the safest medical procedures performed in the United States. Researchers from Gynuity Health Projects and the University of North Carolina School of Medicine found that "between 1998 and 2005, one woman died in childbirth for every 11,000 babies born, compared to one of 167,000 women who died due to abortion complications."[35] Nevertheless, many antiabortion state laws are sold to voters based on phony concern over the "safety" of the procedure.

Laws that demand abortion clinics maintain the same rigorous standards as surgical centers do nothing to improve safety. Instead, they require a number of expensive changes to clinics, such as widening hallways and meeting size minimums for janitor closets, that are often financially prohibitive and force the clinic to close.[36]

Other regulations demand doctors have admitting privileges at local hospitals, again to allegedly increase patient safety. In the rare cases of a complication occurring during an abortion, an ambulance will still transport a patient to the nearest hospital whether the doctor has admitting privileges or not. Like other "safety-based" regulations, these are also designed to restrict abortions. Antiabortion activists know how difficult it is for clinics to meet the requirements. As *The Washington Post* reported: "Their doctors often live too far away from the hospitals or cannot commit to admitting the minimum number of patients required for such a relationship. In other cases, hospitals have religious objections or have been reluctant to become embroiled in such a politically charged issue." When doctors performing abortions do have admitting privileges, antiabortion activists will often seek to disrupt business at the hospital, causing the hospital to revoke a doctor's status in at least one instance.[37]

In his opinion about the strict architectural requirements in the restrictive antiabortion law in Texas, Federal District Court judge Lee Yeakel exposed the lie at the heart of the legislation and of the arguments in support of it. When opponents of the law rightfully pointed out that closing abortion clinics would hurt women, the state argued that women seeking abortions would not be harmed if a local clinic shut down because they could go to other states to seek out the procedure. Judge Yeakel pointedly called the state's motivation into question: "If the State's true purpose in enacting the ambulatory-surgical-center requirement is to protect the health and safety of Texas women who seek abortions, it is disingenuous and incompatible with that goal to argue that Texas women can seek abortion care in a state with lesser regulations." Judge Yeakel continued, "If, however, the State's underlying purpose in enacting the requirement was to reduce or eliminate abortion in parts or all of Texas, the State's position is perfectly congruent with such a goal."[38]

The other provision in the highly restrictive antiabortion law in Texas is a twenty-week ban on abortion. Efforts to pass twenty-week bans in Texas and elsewhere are based on research findings that conclude a fetus might feel pain as early as twenty weeks. But that work is still very much under way. The doctor responsible for much of that research, Dr. Kanwaljeet "Sunny" Anand, is not wholly opposed to abortion and acknowledges more work must be done. His research and appearance—as a member of the Sikh faith he has been referred to as "not a stereotypical Bible-thumping pro-lifer"—have been used by the antiabortion movement for years to justify twenty-week bans.[39]

The existence of fetal pain has been called into question by several other researchers. *The Journal of the American Medical Association* concluded that "evidence regarding the capacity for fetal pain is limited but indicates that fetal perception of pain is unlikely before the third trimester."[40] Additionally, the U.K. Royal College of Obstetricians and Gynaecologists found "fetuses aged 24 weeks or less do not have the brain connections to feel pain."[41] This has not stopped dozens of lawmakers from citing fetal pain as a principal reason to establish a twenty-week ban.

The lies of the antiabortion movement have been a critical part of judicial cases having a far-reaching impact on public policy. This was the case with Hobby Lobby, the nationwide chain of craft superstores that thrust itself into the center of the debate over health care and abortion when they sued the Obama administration over Obamacare. Hobby Lobby owners "challenged the contraception mandate on the grounds that it violates their religious freedom by requiring them to pay for methods of contraception they find morally objectionable." The Green family, which owns Hobby Lobby, runs it in accordance with their Christian faith.[42] Specifically, the family was opposed to coverage of all forms of birth control under Obamacare, due to their belief that "some forms of birth control—emergency contraception and intrauterine devices—are forms of abortion because they could prevent a fertilized egg from implanting in the uterus."[43]

The Hobby Lobby case primarily hinged on the question of whether the contraception mandate infringed upon the religious beliefs of the corporation's ownership. But a factual question also plagued the case: Were these commonly prescribed methods of birth control, including IUDs, ella, and Plan B (the morning-after pill), actually abortifacients? More than ten nationally renowned medical organizations signed an amicus brief in support of the contraception mandate, in which they clearly state the facts: "There is no scientific evidence that emergency contraceptives available in the United States and approved by the FDA affect an existing pregnancy."[44]

The Supreme Court ruled that because Hobby Lobby's owners had a deeply held religious belief about the impact of these contraceptives, they could not be forced to fund the coverage.[45] Neither the truth nor scientific evidence mattered. Instead, the deeply held beliefs of a single individual could control the health care of thousands of employees and potentially millions of Americans.

What makes the antiabortion movement unique is that in addition to spreading their message in the press and affecting the lawmaking process, the activists peddling these lies make earnest attempts to directly interfere in the relationship between a woman and her doctors.

Women seeking abortions in the United States must run the gauntlet, and not just outside clinics where protestors will line up to aggressively confront those in need of medical care. Some end up in a network of crisis pregnancy centers, often posing as health clinics, that are designed with one purpose—to discourage women from seeking abortions. Most shockingly, the federal government has funded some of these centers, several of which have strict religious litmus tests for their employees.[46]

Crisis pregnancy centers are not in the business of providing care and information; they are only interested in preventing abortions—no matter how many lies they have to tell. In Ohio, an activist went to a crisis pregnancy center and secretly filmed her experience. When she asked about Plan B, the emergency contraceptive, the clinic staffer discouraged her from taking the medicine. "It sounds like the morning-after pill," the staffer stated. "If you have intercourse and then take this pill, and it causes a period to come on or something, or bleeding. . . it's like having kind of an abortion." The clinic worker also told the patient, "That could harm you. It really could harm you. . . . You could hemorrhage from anything like that."[47]

Another activist visited a crisis pregnancy center in Virginia and was told birth control pills cause cancer, condoms don't work, having an abortion would ruin her life, and finally was both judged for her sexual history and blamed for a date rape.[48]

None of what these women were told is true. Plan B prevents fertilization from occurring; if a fertilized egg is already implanted, the drug will not stop the pregnancy. This is a common, if new, lie told to women. A much older lie, and one that has taken many forms, is that abortions cause breast cancer.

Often using out-of-context, debunked, or falsified research, anti-choice activists routinely claim that abortion causes breast cancer. It is just yet another blatant lie easily disproved by facts from reputable sources. The American Cancer Society's answer is unambiguous: "Scientific research studies have not found a cause-and-effect relationship between abortion and breast cancer."[49]

The Susan G. Komen organization is likewise clear on the connection: "Research clearly shows abortion (also called induced abortion) does not increase the risk of breast cancer." The organization goes further and explains the problem with studies that come to another conclusion: "Some case-control studies have suggested abortion may increase the risk of breast cancer. However, the design of case-control studies makes the accuracy of these results questionable."[50]

In some states, laws that force health care professionals and educators to knowingly tell lies about abortion have actually been introduced and passed. North Carolina public school health teachers have to lie and tell students that "having an abortion will endanger future pregnancies." Multiple medical organizations have concluded that this is not true.

In Ohio, "no rape crisis center that receives state funding can counsel rape survivors about abortion"—meaning rape survivors who are pregnant will not have professional guidance if they do not want to carry their rapist's child.

Under Kansas law, doctors "must tell patients that 'the abortion will terminate the life of a whole, separate, unique, living human being,'" that "after 20 weeks of gestation, fetuses can feel pain," and that there is "a link between abortion and breast cancer," something that is categorically untrue.[51]

A similar law in South Dakota went further, instructing doctors to "give pregnant women a description of 'medical and statistically significant' risks of abortion, among which it includes depression and other psychological distress, suicide, danger to subsequent pregnancies, and death."[52]

This is nothing short of forcing doctors to lie to women, and, like other pervasive lies, it is based on faulty research from a 2009 study out of Bowling Green State University in Ohio. The study was published in the *Journal of Psychiatric Research* and "suggested that abortion was associated with long-term mental health problems like panic attacks, depression, substance abuse and post-traumatic stress disorder."

Time Magazine reported that "seven states . . . used the study to support laws that require women seeking abortions to be counseled on the mental health risks."[53]

However, according to *Time,* "one of the fundamental errors that plagues [the] study is that the researchers did not distinguish whether mental health problems occurred before or after abortion. Indeed, in many cases, mental illness preceded abortions, weakening the argument that abortion can increase women's mental health risks."[54]

Professor of psychiatry at the University of California Julia Steinberg, who challenged the original study, said: "This is not a scholarly difference of opinion; their facts were flatly wrong. This was an abuse of the scientific process to reach conclusions that are not supported by the data. . . . The shifting explanations and misleading statements that they offered over the past two years served to mask their serious methodological errors."[55] Ultimately, the *Journal of Psychiatric Research* acknowledged the research "does not support assertions that abortions led to psychopathology."[56]

After a review of twenty years of studies, the United Kingdom's National Collaborating Centre for Mental Health concluded: "Abortion does not increase a woman's chance of developing mental health problems. . . . Among women with unwanted pregnancies, those who had abortions were no more likely to suffer from problems including anxiety or depression than women who gave birth."[57]

To contradict these widely accepted findings, the antiabortion movement will point to studies paid for by allied groups. Regardless, the overwhelming majority of research has found that making the decision to terminate a pregnancy does not harm a patient's mental well-being. State laws mandating doctors misinform patients about the link between abortion and mental illness are simply passed in the hope that women will be discouraged from going through with the procedure.

The debate over abortion is not simply the clash of progressive and conservative moralities as portrayed by the media. Instead, like every other current political debate in this country, it is about the contrast between lies and truth.

Lies about women's health care give justification for legislatures to pass laws that are harmful to women and allow friendly courts to uphold these dangerous regulations. Laws that demand doctors lie to patients are bound to create poor health care outcomes. And lies that are a work-around designed to prevent people from accessing safe and legal medical care are another symptom of a broken democratic process.

Yet lies do not always succeed in halting progress. In the debate over gay marriage, religious conservatives saw their falsehoods fail to take hold as public opinion on the issue shifted rapidly. While they deployed a similarly active infrastructure to defend their definition of marriage, they ultimately failed, not only to sway the courts but the American public as well.

Chapter 9

A Lie's Last Gasp: Gay Marriage

In the middle of the last decade, many Democratic Party strategists viewed gay marriage as a cultural third rail. When San Francisco mayor Gavin Newsom began issuing marriage licenses to same-sex couples in 2004, it was seen as a move that could damage John Kerry's chances of winning the White House. Rumors swirled that Karl Rove sought to exploit this by placing "marriage" amendments on the ballot across the country as a wedge issue designed to draw conservative voters to the polls.

Democrats feared the marriage debate would reignite the culture wars and activate a conservative Christian voting base that was sure to support Republicans.

The last gasp of the anti-gay-marriage movement came in 2008 with the passage of Proposition 8 in California, which amended the state's constitution to recognize only marriages between heterosexual couples.[1] While many progressives and members of the LGBT community were shocked and saddened by the outcome of the election, this defeat would soon lead to some big victories for the marriage equality movement.

A lawsuit to overturn Proposition 8 was filed by two legal heavyweights: David Boies, a Democrat who previously represented the U.S. government in its successful antitrust case against Microsoft and Al Gore's presidential campaign at the Supreme Court; and Ted Olson, a Republican who served as George W. Bush's solicitor general and Boies's opposition in *Bush v. Gore*. To have a conservative litigator as distinguished as Olson advocating for same-sex marriage signaled a coming sea change on the issue.[2]

In 2012, as a result of the forceful work of gay rights activists, three states voted to legalize same-sex marriage and a fourth rejected an anti-gay ballot initiative. This was only the beginning of a period of rapid advancement for the gay rights movement. The following year brought two major cases to the Supreme Court, the aforementioned challenges to Proposition 8 and to the federal Defense of Marriage Act. The Clinton-era law known as DOMA, which barred the federal government from in any way acknowledging the relationships of gay Americans, had sweeping ramifications, affecting Social Security payments, hospital visits, survivor benefits, and the treatment of the children of LGBT couples. The plaintiff in the case, Edith Windsor, was denied an estate-tax exemption after the death of her spouse, whom she'd wed in Canada two years earlier.

The court's decision in the Windsor case was significant, setting a tone for the next several years of equality litigation. In striking down DOMA, the majority opinion wrote the "differentiation" of marriages based on sexual orientation "demeans the couple, whose moral and sexual choices the Constitution protects."[3]

In the Prop 8 case, the Supreme Court justices avoided making a sweeping ruling on marriage and instead held that proponents did not have standing to bring the case, because they did not "suffer injury."

In June 2015, the Supreme Court settled the issue of gay marriage with Justice Anthony Kennedy writing that the LGBT community "ask[s] for equal dignity in the eyes of the law" and "the Constitution grants them that right."[4]

The conservative movement's objection to same-sex marriage and gay culture in general is deeply rooted in conservative Christian dogma. In messages broadcast nationwide from church pulpits, Christian radio stations, and the Internet, the religious right has characterized society's increasing acceptance of gay couples as not only anathema to biblical values but as an outright attack on Christianity.[5]

While right-wing positions on social issues are usually based primarily on moral values, conservatives acknowledge that mere religious dogma is not enough to justify laws that discriminate based on sexual orientation. To win Proposition 8, DOMA, and the LGBT marriage cases that followed in various states, conservatives knew they would have to establish, in legal terms, a "rational basis" for the government's discrimination against same-sex couples. The right wing's typical rhetoric suggesting there was a slippery slope from gay marriage to legalized bestiality and incest would not pass constitutional muster.[6]

Ultimately, the supporters of "traditional" marriage settled on an argument that marriage plays a unique role in the rearing of children. If conservatives could demonstrate that families with gay and lesbian parents harm children in their care, it could provide the legal rationale for the government's discrimination against gay couples.[7] However, the vast preponderance of scholarly research indicates this is not the case. According to the American Sociological Association, "decades of methodologically sound social science research" confirm "whether a child is raised by same-sex or opposite-sex parents has no bearing on a child's wellbeing."[8]

The Witherspoon Institute, a socially conservative think tank, decided to commission research to address what they viewed as a deficit of scholarly research on the subject. Although it is not widely known in mainstream or progressive circles, the Wither-spoon Institute is at the epicenter of the conservative religious movement. One of its founders, Robert George, the McCormick Professor of Jurisprudence at Princeton University, has for more than two decades been a leader of anti-gay political organizations, most prominently as the former chairman of the National Orga-nization for Marriage.[9]

A bookish professor, George received his undergraduate degree in political philosophy from Swarthmore College before completing a master's in theology at Harvard, where he also earned a law degree. He later received a doctorate in philosophy from Oxford University.[10]

Outside of the classroom, George has focused much of his scholarship on Catholic "natural law." His academic writing con-tains arguments against same-sex marriage and abortion, as well as embryonic stem cell research, birth control, adultery, divorce, pornography, and masturbation, which he contends is "objec-tively morally wrong."[11] George currently serves on the U.S. Com-mission on International Religious Freedom, to which he was appointed by House Speaker John Boehner.[12]

George's government service spans three decades. In the wan-ing days of his presidency, George H. W. Bush appointed him to the U.S. Commission on Civil Rights, where he became a thorn in the side of the Clinton administration, winning a lawsuit that declared a Clinton administration staff appointment "illegal" in addition to sponsoring "a landmark examination of discrimina-tion against religion in the public schools."[13] George also used his position to attack Surgeon General Joycelyn Elders, a Clin-ton appointee, after she made pro-masturbation remarks.[14] Later, George was one of George W. Bush's principal advisers, helping him design the federal policy to limit the use of embryonic stem cells in scientific research, despite their potential to help cure a variety of ailments.[15] George also worked with Senate Republicans in the early 2000s to author a federal constitutional amendment outlawing same-sex marriage, the passage of which would have explicitly written discrimination into the U.S. Constitution for the first time since slavery.[16]

In conservative circles, Robert George is highly regarded. Glenn Beck described him as "one of the biggest brains in America" and "Superman of the Earth."[17] Supreme Court Justice Antonin Scalia identifies George as one of the most talked-about figures in conservative law. A Catholic journal wrote: "If there really is a vast right-wing conspiracy, its leaders probably meet in George's kitchen."[18] George's influence, however, extends well beyond political circles and the conservative media. "Whenever I venture out into the public square, I would almost invariably check it out with Robby first," said Archbishop John Myers of Newark, a leading church conservative, in an interview with *The New York Times*.[19]

When Pope Benedict XVI visited the United States in 2008, Robert George "implied he'd be meeting privately with the pope in Washington but refused to divulge details."[20]

While taking a hard line on issues like abortion and same-sex marriage, George's adherence to Catholic doctrine is less strict when it comes to other issues. A *New York Times* profile retold the story of a speech the Princeton professor gave at an event in Washington, where the audience included many bishops. "He told them with typical bluntness that they should stop talking so much about the many policy issues they have taken up in the name of social justice," the paper reported. "They should concentrate their authority on 'the moral social' issues like abortion, embryonic stem-cell research and same-sex marriage, where, he argued, the natural law and Gospel principles were clear."[21]

While telling the audience he did not object if Catholic church leaders made "utter nuisances of themselves" on economic issues such as confronting poverty, they should not recommend specific policy solutions.[22]

Practically, this meant eliminating any advocacy from their pulpits for policies that might be mistaken as progressive. Specifically, they should avoid issues such as taxation, wages, health care, and, according to George, "matters of public policy upon which Gospel principles by themselves do not resolve differences of opinion among reasonable and well-informed people of good will."[23]

George opposes capital punishment but "considers it a matter of interpretation about which Catholics can disagree."[24] While the Vatican opposed the war in Iraq, George authored a column in *The Wall Street Journal* in support of George W. Bush. "Preemptive action is 'defensive' when it is motivated by a reasonable belief that a proven aggressor is in the process of equipping himself with the military means to carry out further aggression with impunity," he wrote. "Few people doubt that Saddam is seeking to enhance his chemical and biological arsenal, and (even more ominously) to acquire nuclear weapons. Few deny that he will, if successful, use these weapons to terrorize other nations in the region and force them to bend to his will."[25]

He also contends, however, that some issues "go beyond the application of moral principles." George has asked, "Is it better for education and health care to be provided by governments under socialized systems or by private providers in markets or by some combination?" He added, "You can get all the moral principles dead right and not have an answer to any of those questions."[26]

George's standing in the American conservative movement is the result of not only his scholarship and intellectual ability but also an incredible work ethic. He has been a fellow at the Hoover Institution,[27] and his name is ubiquitous on the boards and leadership rosters of conservative institutions, including:

- The Lynde and Harry Bradley Foundation
- Ethics and Public Policy Center
- Institute for American Values
- Family Research Council
- Institute for Marriage and Public Policy
- Marriage Savers[28]
- The Becket Fund for Religious Liberty[29]
- Catholic Education Resource Center[30]
- Love and Fidelity Network[31]

Each of these groups played critical roles in Christian-right organizing and activism: The Bradley Foundation has contributed nearly $830 million to various causes.[32] The Becket Fund for Religious Liberty was the organization that brought the Hobby Lobby case to the Supreme Court on behalf of the Green family.[33]

George also cowrote the Manhattan Declaration, a manifesto signed by more than 150 evangelical, Catholic, and Orthodox leaders,[34] which declared: "No one has a civil right to have a non-marital relationship treated as a marriage. Marriage is an objective reality—a covenantal union of husband and wife—that it is the duty of the law to recognize and support for the sake of justice and the common good. If it fails to do so, genuine social harms follow."[35]

None of the efforts or groups George has been associated with are more influential in the anti-gay-marriage debate than the National Organization for Marriage (NOM) and the Witherspoon Institute. George was involved in the founding of the two organizations, which provide the "pro-family" movement with both intellectual heft and the grassroots muscle necessary to mobilize activists in opposition to gay rights.

In 2012, some of NOM's internal documents became public as part of a campaign finance lawsuit in Maine. In August 2009, while George was chairman,[36] NOM released a "confidential" document, "National Strategy for Winning the Marriage Battle," revealing the strategies NOM planned to use in its fight against the expansion of civil rights for LGBT Americans. Key to the effort was identifying various communities to spread NOM's anti-gay-marriage message throughout the United States.

As part of the "Expert Witness Project," NOM would "identify and nurture a worldwide community of highly credentialed intellectuals and professional scholars, physicians, psychiatrists, social workers, and writers to credential our concerns and to interrupt the silencing that takes place in the academy around gay marriage and related family issues." The section declared, "Marriage as the union of husband and wife has deep grounding in human nature and is supported by serious social science."[37]

NOM also sought to recruit Latinos to their movement by convincing them the way to stay true to their heritage would be to fight marriage equality: "The Latino vote in America is a key swing vote, and will be even more so in the future because of demographic growth. Will the process of assimilation to the dominant Anglo culture lead Hispanics to abandon traditional family values?" they wrote. "We can interrupt this process of assimilation by making support for marriage a key badge of Latino identity."[38]

Finally, under the header "Not a Civil Right Project," NOM outlined the plan to train black people to explain why their community should oppose marriage equality: "The majority of African-Americans, like the majority of Americans, oppose gay marriage, but Democratic power bosses are increasingly inclined to privilege the concerns of gay rights groups over the values of African-Americans. A strategic goal of this project is to amplify the voice and the power of black Americans within the Democratic Party. We aim to find, equip, energize and connect African-American spokespeople for marriage; develop a media campaign around their objections to gay marriage as a civil right." NOM continued with a key insight as to why these message surrogates were so critical to their effort: "No politician wants to take up and push an issue that splits the base of the party."[39]

NOM's plan was to identify, train, and activate minorities to speak out against marriage equality—intentionally drawing attention away from the rest of the debate. The organization was explicitly calling for the use of divisive racial tactics in order to further the cause of discriminating against the gay community.

Robert George was NOM's chairman when these documents were drafted. He subsequently left the organization's board in 2010.

While NOM was laying out detailed plans to prevent national marriage equality, another Robert George group was mobilizing its own resources to assist in the fight. Located in Princeton, New Jersey, the Witherspoon Institute was careful to both highlight its connections to the university and officially maintain its independence. A number of its fellows and employees, including George, hold positions at the school.[40] Additionally, the think tank is named for John Witherspoon, a signer of the Declaration of Independence and Princeton's sixth president, who taught both James Madison and Aaron Burr. A Scottish minister, Witherspoon was recruited in the 1760s to head the College of New Jersey, which later became known as Princeton. The Witherspoon Institute's current president, Luis Tellez, is a former officer of the controversial Catholic organization Opus Dei and worked in the chemical industry before joining with George to form the think tank.

As NOM sought experts to speak about the "dangers" of same-sex marriage, Tellez made plans to demonstrate in court that the LGBT "lifestyle" was harmful to children to counteract social science research that, in the minds of many conservatives, had normalized gay behavior. To this end, the Witherspoon Institute made a grant of nearly $700,000 to University of Texas sociologist Mark Regnerus to conduct research that would ultimately be known as the New Family Structures Study (NFSS). This comprehensive "research" consisted of a large sample survey to compare the "outcomes" of children raised by LGBT individuals to those raised by heterosexual parents. These "outcomes" included factors such as level of education, the use of public assistance programs, drug use, sexual abuse, unemployment, the rate of sexually transmitted infections, and even the suicide rate of respondents.[41]

Recognizing the potential for controversy, Regnerus sought to disarm critics who would claim that he conducted research to support predetermined conclusions. "The NFSS was supported in part by grants from the Witherspoon Institute and the Bradley Foundation," he wrote in the study. "While both of these are commonly known for their support of conservative causes—just as other private foundations are known for supporting more liberal causes—the funding sources played no role at all in the design or conduct of the study, the analyses, the interpretations of the data, or in the preparation of this manuscript."[42]

However, private emails unearthed by an open-records request reveal that the study's purpose was not purely academic. Witherspoon president Luis Tellez wrote to Regnerus, encouraging him not to "dilly-dolly" [*sic*]: "It would be great to have this before major decisions of the Supreme Court"—clearly demonstrating the nonacademic political motivation behind the study. Tellez did attempt to couch this within standard research norms, stating that this goal was "secondary to the need to do this and do it well." He told Regnerus, "I would like you to take ownership and think of how would you want it done, rather than someone like me dictating parameters but of course, here to help."[43]

As Tellez turned to donors to cover the cost of the study, the ideological motivations behind it became more transparent. In a fund-raising letter written by Tellez to the Lynde and Harry Bradley Foundation, an organization that frequently is a financial supporter of anti-gay activism, he explained that "the future of the institution of marriage at this moment is very uncertain. . . . It is essential that the necessary data be gathered to settle the question in the forum of public debate about what kinds of family arrangement are best for society. That is what the NFSS is designed to do."[44]

While claiming that Witherspoon's "first goal is to seek the truth, whatever that may turn out to be," Tellez was "confident that the traditional understanding of marriage will be vindicated by this study as long as it is done honestly and well."[45]

Even after the emails were made public, Regnerus denied that his relationship with the Witherspoon Institute or the Bradley Foundation had influenced the results of the study. "I have always acted without strings from either organization," he said, declaring any such allegations "simply false."[46] This statement of independence was indisputably undermined by the fact that Regnerus brought on Brad Wilcox, who served as director of Witherspoon's "Program on Family, Marriage, and Democracy" as a consultant on the study.[47] By hiring a person who worked for his study's funder and clearly had a biased interest in the results, he could no longer credibly claim impartiality.

For its part, Witherspoon claimed that Wilcox was a fellow, not a staff member, and that he left the organization as the New Family Structures Study was about to go into the field. "In his capacity as director of the program in Family, Marriage and

Democracy, Prof. Wilcox offered advice and assistance in various family related events or projects that the Witherspoon Institute decided to undertake," wrote Tellez. "Never did Prof. Wilcox represent in any way the Witherspoon Institute when dealing with other scholars or the public. Prof. Wilcox, like any other fellow of the Institute, never was involved in the decision-making of the Witherspoon Institute." He continued, "More specifically, he was never involved in any decision making at the Witherspoon Institute in matters related to the New Family Structure Study."[48]

Tellez acknowledged, however, that Wilcox's "role was to help assemble an initial group of scholars, Mark Regnerus included, out of which came the idea of the NFSS," but he insisted that this had no impact on his grantee's work. Yet he did admit, "I would inquire with him occasionally as to whether this [sic] standards were being applied. Just to be sure all was well."[49]

Emails released in an open-records request indicate the involvement of funders in the construction of the project. In one email to Wilcox, Regnerus asks for confirmation to proceed with a variety of research parameters and goals. Regnerus also expresses his desire for direct input from two influential people: "I would like, at some point, to get more feedback from Luis and Maggie about the 'boundaries' around this project, not just costs but also their optimal timelines (for the coalition meeting, the data collection, etc.), and their hopes for what emerges from this project, including the early report we discussed in D.C."[50] The "Luis" Regnerus refers to is likely Witherspoon Institute president Luis Tellez; it is reasonable to assume the "Maggie" mentioned is Maggie Gallagher, cofounder and board member of NOM. This was not academic inquiry; it was research bought and paid for by a conservative institute to achieve a designed outcome.

Furthermore, Wilcox served on the editorial board of *Social Science Research,* the journal that published the study.[51]

The rigged study gave conservatives the ammunition they desired. According to Regnerus, his data showed that children of gay parents faced negative economic, social, and psychological consequences as a result of their upbringing. In an article summarizing and introducing the study, Regnerus wrote:

> Instead of relying on small samples, or the challenges of discerning sexual orientation of household residents using census data, my colleagues and I randomly screened over 15,000 Americans aged 18–39 and asked them if their biological mother or father ever had a romantic relationship with a member of the same sex. . . .
>
> On 25 of 40 different outcomes evaluated, the children of women who've had same-sex relationships fare quite differently than those in stable, biologically-intact mom-and-pop families, displaying numbers more comparable to those from heterosexual stepfamilies and single parents. Even after including controls for age, race, gender, and things like being bullied as a youth, or the gay-friendliness of the state in which they live, such respondents were more apt to report being unemployed, less healthy, more depressed, more likely to have cheated on a spouse or partner, smoke more pot, had trouble with the law, report more male and female sex partners, more sexual victimization, and were more likely to reflect negatively on their childhood family life, among other things.
>
> Why such dramatic differences? I can only speculate, since the data are not poised to pinpoint causes. One notable theme among the adult children of same-sex parents, however, is household instability, and plenty of it.[52]

Almost immediately, other researchers began to note significant flaws in the study. One of the first problems identified was the question Regnerus asked to establish if a respondent's parents qualified as gay.

> From when you were born until age 18 (or until you left home to be on your own), did either of your parents ever have a romantic relationship with someone of the same sex?
> A. Yes, my mother had a romantic relationship with another woman
> B. Yes, my father had a romantic relationship with another man
> C. No[53]

Professor John Corvino, chairman of the Philosophy Department at Wayne State University in Michigan, explained the error behind this approach in *The New Republic*. Instead of studying children raised in a household with gay parents, Regnerus could have included in his sample group a "heterosexually married female prostitute who on rare occasion services women," or "a never-married straight male prison inmate who sometimes seeks sexual release with other male inmates," or even "Ted Haggard, the disgraced evangelical pastor who was caught having drug fueled-trysts with a male prostitute over a period of several years."[54]

Further inspection of the data collected by Regnerus revealed another obvious problem. Regnerus did not study the long-term effects of same-sex parentage in stable households. Instead, according to Nathaniel Frank, then a visiting scholar at Columbia's Center for Gender and Sexuality Law, the study compared intact homes with broken families. Thus, according to Frank, Regnerus "fails the most basic requirement of social science research—assessing causation by holding all other variables constant."[55]

With his work coming under attack, many on the right aggressively defended Regnerus. In a blog post at *National Review Online,* former Heritage Foundation researcher Jason Richwine defended the Texas professor. Writing just a few months after resigning after his own research was questioned, Richwine dismissed the criticism of Regnerus as "hysterical condemnations in the press, a frivolous 'scientific misconduct' investigation conducted at the behest of a blogger (!), emotion-laden joint statements, evidence-free accusations of corruption on the part of the journal, and more."[56]

Ultimately, *Social Science Research*'s editor tasked Darren Sherkat, a professor of sociology at Southern Illinois University at Carbondale, and board member of the journal to investigate the paper and its publication. Sherkat's determination was blunt: Regnerus's study was "bullshit."[57]

Sherkat's audit also found that "the peer-review system failed because of 'both ideology and inattention' on the part of the reviewers," as half the reviewers were "on record as opposing same-sex marriage." Additionally, the way in which Regnerus defined an LGBT parent for the purpose of the study should have "disqualified [the New Family Structures Study] immediately" from publication.[58]

Regnerus's own department took steps to distance themselves from their faculty member in a statement: "Dr. Regnerus' opinions are his own. They do not reflect the views of the Sociology Department of The University of Texas at Austin."[59] They went on to cite the American Sociological Association's calling the conclusions of the professor's study "fundamentally flawed on conceptual and methodological grounds." They also acknowledged his research was used "inappropriately" in an attempt to "diminish the civil rights and legitimacy of LBGTQ partners and their families."[60]

Throughout the controversy, Regnerus stuck closely to talking points provided by the Witherspoon Institute that positioned him as a neutral academic as opposed to an interested party. "You are a researcher, not an advocate. You are simply reporting on what the data tells us," read a document titled "Mark Regnerus Media Training." Other recommended talking points included:

- This study does not ascribe a cause to the effects, it simply reports the data.
- For many years, gay advocates have claimed that there are no meaningful differences between children of same-sex couples and other children. This study shows this not to be true.
- Young adults raised in a same-sex household are [list key findings such as more likely to have considered suicide, etc.].[61]

Anticipating that the study would be controversial, the document also included a section titled "Points to Avoid/Hard Questions." For example, if asked about his own views on gay marriage, Regnerus was advised to respond:

This study is not about same-sex marriage. It does not attempt to assess the differences between those gay couples who have married and those who have not. It is focused on the differences between young adults raised in a same-sex household and those raised in an [*sic*] intact families.

And on his opinion of adoption by gay parents:

Again, I am a researcher, not an advocate. Our research finds that there are a number of significant differences between young adults raised in a same-sex household and those raised in intact families where their parents are married to each other. I have no position on adoption, gay marriage or any other similar issue.[62]

In fact, this claimed objectivity was deeply misleading. Regnerus acted as an advocate in friend-of-the-court briefs filed in both *Hollingsworth v. Perry* and *United States v. Windsor.* "A persistent claim by those supporting same-sex marriage is that there is 'no difference' in the outcomes of children raised by a biological mother and father and those who have been raised by two women or two men," wrote Regnerus and half a dozen other academics. "But as recent scholarship indicates, the claim is difficult to support because nearly all of the studies upon which the 'no difference' assertion is based are rather limited, involving nonrandom, nonrepresentative samples, often with relatively few participants. Specifically, the vast majority of the studies were based on samples of fewer than one hundred parents (or children), and typically representative only of well-educated, white women (parents), often with elevated incomes."[63] The very act of filing friend-of-court briefs in these politically charged cases points to his role as an advocate and not one of a disinterested academic. He could have simply been content to let others cite his research, which regardless of its flaws, was included in numerous briefs before the Supreme Court.

The United States Conference of Catholic Bishops wrote, "A mother and father each bring something unique and irreplaceable to child-rearing that the other cannot." Citing the study's findings, the bishops claimed, "Children raised by married biological parents fared better in a range of significant outcomes than children raised in same-sex households."[64]

The Bipartisan Legal Advisory Group, the body in the House of Representatives charged with defending DOMA after the Obama administration determined the law was unconstitutional, also touted the University of Texas professor's work as one of the reasons the law should remain in place, writing "unlike virtually all of the previous studies in this area, the Regnerus study included a representative sample that was large enough to draw statistically powerful conclusions regarding comparative outcomes of people whose parents had homosexual relationships and those who were raised by their married biological mothers and fathers—and it discovered that the former group reported significantly worse outcomes on a large number of key indicators."[65]

The repeated citations of Regnerus's work prompted his professional society, the American Sociological Association, to issue its own brief declaring that the New Family Structures Study "provides no support for the conclusions that same-sex parents are inferior parents or that the children of same-sex parents experience worse outcomes."[66]

The condemnation of Regnerus's professional society did not undermine Witherspoon's strategic goals. This sort of debate is exactly what opponents of gay marriage desired when they funded the New Family Structures study. They recognized that it would not change the judgment of most sociologists, but they hoped to confuse the issue, allowing the conservative justices to argue that there were academic doubts about the ramifications of same-sex marriage.

During oral arguments, Justice Elena Kagan asked Charles Cooper, the lawyer defending Proposition 8, how allowing same-sex couples to wed might harm the institution of marriage. Cooper responded, "I would reiterate that we don't believe that's the correct legal question before the Court."[67]

Justice Antonin Scalia then stepped in to bolster the conservative argument. "Mr. Cooper, let me give you one concrete thing. I don't know why you don't mention some concrete things," he said. "If you redefine marriage to include same-sex couples, you must permit adoption by same-sex couples, and there's considerable disagreement among sociologists as to what the consequences of raising a child in a single-sex family, whether that is harmful to the child or not. Some states do not permit adoption by same-sex couples for that reason."[68]

In Scalia's mind, the disagreement about the impact on children raised in same-sex households created enough uncertainty to allow discrimination against gay couples, exactly as the Witherspoon Institute and the funders of the New Family Structures Study intended.

Scalia's argument and Regnerus's study, while debunked, continued to be cited by conservatives in court. Alabama's attorney general cited New Family Structures in a brief filed in district court in November of 2014, claiming it was "one of the most rigorous and exhaustive studies of family structure to date" and that it "found that children raised by two fathers or two mothers are statistically more likely than children raised in intact, biological families to exhibit negative outcomes in several social and economic areas."[69]

Arguments clearly informed by the Regnerus study were made in January 2015 by Idaho governor Butch Otter, who petitioned the Supreme Court to uphold his state's ban on LGBT marriage. Otter claimed his state's law "satisfies any level of constitutional scrutiny" due to the "salutary effects on the children of heterosexual couples."[70]

Before Otter's brief was filed, courts already demonstrated an extremely skeptical attitude toward Regnerus's research. In

Michigan, Federal District Court judge Bernard Friedman wrote
in his decision that "Regnerus's testimony is entirely unbelievable
and not worthy of serious consideration." He continued, "The
evidence adduced at trial demonstrated that his 2012 'study' was
hastily concocted at the behest of a third-party funder, which
found it 'essential that the necessary data be gathered to settle the
question in the forum of public debate about what kinds of family arrangement are best for society.'"[71]

Judge Friedman directly questioned Regnerus's ability to carry
out the study. "While Regnerus maintained that the funding
source did not affect his impartiality as a researcher, the Court
finds this testimony unbelievable," he wrote. "The funder clearly
wanted a certain result, and Regnerus obliged."

He also stated that New Family Structures was "flawed on its
face" and "whatever Regnerus may have found in this 'study,' he
certainly cannot purport to have undertaken a scholarly research
effort to compare the outcomes of children raised by same-sex
couples with those of children raised by heterosexual couples."

He concluded his summation of the scholar's work with, "It is
no wonder that the NFSS has been widely and severely criticized
by other scholars, and that Regnerus's own sociology department
at the University of Texas has distanced itself from the NFSS in
particular and Dr. Regnerus's views in general and reaffirmed the
aforementioned APA position statement."[72]

From bogus studies concluding that gay parenting leads to
poor outcomes for children to baseless comparisons to bestiality and pedophilia, anti-gay conservatives have used a series of
deceptions in an attempt to demonize the gay community and
scare straight Americans into opposing full equality. For a long
time, they succeeded in making their arguments without being
labeled bigots and even passed anti-gay ballot measures around
the country. Once public sentiment turned, they hoped to use a

similar strategy to sway the Supreme Court. Yet they failed in part because Regnerus's lies were exposed to the public.

The story of the acceptance of same-sex marriage provides us with the antidote to the plague of Lies, Incorporated. By June 2015, when the Supreme Court ruled on same-sex marriage, it was telling that none of the conservative justices used the Regnerus research in their dissents. Quite to the contrary, the majority on the court cited the discriminatory effect on the children of LGBT couples as a reason to strike down bans on same-sex marriage.

The debunking of Regnerus's lie is interwoven into the success of the LGBT civil rights movement. The ACLU filed its first gay marriage case, *Baker v. Nelson,* in 1971. After a long period, in a flurry of activity over the course of a few years, marriage equality was achieved. Regnerus was not simply debunked by the facts; his work was rejected because the culture had shifted. The idea that LGBT individuals were fundamentally flawed was not an argument the public would agree with. For this reason, when his research turned out to be false, its debunking was generally accepted.

Chapter 10

Defeating Lies, Incorporated

The impact of lies on our political process is unquestionable, and the damage they cause is shocking. Nearly five and a half years since Betsy McCaughey's lie was debunked, even after the Affordable Care Act was implemented with no evidence of grandmothers and disabled children being murdered by the state, 41 percent of Americans believe the law created death panels, according to a December 2014 poll funded by the Kaiser Family Foundation.[1]

What damage is the "death panel" lie currently wreaking? To this day, it dissuades some Americans from getting health insurance coverage, potentially leading to life-threatening conditions going untreated. In June 2014, *The Washington Post* told the story of a woman and her husband who were employed but receiving no benefits. They "would rather pay a penalty for being uninsured than participate in Obamacare." This is despite serious out-of-pocket monthly medical expenses stemming from chronic conditions.

The *Post* also quoted Carolyn Underwood, who, while a supporter of "expanded" health coverage, was "scared of Obama-care," she said. "We've been hearing too many tales about it. We heard there's doctors who get to decide ..." *The Post* then described the scene: "Before she could put her finger on the term 'death panels,' her sister Nancy Taylor, 62, made a gun gesture with her hand and said, 'Pow!'"[2]

Conservatives lied in an attempt to block passage of Barack Obama's signature piece of legislation. Betsy McCaughey's death panel falsehood even resulted in the president removing from the law coverage for end-of-life counseling that could have been useful to millions of Americans and their families. Now these same lies have frightened people into denying themselves access to the Affordable Care Act's benefits. A November 2014 poll by Gallup found that 35 percent of uninsured Americans would rather pay the fine prescribed by the law than receive health insurance.[3]

The tobacco companies, the fossil fuel industry, and organizations that employ the Richard Bermans of Washington, all recognize the usefulness of lies: their power to halt progress and justify political positions that would otherwise seem cruel, irrational, or extreme.

Like any successful strategy, it can be packaged up and sold, thus creating the business of Lies, Incorporated. But it is not an industry that operates simply based on a monetary benefit. Some rewards are more important. Betsy McCaughey or John Lott can expand their public platform, or a doctor from northern Michigan or a professor at Princeton can steer our national debate on an issue whose outcome they care deeply about.

Naomi Oreskes observed that the tobacco and fossil fuel industries' campaigns of misinformation have "been so successful" in part "because you've got money and ideology lined up together. . . . It's this alignment of the power of the money from the industry side and the authentic belief, the ideology that many of these people are carrying that gives this its tremendous power."[4] The same holds true for the rest of Lies, Incorporated as well.

The purveyors of misinformation have a built-in advantage. Lies are socially sticky, and even after one has been thoroughly debunked, it will still have advocates among those whose worldview it justifies. These zombie lies continue to rise from the dead again and again, impacting political debate and swaying public opinion on a variety of issues.

Misinformation is damaging to those who read and absorb it. Once a lie—no matter how outrageous—is part of the consciousness of a particular group, it is nearly impossible to eliminate, and like a virus it spreads uncontrollably within the affected communities. Richard Berman explained to energy executives that once you "solidify [a] position," in a person's mind, regardless of the truth, you have "achieved something the other side cannot overcome because it's very tough to break common knowledge."[5] That "common knowledge" is repeated on radio, television, in print, and at the water cooler. With each new citation, the lie becomes more entrenched.

Furthermore, belief in lies is not indicative of a lack of intelligence or ignorance. The smarter and better-read you are, the more likely you are to believe and repeat falsehoods. Chris Mooney, a journalist who has made a career of exploring why the Republican base believes and perpetuates lies, has found that with a greater level of education, Republicans actually become "*more* skeptical of modern climate science."[6]

Mooney makes his assertion based on a Pew poll that found 19 percent of Republicans with a college education believe climate change is occurring, compared with 31 percent of those without a college degree.[7]

George Washington University political science professor John Sides found this same pattern existed when looking at Republicans who believed Barack Obama is a Muslim. Mooney explains, "Belief in this falsehood actually increased *more* among better-educated Republicans from 2009 to 2010 than it did among less-educated Republicans."[8]

Mooney found this pattern continued in the debate over health care. Republicans "who thought they knew more about" the bill were "more likely to endorse" the lie that the ACA contained death panels, according to research he cited.[9]

These findings have been replicated in academic studies. According to research funded by the National Science Foundation and led by Dan Kahan, a law and psychology professor at Yale Law School, "greater scientific literacy and numeracy were associated with greater *cultural polarization:* respondents predisposed by their values to dismiss climate change evidence became more dismissive, and those predisposed by their values to credit such evidence more concerned, as science literacy and numeracy increased."[10]

There is no simple counter to Lies, Incorporated's strategy. No law or single piece of legislation can reasonably be passed that will put a halt to the practice. The first step is demanding transparency from our elected leaders as well as the media. On CNBC, it is common for the network to post the stocks its guests own on the screen as they speak. Therefore, viewers can judge guests' opinions in full context.

CNN, MSNBC, Fox, and other news channels should consider the same practices with political commentators. Guests should be forced to publicly disclose financial connections to their policy opinions. Post-truth politics thrives because it can operate in the shadows, covered up by polite Washington society that bristles at the notion that people would take positions on policy issues simply because they were paid to. Or, heaven forbid, people are intentionally distorting the truth for their ideological benefit.

The culture of Washington needs to change so lies are no longer an accepted part of the discourse or treated with a ho-hum attitude. We should not express outrage only in extreme circumstances, as in response to Todd Akin's "shut the whole thing down" remark. Instead we should voice the same anger and belligerence toward every lie. This requires constant vigilance and a willingness to challenge figures, especially those with large media platforms, who allow lies to be told to the public. And it must happen at every level, from monitoring the press to ensuring lies are not spread at the water cooler.

It's telling that in today's political culture, people are more likely to express concern at the social faux pas of calling someone a liar, rather than be concerned about the lie itself. During President Obama's fall 2009 address to Congress, South Carolina representative Joe Wilson screamed, "You lie," after the president told Congress, "There are also those who claim that our [health care] reform effort will insure illegal immigrants. This, too, is false— the reforms I'm proposing would not apply to those who are here illegally."[11]

Democrats and some in the press corps obsessed about the impolitic nature of Joe Wilson's statement, while Republicans and the conservative media turned the previously obscure congressman into a hero. Few paid attention to the truthfulness of President Obama's statement. Page 143, line 3, Section 246 of the health care bill spelled out in plain language: "No Federal Payment for Undocumented Aliens. Nothing in this subtitle shall allow Federal payments for affordability credits on behalf of individuals who are not lawfully present in the United States."[12]

The Joe Wilson incident highlights the need for another change in the culture of Washington: policy makers should not cave to those who peddle falsehoods. In the days following Obama's address to Congress, as the issue gained traction in the right-wing media, the White House and Democrats on Capitol Hill added even tougher anti-immigrant language to the health care law.

As mentioned earlier, Democrats similarly attempted to placate those who believed the death panel falsehood. After the furor died down, in July 2015, Medicare proposed reimbursing doctors who offered end-of-life counseling to patients.[13] Without the health care law hanging in the balance, this change has largely been uncontroversial with limited reporting even in the conservative media.

When trying to pass a piece of legislation like the Affordable Care Act, political leaders will look to the path of least resistance, quickly throwing overboard provisions they view as tangential to save the broader legislation. This strategy is flawed in two regards.

First, it empowers liars, elevating their falsehoods. In the mind of the public, if Betsy McCaughey and Joe Wilson weren't right, then why would the administration be forced to change these provisions? To the media, it is a signal that future accusations from these liars should be taken seriously.

A second strategic flaw is the idea that in today's environment you can placate political opponents. Those who did not want the Affordable Care Act to become law continued to claim the bill contained death panels and would provide health insurance to undocumented immigrants. It seems clear that caving in to liars in an attempt to achieve short-term political gain serves little to no purpose and is potentially quite destructive.

The political media is predisposed to treat public policy like sports, putting liars at an advantage. If every policy fight is simply covered as the blue team versus the red team, then truth invariably sits on the sideline. News organizations and reporters need to be held accountable when they give equal weight to scientists talking about climate change and industry-funded deniers. The same goes for other issues, where experts are pushed to the side in favor of TV-friendly pundits.

Just as those we covered in this book have fought their battle with lies, we need to weaponize truth, wielding it against those who distort it for financial or ideological gain. In *The Fox Effect,* David Brock and I wrote that misinformation is dangerous when it metastasizes. The biggest danger of Fox News is not that it broadcasts lies to its audience, who mainly have their minds made up already, but that these lies then spread to other more mainstream outlets. The same holds true for the members of Lies, Incorporated. If we can isolate the spread of their messages, their impact will be diminished.

News networks must shun John Lott in the wake of mass shootings, and there is no reason Betsy McCaughey should ever be part of a public debate on health care again. Richard Berman should not be permitted to describe himself in the media as executive director of one of his front groups and should be forced to disclose the funders behind his efforts. To put it simply, liars should not be welcome as part of the public conversation. There are important differences between progressives and conservatives that need to be publicly debated. Lies and liars actively prevent those conversations from occurring.

Lies, Incorporated succeeds by taking advantage of the structure of mass media in the Internet age. Bound by the constraint to tell "both sides" of the story, mainstream reporters often give credence to lies. When the press feels obligated to cover both sides of an issue, without regard for factual merit, truth is automatically at a disadvantage. Lies, Incorporated takes advantage of this "he said/she said" approach to covering public policy debates.

Until recently, members of the press were loath to be arbiters of truth. This has changed somewhat with the rise of fact-checking websites such as PolitiFact, *The Washington Post*'s fact-checking blog, and Annenberg's FactCheck.org. While these outlets are far from perfect, their positive impact is felt as others in both print and broadcast media have become less likely to present both truth and lies with equal weight. However, these fact-checkers do not constrain ideologically driven media organizations that believe truth should be a secondary value to victory.

Television news networks have a preference for hosting political debates rather than presenting news. This was clearly illustrated by a Media Matters study of coverage of the 2014 National Climate Assessment, which found "the top cable news networks relied on scientists for a mere 14 percent of all interviews when interpreting the significance of the climate report's findings."[14] Politicians represented another 36 percent of guests, while a smattering of talking heads with limited expertise represented the remaining 50 percent. So instead of discussing solutions to the warming of the planet, or even mitigating its impact, we are stuck debating hot or cold.

We live in isolated communities, not only in the physical world, but online as well, often making it difficult to communicate with others of the opposite perspective. Go to any neighborhood and you are likely to find ideologically homogeneous clusters. It appears that digital platforms, which promised to enlarge our exposure to different viewpoints, have had the opposite effect. The algorithms employed by Google, Facebook, and other technology companies feed us information that we are likely to agree with, because those are the links we are most likely to click, as UpWorthy CEO Eli Pariser explained in his book *The Filter Bubble*.

The post-truth landscape is fueled by a bifurcated media structure, which allows misinformation to rapidly spread in ideological echo chambers. Because it is simply impossible for individuals to track down the primary source for every piece of information they consume, we invariably rely on aggregators to report the news to us. No longer limited to anchors on the three big networks to tell us what we need to know, we flock to the venues that best conform to our own worldview.

Those on the left watch the nightly news and *The Daily Show,* read *The New York Times,* listen to NPR, and perhaps have added MSNBC to their information diets. On the right, conservative media sources dominate the conversation, most prominently Fox News, and in recent years a bevy of new outlets, including Tucker Carlson's *The Daily Caller,* Glenn Beck's TheBlaze.com, and Breitbart.com. While some suggest they simply preach to the converted, these outlets are powerful amplifiers of lies.

Sometimes media outlets are directly connected to the entities responsible for manufacturing the lies. A former executive editor of *The Daily Caller* previously worked for Richard Berman,[15] who himself is a columnist for the site, primarily doing his clients' bidding by attacking organized labor and defending the food industry.[16]

The lobbyists, ideological warriors, and communications strategists who create and traffic in lies no longer have to convince others to transmit the false information they produce. With a relatively small budget, they can create their own media outlets. Recently, the conservative Heritage Foundation launched *The Daily Signal* to help push their views on public policy, and a group of neoconservative hawks founded *The Washington Free Beacon* to serve their ideological interests. These media entities, which once would have been considered fringe venues, are growing in power and influence to the point where we see information reported by them repeated as gospel by powerful politicians.

As noted above, just because a lie has been thoroughly debunked doesn't mean it goes away. These zombie lies continue to rise from the dead again and again, impacting political debate and swaying people's opinions on a variety of issues. The emotional resonance of the "death panels" lie meant it would continue to be repeated to this day, years after being thoroughly debunked.

These vulnerabilities in our political and media ecosystems contribute to the playbook Lies, Incorporated uses to hack the policy process, giving extreme positions at least a thin veneer of respectability.

At its most basic level, Lies, Incorporated exists because, as cynical and corrupt as our politics have become, elected officials still feel the need to have a plausible rationale behind their decisions that appeals to voters. They need the facade of a benefit to consumers or the false fear of government overreach, sowing confusion about the issues of the day to justify their political positions and short-circuit progress.

Too often, we are blasé about the impact lies have on politics and public policy. Politicians lie during campaigns, they lie to get elected, and they lie in office. Pundits are paid for their partisan warfare, not their truth telling. We have become a society and a political class that has become desensitized to the impact of falsehoods. But lies have consequences.

Barack Obama was elected with a clear mandate. Americans facing the worst recession in decades and weary from seven years of war desperately wanted change. He was empowered with a grassroots army of more than ten million Americans ready to stand by his side.

Lies, Incorporated aggressively responded to this challenge. No policy—from health care, to climate, to Wall Street reform—went unopposed by these practitioners. In many ways, even when Lies, Incorporated failed, they succeeded by helping to prevent the full implementation of anti-industry policies. Any president seeking to challenge the status quo will face the same coordinated attack from Lies, Incorporated, which is why its defeat is so critical.

John Lott's lies have helped to maintain policies that put more dangerous weapons on the streets, making our country less safe. Hans von Spakovsky's lies have helped to disenfranchise significant numbers of Americans, doing untold damage to our democracy. People are refusing health coverage because they believe Betsy McCaughey's lie that they could be subjected to a death panel. Reinhart and Rogoff's study justifying austerity policies led to layoffs and a downgrade of public services around the world. Each of these liars, and the policies they advocate for, causes real and unnecessary pain for millions of people. As long as Lies, Incorporated continues to operate without public scrutiny or consequence, we will continue to have a damaged system for discussing, debating, and creating policy that is essential to the success of our nation.

Notes

Lies, Incorporated owes a special debt of gratitude to a number of seminal works that were critical to our thinking while writing this book. They include Lee Drutman's *The Business of America is Lobbying*, Naomi Oreskes and Erik M. Conway's *Merchants of Doubt*, David Michaels's *Doubt Is Their Product*, Jane Mayer's profile of Hans von Spakovsky, Sofia Resnick's reporting on Mark Regnerus, and Andy Birkey's reporting on Robert George for *The American Independent*.

Preface

1. Schorn, Daniel, "Meet Rick Berman, A.K.A. 'Dr. Evil,'" CBS News, February 25, 2011, www.cbsnews.com/news/meet-rick-berman-aka-dr-evil/.
2. Ibid.
3. Center for Consumer Freedom, "Wayne Pacelle and The HSUS Scam," www.youtube.com/watch?v=4hN0ai9WzBQ.
4. The Humane Society of the United States Annual Report, www.humanesociety.org/about/overview/annual_reports_financial_statements.html.
5. The Humane Society of the United States, "Celebrating Animals, Confronting Cruelty: Annual Report 2014," www.humanesociety.org/assets/pdfs/about/2014-hsus-annual-report.pdf.
6. *The Colbert Report*, October 2007, www.cc.com/video-clips/pmtsjp/the-colbert-report-richard-berman.
7. *The Rachel Maddow Show*, "Meet Rick Berman," March 2010; "Rachel Maddow Confronts Notorious Corporate Lobbyist Rick Berman," *Huffington Post*, March 28, 2010, www.huffingtonpost.com/2009/10/07/rachel-maddow-confronts-n_n_312334.html.
8. Craig Harrington, "Fox Fails to Disclose Corporate Ties of Lobbyist Dismissing Fast Food Worker Strike," MediaMatters.org, July 29, 2013,

mediamatters.org/blog/2013/07/29/fox-fails-to-disclose-corporate-ties
-of-lobbyis/195112.

9. Eric Lipton, "Fight Over Minimum Wage Illustrates Web of Industry Ties,"
   New York Times, February 9, 2014, www.nytimes.com/2014/02/10/us/
   politics/fight-over-minimum-wage-illustrates-web-of-industry-ties.html.

10. Employment Policies Institute, 2013 IRS Form 990. Filed November 20,
    2014, 990s.foundationcenter.org/990_pdf_archive/521/521902264/
    521902264_201312_990.pdf?_ga=1.43879271.310218252.1440786558.

11. Eric Morath, "Is Economy Too Fragile to Raise the Minimum Wage?," *Wall
    Street Journal,* February 3, 2014, blogs.wsj.com/economics/2014/02/03/is
    -economy-too-fragile-to-raise-the-minimum-wage/.

12. Employment Policies Institute, 2013 IRS Form 990.

13. Employment Policies Institute, 2013 IRS Form 990.

14. "Who is Richard Berman," Berman Exposed, bermanexposed.org/
    associate/richard-berman/.

15. "About Us," Berman and Company, www.bermanco.com/about-us/.

16. The Center for Organizational Research and Education, 2013 IRS Form
    990, www.guidestar.org/FinDocuments/2013/260/006/2013-260006579
    -0af5d15d-9.pdf.

17. Core, coreprojects.com.

18. Environmental Policy Alliance, environmentalpolicyalliance.org.

19. Big Green Radicals, www.biggreenradicals.com.

20. EPA Facts, epafacts.com.

21. Green Decoys, www.greendecoys.com.

22. LEED Exposed, www.leedexposed.com.

23. Humane Watch, www.humanewatch.org.

24. The Facts About Maternity Pens, maternitypens.com.

25. PETA Kills Animals, www.petakillsanimals.com/contact/.

26. Prop 65 Scam, prop65scam.com.

27. Center for Accountability in Science, www.accountablescience.com.

28. "About Us," Activist Facts, www.activistfacts.com/about/.

29. "About Us," CREW Exposed, crewexposed.com/about-us/.

30. "About," Humane Society for Shelter Pets, humaneforpets.com/about/.

31. Employment Policies Institute Foundation, 2013 IRS Form 990, www
    .guidestar.org/FinDocuments/2013/521/902/2013-521902264-0af5d135
    -9.pdf.

32. "EPI Projects," Employment Policies Institute, www.epionline.org/epi
    -projects/.

33. About MinimumWage.com, MinimumWage.com, www.minimumwage
    .com/about/.

34. "About Us," TippedWage.com, tippedwage.com/about-us/.

35. Bad Idea New Jersey, badideanj.com.

36. Bad Idea California, badideaca.com.

37. Ari Phillips, "Mastermind of the World's Most Despicable PR Cam-
    paigns Has a New Job," ThinkProgress.org, March 5, 2015, thinkprogress
    .org/climate/2015/03/05/3627572/richard-bermans-incredible-public
    -relations-machine/.

38. Econ4U.org, econ4u.com/contact.php.
39. "About Us," Rethink Reform, www.rethinkreform.com/about-us/.
40. "Defeat the Debt," Activist Facts, www.activistfacts.com/organizations/498-defeat-the-debt/.
41. American Beverage Institute, 2013 IRS Form 990, www.guidestar.org/FinDocuments/2013/521/730/2013-521730954-0af7580d-9O.pdf.
42. American Beverage Institute, abionline.org.
43. InterLockFacts.org, interlockfacts.com/about/. Via: web.archive.org/web/20150801142229/http://interlockfacts.com/.
44. No Drink Tax, nodrinktax.com/about-us/. Via: web.archive.org/web/20150801222157/http://nodrinktax.com/.
45. "Know Your Limits, Know the Law," ResponsibleLimits.com, www.responsiblelimits.com. Via: web.archive.org/web/20150418072125; www.responsiblelimits.com/.
46. "Negligent Driving," NegligentDriving.com, www.negligentdriving.com/about.php. Via: web.archive.org/web/20150910040001/http://negligentdriving.com/.
47. "The New Prohibition," TheNewProhibition.com, thenewprohibition.com/contact-us.php. Via: web.archive.org/web/20150305132443/; thenewprohibition.com/.
48. "About the Center for Union Facts," Center for Union Facts, www.unionfacts.com/article/about-us/.
49. Center for Union Facts, 2013 IRS Form 990, www.guidestar.org/FinDocuments/2013/204/036/2013-204036946-0af8b6a2-9.pdf.
50. "About the Center for Union Facts," TeachersUnionsExposed.com, www.teachersunionexposed.com/about.php.
51. "DC Teachers Union Exposed," TeachersUnionExposed.com, teachersunionexposed.com/dc/.
52. "About Us," AFTFacts.com, www.aftfacts.com/about-us/.
53. "EmployeeRightsAct.com," employeerightsact.com.
54. "About," WorkerCenters.com, workercenters.com/about/.
55. ProtectingBadTeachers, protectingbadteachers.com.
56. "Center for Union Facts," ActivistFacts.com, www.activistfacts.com/organizations/495-center-for-union-facts/.
57. LaborPains.org, laborpains.org.
58. Will Evans, "Profile: Employee Freedom Action Committee," National Public Radio, September 8, 2008. www.npr.org/templates/story/story.php?storyId=94395162.
59. Enterprise Freedom Action Committee, 2013 IRS Form 990, www.guidestar.org/FinDocuments/2013/260/563/2013-260563406-0af4d0e5-9O.pdf.
60. Richard Berman Speech Transcript, s3.amazonaws.com/s3.documentcloud.org/documents/1349204/berman-at-western-energy-alliance-june-2014-doc.pdf; Eric Lipton, "Hard-Nosed Advice From Veteran Lobbyist: 'Win Ugly or Lose Pretty,'" *New York Times,* October 30, 2014, www.nytimes.com/2014/10/31/us/politics/pr-executives-western-energy-alliance-speech-taped.html.

61. Tobacco Legacy Documents Library, Memo to Denise Keane, March 28, 1996, industrydocuments.library.ucsf.edu/tobacco/docs/#id=fjhv0083. Also see: "Center for Consumer Freedom," Source Watch, www .sourcewatch.org/index.php/Center_for_Consumer_Freedom.

62. Caroline E. Mayer and Amy Joyce, "The Escalating Obesity Wars," *Washington Post,* April 27, 2005, www.washingtonpost.com/wp-dyn/content/article/2005/04/26/AR2005042601259.html.

63. Tobacco Legacy Documents Library, Letter to Richard Berman, August 26, 1999, industrydocuments.library.ucsf.edu/tobacco/docs/#id=zzgx0085.

64. Tobacco Legacy Documents Library, Letter from Richard Berman to Barbara Trach, September 5, 1995, industrydocuments.library.ucsf.edu/tobacco/docs/#id=jqjx0053.

65. Ibid. Also see: "Center for Consumer Freedom," SourceWatch.org. www .sourcewatch.org/index.php/Center_for_Consumer_Freedom.

66. Sam Stein, Amanda Terkel, "Private Documents Show Coca-Cola Played Both Sides of the Drunk Driving Debate," *Huffington Post,* May 13, 2014, www.huffingtonpost.com/2014/05/13/american-beverage-institute_n _5310917.html.

67. Lipton, February 9, 2014.

68. Jane Wells, "Sugar v. Corn Syrup: Sweeteners Clash in Court," CNBC, January 23, 2014, www.cnbc.com/2014/01/23/legal-fight-between-sugar-and -corn-syrup-groups-rages-on.html.

69. Scott Lapatine, "Silver Jew Calls It Quits, Exposes Dad," StereoGum, January 23, 2009, www.stereogum.com/47621/silver_jew_calls_it_quits _exposes_dad/news/.

70. Lipton, October 30, 2014.

Introduction: Lies, Incorporated

1. "National Rifle Assn," Open Secrets, www.opensecrets.org/lobby/clientsum.php?id=D000000082&year=2013.

2. "Statement by the President," April 17, 2013, White House, www .whitehouse.gov/the-press-office/2013/04/17/statement-president.

3. David Frum, "Waterloo," Frum Forum, March 21, 2010, www.frumforum .com/waterloo/.

4. Lipton, October 30, 2014.

5. Lipton, February 9, 2014.

6. "Appendix 4: The Federal Election Campaign Laws: A Short History," Federal Election Commission, www.fec.gov/info/appfour.htm.

7. "Federal Law," The Campaign Finance Institute, www.cfinst.org/law/federal.aspx.

8. U.S. Supreme Court, *Buckley v. Valeo,* January 30, 1976, caselaw.findlaw .com/us-supreme-court/424/1.html.

9. Seth Getell, "Making Sense of McCain-Feingold and Campaign-Finance Reform," *The Atlantic,* July/August 2013, www.theatlantic.com/magazine/archive/2003/07/making-sense-of-mccain-feingold-and-campaign -finance-reform/302758/.

10. Morton Mintz, "Will McCain-Feingold Survive Another Court Test?" *The*

Nation, June 19, 2007. www.thenation.com/article/will-mccain-feingold -survive-another-court-test/.

11. John Dunbar, "The 'Citizens United' Decision and Why It Matters," The Center for Public Integrity, October 18, 2012, www.publicintegrity.org/ 2012/10/18/11527/citizens-united-decision-and-why-it-matters.

12. "Summary of Supreme Court Decision in *FEC v. Wisconsin Right to Life,*" Brennan Center for Justice, www.brennancenter.org/analysis/summary -supreme-court-decision-fec-v-wisconsin-right-life.

13. "Summary of Supreme Court Decision in *FEC v. Wisconsin Right to Life,*" Brennan Center for Justice, July 5, 2007, www.oyez.org/cases/2000-2009/ 2007/2007_07_320.

14. Lee Drutman, *The Business of America is Lobbying: How Corporations Became Politicized and Politics Became More Corporate* (New York: Oxford University Press, 2015), 16.

15. Robert C. Byrd, "Lobbyists," September 28, 1987 (updated 1989), www .senate.gov/legislative/common/briefing/Byrd_History_Lobbying.htm.

16. Bethanne Kelly Patrick, "Gen. William Hull." Millitary.com, www.military .com/Content/MoreContent?file=ML_whull_bkp.

17. Byrd, September 1987.

18. Ibid.

19. Ibid.

20. Del Quentin Wilber and Carrie Johnson, "Abramoff Gets Reduced Sentence of Four Years in Prison," *Washington Post,* September 5, 2008, www.washingtonpost.com/wp-dyn/content/article/2008/09/04/ AR2008090402321_2.html?sid=ST2008090403024.

21. Susan Schmidt and James V. Grimaldi, "Panel Says Abramoff Laundered Tribal Funds," *Washington Post,* June 23, 2005, www.washingtonpost.com/ wp-dyn/content/article/2005/06/22/AR2005062200921_pf.html.

22. Lou Dubose, "Inside the A-List Event Where 2016 GOPers Are More Christian-Than-Thou," *TPM Cafe,* July 27, 2015, talkingpointsmemo.com/ cafe/ted-cruz-faith-and-freedom-coalition-conference.

23. John B. Judis, *The Paradox of American Democracy* (New York: Pantheon Books, 2000), 112.

24. Judis, 2000, 132–133.

25. Lewis Powell, "Confidential Memorandum: Attack of American Free Enterprise System," August 23, 1971, reclaimdemocracy.org/powell _memo_lewis/.

26. Ibid.

27. Lee Drutman, "How Corporate Lobbyists Conquered American Democracy," *The Atlantic,* April 20, 2015, www.theatlantic.com/business/archive/ 2015/04/how-corporate-lobbyists-conquered-american-democracy/ 390822/.

28. Drutman, 2015, 13.

29. Drutman, 2015, 78.

30. "Honest Leadership and Open Government Act of 2007," Congress.gov, www.congress.gov/bill/110th-congress/house-bill/2316.

31. "Executive Order 13490—Ethics Commitments by Executive Branch

Personnel," WhiteHouse.gov, January 21, 2009, www.whitehouse.gov/the
-press-office/ethics-commitments-executive-branch-personnel.

32. Lee Fang, "Where Have All the Lobbyists Gone?," *The Nation,* February 19, 2014, www.thenation.com/article/shadow-lobbying-complex/.

33. Ibid.

34. Drutman, 2015, 37.

35. Ibid.

36. Arthur M. Schlesinger, Jr., *The Politics of Upheaval: 1935–1936, The Age of Roosevelt,* vol. 3 (New York: Mariner Books, 2003), 315.

37. Schlesinger, Jr., 318–320.

38. Tony Romm, "Net Neutrality Emails Raise Suspicions," *Politico,* March 31, 2015, www.politico.com/story/2015/03/net-neutrality-email-american
-commitment-116553.

39. Whitfield to Rick Rodgers, Washington, D.C., June 30, 2009, www.politico
.com/static/PPM130_fedex_grassroots_proposal_6-30-09_final.html;
Mike Allen, "Exclusive: Conservative Group Offers Support for $2M,"
Politico, July 17, 2009, dyn.politico.com/printstory.cfm?uuid=87F6C993
-18FE-70B2-A8801E4FA12982D9.

40. Ibid.

41. Michelangelo Signorile, "How Gay Media Helped Sink the AT&T/
T-Mobile Merger," *Huffington Post,* February 19, 2012, www.huffingtonpost
.com/michelangelo-signorile/how-gay-media-helped-sink_b_1160449
.html.

42. Ibid.

43. "Politico Influence," *Politico,* www.politico.com/tipsheets/politico-influence.

Chapter 1: The Birth of Lies, Incorporated: *Tobacco*

1. Naomi Oreskes and Erik M. Conway, *Merchants of Doubt: How a Handful of Scientists Obscured the Truth on Issues from Tobacco Smoke to Global Warming* (New York: Bloomsbury Press, 2010), 10–35.

2. Ibid, 14.

3. Ibid.

4. Ibid, 15.

5. Barnaby Feder, "THE MEDIA BUSINESS; Hill & Knowlton Chief Makes an Abrupt Exit," *New York Times,* September 27, 1991, www.nytimes.com/
1991/09/27/business/the-media-business-hill-knowlton-chief-makes-an
-abrupt-exit.html.

6. Kevin Moloney, *Rethinking Public Relations: PR Propaganda and Democracy* (London: Routledge, 2006), 89.

7. Robert N. Proctor, "The History of the Discovery of the Cigarette–Lung Cancer Link: Evidentiary Traditions, Corporate Denial, Global Toll," *Tobacco Control,* November 2011, tobaccocontrol.bmj.com/content/21/2/87.full.

8. Ibid.

9. Ibid.

10. Oreskes and Conway, 2010, 15–16.

11. Tobacco Archive, December 24, 1953, archive.tobacco.org/Documents/
531224hill&knowlton.html.

12. Oreskes and Conway, 2010.

13. Tobacco Archive, December 24, 1953.

14. "United States of America et. al. vs. Phillip Morris USA Inc., Final Opinion," TobaccoFreeKids.org, Page 37, https://www.tobaccofreekids.org/content/what_we_do/industry_watch/doj/FinalOpinion.pdf.

15. "Regulation of Tobacco Products," hearings before the Subcommittee on Health and the Environment of the Committee on Energy and Commerce, House of Representatives, One Hundred Third Congress, second session, April 28, May 17, May 26, 1994, archive.org/stream/regulationoftoba02unit/regulationoftoba02unit_djvu.txt.

16. "A Frank Statement to Cigarette Smokers," Tobacco Archive, archive.tobacco.org/History/540104frank.html.

17. "Regulation of Tobacco Products."

18. Oreskes and Conway, 2010, 16.

19. Martha N. Gardner and Allan M. Brandt, "The Doctors' Choice Is America's Choice," *American Journal of Public Health,* February 2006, www.ncbi.nlm.nih.gov/pmc/articles/PMC1470496/.

20. David Michaels, "Doubt Is Their Product: How Industry's Assault on Science Threatens Your Health," (London: Oxford University Press, 2008), 5.

21. "Regulation of Tobacco Products."

22. Alcoholic Beverage Executive Newsletter, Tobacco Archive, industrydocuments.library.ucsf.edu/tobacco/docs/#id=hkgm0027.

23. David D. Rutstein, "An Open Letter to Dr. Clarence Cook Little," *The Atlantic,* October 1957, www.theatlantic.com/past/docs/unbound/flashbks/smoking/rutsteinf.htm.

24. Ibid.

25. Christopher Zbrozek, "The strange career of C.C. Little," *The Michigan Daily,* September 26, 2006, www.michigandaily.com/content/christopher-zbrozek-strange-career-cc-little.

26. Oreskes and Conway, 2010.

27. Interview with Naomi Oreskes by author, SiriusXM Satellite Radio, March 6, 2015.

28. "Regulation of Tobacco Products."

29. Ibid.

30. Public Relational Report to the Tobacco Industry Research Committee, Tobacco Archive, industrydocuments.library.ucsf.edu/tobacco/docs/#id=znyp0042.

31. "Regulation of Tobacco Products."

32. Majority Staff of the Subcommittee on Health and the Environment, "The Hill and Knowlton Documents: How the Tobacco Industry Launched Its Disinformation Campaign," Tobacco Archive, May 26, 1994, industrydocuments.library.ucsf.edu/tobacco/docs/#id=krjp0058.

33. Tobacco Archive, 1953, industrydocuments.library.ucsf.edu/documentstore/r/r/m/c//rrmc0142/rrmc0142.pdf.

34. History of the Surgeon General's Reports on Smoking and Health, Centers for Disease Control, http://www.cdc.gov/tobacco/data_statistics/sgr/history/.

35. Tobacco Industry Records, New York State Archives, http://nysa32.nysed
.gov/a/research/res_topics_bus_tobacco_adminctr.shtml.

36. John Hill, "Health and Morality: Tobacco's Counter Campaign," Tobacco
Archive, industrydocuments.library.ucsf.edu/tobacco/docs/#id=snjg0128.
"Hill & Knowlton," Source Watch, www.sourcewatch.org/index.php/Hill
_%26_Knowlton.

37. Ibid.

38. Michaels, 2008, 18.

39. Ibid, 45.

Chapter 2: Tobacco's Sequel: *Climate Change*

1. John Cushman, "Industry Group Plans to Battle Climate Treaty," *New York
Times,* April 26, 1998, www.nytimes.com/1998/04/26/us/industrial-group
-plans-to-battle-climate-treaty.html.

2. "Kyoto Protocol," United Nations Framework Convention on Climate
Change, unfccc.int/kyoto_protocol/items/2830.php.

3. Robert Kenner, *Merchants of Doubt,* Sony Pictures Classics, December
2014.

4. Oreskes and Conway, 2010, 5.

5. Neela Banerjee, Lisa Song, and David Hasemyer, "Exxon's Own Research
Confirmed Fossil Fuels' Role in Global Warming Decades Ago," Inside-
Climate News, September 16, 2015, insideclimatenews.org/news/
15092015/Exxons-own-research-confirmed-fossil-fuels-role-in-global
-warming.

6. Ibid.

7. Ibid.

8. Suzanne Goldenberg, "Exxon Knew of Climate Change in 1981, Email
Says—but It Funded Deniers for 27 More Years," *Guardian,* July 8, 2015,
www.theguardian.com/environment/2015/jul/08/exxon-climate-change
-1981-climate-denier-funding.

9. "Exxon Chairman Calls Poverty Most Pressing Environmental Problem in
Developing Countries," PR Newswire, October 13, 1997, www.prnewswire
.com/news-releases/exxon-chairman-calls-poverty-most-pressing
-environmental-problem-in-developing-countries-77530627.html.

10. Cushman, April 26, 1998.

11. Ibid.

12. Joe Walker to Global Climate Science Team, memo on Global Science Communications Action plan, American Petroleum Institute, April
1998, research.greenpeaceusa.org/?a=view&d=4383; Greenpeace, www
.greenpeace.org/international/Global/international/planet-2/report/
2010/3/dealing-in-doubt.pdf.

13. Ibid.

14. Mark Hertsgard, "While Washington Slept," *Vanity Fair,* May 2006, www
.vanityfair.com/news/2006/05/warming200605.

15. Interview with Naomi Oreskes by author, SiriusXM Satelite Radio, March 6,
2015.

16. "Fred Seitz," August 31, 1989, Tobacco Archive, tobaccodocuments.org/

pm/2023266534.html?pattern=fred%5Ba-z%5D%2A%5CW%2Bseitz
%5Ba-z%5D%2A&#p1; Oreskes and Conway, 2010, 36.

17. Fred Seitz, "Do People Cause Global Warming?" The Heartland Institute, December 1, 2001, news.heartland.org/newspaper-article/2001/12/01/do-people-cause-global-warming.

18. "The Science of Climate Change," *Science,* May 18, 2001, www.sciencemag.org/content/292/5520/1261.short.

19. Oreskes and Conway, 2010, 36–38.

20. Kenner, 2014.

21. Paul Feine, "Green on the Outside, Red on the Inside," *Reason Magazine,* January 2012, reason.com/archives/2011/11/20/green-on-the-outside-red-on-the-inside.

22. "Thoughts on TASSC Europe," March 25, 1994, Tobacco Archive, industrydocuments.library.ucsf.edu/documentstore/s/j/c/f//sjcf0114/sjcf0114.pdf.

23. Ibid.

24. Global Warming Basics, Natural Resources Defense Council, http://www.nrdc.org/globalwarming/f101.asp

25. Dana Nuccitelli, "Survey Finds 97% of Climate Science Papers Agree Warming Is Man-Made," *Guardian,* May 16, 2013, www.theguardian.com/environment/climate-consensus-97-per-cent/2013/may/16/climate-change-scienceofclimatechange.

26. Richard Muller, "The Conversion of a Climate-Change Skeptic," *New York Times,* July 28, 2012, www.nytimes.com/2012/07/30/opinion/the-conversion-of-a-climate-change-skeptic.html.

27. "Financial Support," Berkley Earth, http://berkeleyearth.org/funders/.

28. Ross Gelbspan, *The Heat Is On* (New York: Basic Books, 1998); "Dealing in Doubt," Greenpeace, March 24, 2010, www.greenpeace.org/international/en/publications/reports/dealing-in-doubt/.

29. "Dealing in Doubt."

30. Tom Hamburger, "Sen. Inhofe, Denier of Human Role in Climate Change, Likely to Lead Environment Committee," *Washington Post,* November 5, 2014, www.washingtonpost.com/politics/inhofe-an-epa-foe-likely-to-lead-senate-environment-committee/2014/11/05/d0b4221e-64f4-11e4-836c-83bc4f26eb67_story.html.

31. Kenner, 2014.

32. "About," Climate Depot, www.climatedepot.com/about/.

33. Kenner, 2014.

34. Ibid.

35. Ibid.

36. Suzanne Goldberg, "Rockefeller Family Tried and Failed to Get Exxon-Mobil to Accept Climate Change," *Guardian,* March 27, 2015, www.theguardian.com/environment/2015/mar/27/rockefeller-family-tried-and-failed-exxonmobil-accept-climate-change.

37. Kate Sheppard, "Everything You Always Wanted to Know About the Waxman-Markey Energy/Climate Bill—in Bullet Points," *Grist,* June 4, 2009, grist.org/article/2009-06-03-waxman-markey-bill-breakdown/.

38. "Issues and Policy," America's Power, www.americaspower.org/issues
    -policy.
39. "American Cltn for Clean Coal Electricity," Open Secrets, www.opensecrets
    .org/lobby/clientsum.php?id=D000046880&year=2009.
40. Lee Fang, *The Machine: A Field Guide to the Insurgent Right,* American Coalition
    for Clean Coal Electricity 2009 IRS Form 990 (New York: The New Press,
    2013), 126.
41. Ibid, 125. Also see Alex Kaplun: "Coal Industry Group Linked to a
    Dozen Forged Cap-and-Trade Letters," *New York Times,* August 4, 2009,
    www.nytimes.com/gwire/2009/08/04/04greenwire-coal-industry-group
    -linked-to-a-dozen-forged-ca-2624.html.
42. Letters to Representative Tom Perriello, thinkprogress.org/wp-content/
    uploads/2009/07/090731_bonner_forged_aces_documents.pdf.
43. Brad Johnson, "Rep. Perriello: Coal Fraudster Impersonated Women's and
    Seniors' Groups As Well," ThinkProgress.org, August 5, 2009, thinkprogress
    .org/politics/2009/08/05/54769/perriello-women-seniors/.
44. Lisa Lerer, "Coal Industry Knew About Fake Letters," *Politico,* October 29,
    2009, www.politico.com/story/2009/10/coal-industry-knew-about-fake
    -letters-028885.
45. Hearing Before the Select Committee on Energy Independence and
    Global Warming, October 29, 2009, www.gpo.gov/fdsys/pkg/CHRG
    -111hhrg62519/html/CHRG-111hhrg62519.htm.
46. "EPA Analysis of the American Power Act in the 111th Congress," June 14,
    2010, http://www3.epa.gov/climatechange/Downloads/EPAactivities/
    EPA_APA_Analysis_6-14-10.pdf.
47. Kevin Boland, "Ohio Manufacturer Says National Energy Tax Spells Disas-
    ter for Jobs," Speaker.gov, www.speaker.gov/general/ohio-manufacturer
    -says-national-energy-tax-spells-disaster-jobs#sthash.4fWT2IjR.dpuf.
48. Letter from John M. Reilly, Massachusetts Institute of Technology, April 1,
    2009, d35brb9zkkbdsd.cloudfront.net/wp-content/uploads/2009/04/
    republican.pdf.
49. Alexander Lane, "GOP Full of Hot Air About Obama's 'Light Switch
    Tax,'" PolitiFact, March 30, 2009, www.politifact.com/truth-o-meter/
    statements/2009/mar/30/house-republicans/GOP-full-of-hot-air-about
    -Obamas-light-switch-tax/.
50. Ibid.
51. Ben Armbruster, "Joining Their 11 Colleagues, Eight More Republicans
    Advance Cap-and-Trade Tax Myth," ThinkProgress.org, April 2, 2009,
    thinkprogress.org/politics/2009/04/02/37257/eight-republicans-tax
    -myth/.
52. Dianna Parker, "Fox Still Peddling Debunked Cap-and-Trade Cost Figure,"
    MediaMatters.org, June 26, 2009, mediamatters.org/research/2009/06/
    26/fox-still-peddling-debunked-cap-and-trade-cost/151556.
53. Bryan Walsh, "Cap and Trade Is Dead (Really, Truly, I'm Not Kidding).
    Who's to Blame?" *Time,* July 22, 2010, http://science.time.com/2010/07/
    22/cap-and-trade-is-dead-really-truly-im-not-kidding-whos-to-blame/.
54. "Regulatory Initiatives," United States Environmental Protection Agency,

www3.epa.gov/climatechange/EPAactivities/regulatory-initiatives
.html.

55. "Climategate," FactCheck.org, December 10, 2009, www.factcheck.org/
2009/12/climategate/.

56. Christopher Booker, "Climate Change: This Is the Worst Scientific Scandal
of Our Generation," *Telegraph,* November 28, 2009, www.telegraph.co.uk/
comment/columnists/christopherbooker/6679082/Climate-change-this
-is-the-worst-scientific-scandal-of-our-generation.html.

57. James Delingpole, "Climategate: The Final Nail in the Coffin of 'Anthropogenic Global Warming'?" *Telegraph,* November 20, 2009, blogs.telegraph
.co.uk/news/jamesdelingpole/100017393/climategate-the-final-nail-in
-the-coffin-of-anthropogenic-global-warming/.

58. Booker, 2009.

59. Anthony Watts, "'Climategate' Surpasses 'Global Warming' on Google,"
WattsUpWithThat.com, November 28, 2009, wattsupwiththat.com/2009/
11/28/climategate-surpasses-global-warming-on-google-autosuggest-still
-blocked/.

60. Leiserowitz, A., Maibach, E., and Roser-Renouf, C. (2010) *Climate Change
in the American Mind: Americans' Global Warming Beliefs and Attitudes in January 2010* (New Haven, CT: Yale University and George Mason University), Yale Project on Climate Change, e360.yale.edu/images/digest/
AmericansGlobalWarmingBeliefs2010.pdf.

61. Leiserowitz, A., Maibach, E., Roser-Renouf, C., Smith, N., and Dawson, E.,
"Climategate, Public Opinion, and the Loss of Trust," *American Behavioral
Scientist,* Yale Project on Climate Communication, 2012, environment.yale
.edu/climate-communication/article/climategate-public-opinion-and-the
-loss-of-trust.

62. Ben Dimiero, "FOXLEAKS: Fox Boss Ordered Staff to Cast Doubt on
Climate Science," MediaMatters.org, December 15, 2010, mediamatters
.org/blog/2010/12/15/foxleaks-fox-boss-ordered-staff-to-cast-doubt-o/
174317.

63. FactCheck.org, December 2009.

64. "Trenberth Can't Account for the Lack of Warming," SkepticalScience
.com, Updated July 2015, www.skepticalscience.com/Kevin-Trenberth
-travesty-cant-account-for-the-lack-of-warming.htm.

65. Jocelyn Fong, Jeremy Holden, and Dianna Parker, "Climategate Exposed:
Conservative Media Distort Stolen Emails in Latest Attack on Global
Warming Consensus," MediaMatters.org, December 1, 2009, mediamatters
.org/research/2009/12/01/climategate-exposed-conservative-media
-distort/157590.

66. Eric Schroeck, "Will Distorted Stolen CRU Emails to Argue Against
Climate Change Legislation," MediaMatters.org, November 30, 2009,
mediamatters.org/research/2009/11/30/will-distorted-stolen-cru-emails
-to-argue-again/157549.

67. Kim Zetter, "Hacked Emails Fuel Global Warming Debate," *Wired,*
November 20, 2009, www.wired.com/2009/11/climate-hack/.

68. Ibid.

69. David Appell, "Behind the Hockey Stick." *Scientific American,* March 2005, www.scientificamerican.com/article/behind-the-hockey-stick/.

70. "Clearing up Misconceptions Regarding 'Hide the Decline,'" Skeptical Science.com, Updated July 2015, www.skepticalscience.com/Mikes-Nature -trick-hide-the-decline.htm.

71. J. R. Pegg, "GOP Senators Blame Nature for Climate Change," Environment News Service, July, 29 2003, www.ens-newswire.com/ens/jul2003/ 2003-07-29-10.html.

72. "20th Century Climate Not So Hot," Harvard-Smithsonian Center for Astrophysics, March 31, 2003, www.cfa.harvard.edu/news/archive/pr0310 .html.

73. "Political Interference with Climate Change Science Under the Bush Administration," Committee on Oversight and Government Reform, December 2007, www.climatesciencewatch.org/wp-content/uploads/2014/ 01/House_Oversight_MajRpt_10dec07.pdf. As cited in Andrew Revkin, "Bush Aide Softened Greenhouse Gas Links to Global Warming," *New York Times,* June 8, 2005, www.nytimes.com/2005/06/08/politics/bush -aide-softened-greenhouse-gas-links-to-global-warming.html.

74. Richard Monastersky, "Storm Brews Over Global Warming," *Chronicle of Higher Education,* September 5, 2003, chronicle.com/article/Storm-Brews -Over-Global/27779/.

75. Andrew Revkin, "Politics Reasserts Itself in the Debate Over Climate Change and Its Hazards," *New York Times,* August 5, 2003, www.nytimes .com/2003/08/05/science/politics-reasserts-itself-in-the-debate-over -climate-change-and-its-hazards.html.

76. Ibid.

77. "Dr. Willie Soon, a Career Fueled by Big Oil and Coal," Greenpeace, updated February 2015, www.greenpeace.org/usa/global-warming/climate -deniers/koch-industries/dr-willie-soon-a-career-fueled-by-big-oil-and -coal/.

78. Timothy Gardner, "American Climate Skeptic Soon Funded by Oil, Coal Firms," Reuters, June 28, 2011, www.reuters.com/article/2011/06/28/us -usa-climate-skeptic-idUSTRE75R2HD20110628.

79. Interview with Naomi Oreskes by author, SiriusXM Satelite Radio, March 6, 2015.

80. Leo Hickman and James Randerson, "Climate Sceptics Claim Leaked Emails Are Evidence of Collusion Among Scientists," *Guardian,* November 20, 2009, www.theguardian.com/environment/2009/nov/20/climate -sceptics-hackers-leaked-emails.

81. Kate Sheppard, "Climategate: What Really Happened?" *Mother Jones,* April 21, 2011, www.motherjones.com/environment/2011/04/history-of -climategate.

82. Jim Efstathiou, Jr., "No 'Research Misconduct' by Climate-Change Scientist, U.S. Says," *Bloomberg,* April 22, 2011, www.bloomberg.com/news/ articles/2011-08-22/climate-change-scientist-cleared-in-u-s-data-altering -inquiry.

83. Brendan DeMelle, "Penn State Completely Exonerates Climate Scien-

tist Michael Mann On Bogus Climategate Accusations," *Huffington Post,* May, 25, 2011, www.huffingtonpost.com/brendan-demelle/penn-state -completely-exo_b_632810.html.

84. Anita Kumar, "Va. Supreme Court Rejects Cuccinelli's Bid for U-Va. Documents," *Washington Post,* March 2, 2012, www.washingtonpost.com/local/ dc-politics/va-supreme-court-rejects-cuccinellis-bid-for-u-va-documents/ 2012/03/02/gIQAmo8inR_story.html.

85. Michael E. Mann, "Get the Anti-science Bent out of Politics," *Washington Post,* October 8, 2010, www.washingtonpost.com/wp-dyn/content/ article/2010/10/07/AR2010100705484.html.

86. "Cato's Pat Michaels at Center of 'Climategate' Controversy That Rocks Climate Change Establishment," Cato Policy Report, January/February 2010, www.cato.org/policy-report/januaryfebruary-2010/catos-pat-michaels -center-climategate-controversy-rocks-climate.

87. Rand Simberg, "The Other Scandal in Unhappy Valley," Competitive Enterprise Institute, July 13, 2012, cei.org/blog/other-scandal-unhappy -valley.

88. Anne-Marie Blackburn and Dana Nuccitelli, "Hockey Stick Scores Another Point in Climate Study: Op-Ed," *Live Science,* April 25, 2013. www.livescience .com/29068-hockey-stick-climate.html.

Chapter 3: Lie Panel: *Health Care*

1. David Whelan, "ObamaCare Dives into End-of-Life Debate," *Forbes,* July 24, 2009, www.forbes.com/2009/07/24/obamacare-medicare-death -business-healthcare-obamacare.html.

2. Fred Thompson Show, July 16, 2009, mediamatters.org/research/2009/ 07/31/media-echo-serial-misinformer-mccaugheys-false/152759.

3. Clifford Kraus, "CLINTON'S HEALTH PLAN: Interest Groups; Lobbyists of Every Stripe Turning to the Grass Roots on Health Care," *New York Times,* September 24, 1993, www.nytimes.com/1993/09/24/us/clinton -s-health-plan-interest-groups-lobbyists-every-stripe-turning-grass-roots .html?pagewanted=all.

4. Elizabeth McCaughey, "No Exit," *New Republic,* February 7, 1994, www .newrepublic.com/article/health-care/no-exit.

5. Ibid.

6. Benjamin Sarlin, "The Woman Who Killed Health Care," *Daily Beast,* May 15, 2009, www.thedailybeast.com/articles/2009/05/15/the-woman -who-killed-health-care.html.

7. Ann Devroy, "President Insists Congress Enact Reforms in Welfare, Health Care," *Washington Post,* January 26, 1994, www.washingtonpost.com/wp -srv/politics/special/states/stories/sou012694.htm.

8. Josh Marshall, "The 1993 Kristol Memo on Defeating Health Care Reform," *Talking Points Memo,* September 24, 2013, talkingpointsmemo .com/edblog/the-1993-kristol-memo-on-defeating-health-care-reform.

9. James Fallows, "A Triumph of Misinformation," *Atlantic,* January, 1995, www.theatlantic.com/magazine/archive/1995/01/a-triumph-of -misinformation/306231/.

10. James Fallows, "Let's Stop This Before It Goes Any Further," *Atlantic,* February 12, 2009, www.theatlantic.com/technology/archive/2009/02/lets -stop-this-before-it-goes-any-further/555/.

11. Fallows, 1995.

12. The Editors, "Moral Imperative," *New Republic,* March 20, 2006, www .newrepublic.com/article/moral-imperative.

13. Tim Dickinson, "Betsy McCaughey Philip Morris Shill," *Rolling Stone,* September 14, 2009, www.rollingstone.com/politics/news/betsy-mccaughey -br-philip-morris-shill-20090914#ixzz3nG0gpRFu.

14. "Tobacco Strategy," Tobacco Archive: industrydocuments.library.ucsf.edu/ tobacco/docs/#id=qkfw0114.

15. Ibid.

16. Ibid.

17. James Fallows, "One Crucial B. McCaughey Update," *Atlantic,* September 28, 2009, www.theatlantic.com/technology/archive/2009/09/one -crucial-b-mccaughey-update/27320/.

18. "Manhattan Institute Statement: Betsy McCaughey Was Not Paid or Influenced by Philip Morris," PR Newswire, September 28, 2009, www .prnewswire.com/news-releases/manhattan-institute-statement-betsy -mccaughey-was-not-paid-or-influenced-by-philip-morris-62426742.html.

19. Michelle Cottle, "No Exit," *New Republic,* October 5, 2009, www.newrepublic .com/article/politics/no-exit.

20. Ibid.

21. Ibid.

22. Ibid.

23. Ibid.

24. Ezra Klein, "What Betsy McCaughey Knows," *Washington Post,* October 9, 2005, voices.washingtonpost.com/ezra-klein/2009/10/what_betsy _mccaughey_knows.html.

25. Betsy McCaughey, "Deadly Doctors," *New York Post,* July 24, 2009, nypost .com/2009/07/24/deadly-doctors/.

26. Michelle Bachman, Floor Speech, House of Representatives, July 27, 2009, thomas.loc.gov/cgi-bin/query/z?r111:H27JY9-0057.

27. Catharine Richert, "McCaughey Claims End-of-Life Counseling Will Be Required for Medicare Patients," PolitiFact, July 23, 2009, www.politifact .com/truth-o-meter/statements/2009/jul/23/betsy-mccaughey/ mccaughey-claims-end-life-counseling-will-be-requi/.

28. Sarah Palin, "Statement on the Current Health Care Debate," Facebook.com, August 7, 2009, www.facebook.com/note.php?note_id= 113851103434.

29. Hannah Dreier, "Fox News Personalities Advance Palin's 'Death Panel' Claim," MediaMatters.org, August 10, 2009, mediamatters.org/research/ 2009/08/10/fox-news-personalities-advance-palins-death-pan/153138.

30. Jocelyn Fong, "*Special Report* Portrays 'Death Panels' Falsehood as He Said/She Said Issue," MediaMatters.org, August 14, 2009, mediamatters .org/research/2009/08/14/special-report-portrays-death-panels -falsehood/153345.

31. Adam Shah, "Jon Stewart Corrects Serial Misinformer McCaughey's Latest End-of-Life Counseling Falsehood," MediaMatters.org, August 21, 2009, mediamatters.org/research/2009/08/21/jon-stewart-corrects-serial-misinformer-mccaugh/153653.

32. Jeremy Holden, "Dobbs, Beck Allow McCaughey to Advance Health IT Falsehood," MediaMatters.org, February 11, 2009, mediamatters.org/research/2009/02/11/dobbs-beck-allow-mccaughey-to-advance-health-it/147413.

33. "AARP Responds to Health Reform Scare Tactics," PR Newswire, August 3, 2009, www.prnewswire.com/news-releases/aarp-responds-to-health-reform-scare-tactics-62126477.html.

34. Glenn Thrush, "Poll: 41 Percent Believe in Death Panels," *Politico,* September 14, 2009, www.politico.com/blogs/on-congress/2009/09/poll-41-percent-believe-in-death-panels-021365.

35. Frum, 2010.

36. Soon after writing the post, he was fired from the American Enterprise Institute. *Politico*'s Mike Allen reported in his Playbook email newsletter, "David Frum told us last night that he believes his axing from his $100,000-a-year resident 'scholar' gig at the conservative American Enterprise Institute was related to DONOR PRESSURE following his viral blog post arguing Republicans had suffered a devastating, generational 'Waterloo' in their loss to President Obama on health reform." Mike Allen, "Frum thinks critique of GOP led to boot—2 big bipartisan bashes—Chris Matthews, cornered—HHS Secretary is vastly more powerful—Jackie Calmes to White House beat—Kimberly Dozier to AP," Politico Playbook, *Politico,* March 26, 2010, www.politico.com/tipsheets/playbook/2010/03/frum-thinks-critique-of-gop-led-to-boot-2-big-bipartisan-bashes-chris-matthews-cornered-hhs-secretary-is-vastly-more-powerful-jackie-calmes-to-white-house-beat-kimberly-dozier-to-ap-002682#ixzz3ldePYo79.

Chapter 4: Growth in a Time of Lies: *Debt*

1. Carmen M. Reinhart, Kenneth S. Rogoff, "Growth in a Time of Debt," NBER Working Paper No. 15639, January 2010, www.nber.org/papers/w15639.

2. Rob Wile, "JOURNAL EDITOR: The Famous Reinhart-Rogoff Debt Paper Did Not Go Through the Normal Refereeing Process," *Business Insider,* April 18, 2013, www.businessinsider.com/editor-talks-reinhart-rogoff-excel-error-2013-4.

3. Joe Weisenthal, "Meet the Two Most Dangerous Economists in the World Right Now," *Business Insider,* August 2, 2011, www.businessinsider.com/reinhart-and-rogoff-dangerous-debt-ceiling-2011-8.

4. "Thousands of Anti-tax 'Tea Party' Protesters Turn Out in U.S. Cities," FoxNews.com, April 15, 2009, www.foxnews.com/politics/2009/04/15/thousands-anti-tax-tea-party-protesters-turn-cities/.

5. Graeme Wearden, "Greece Debt Crisis: Timeline," *Guardian,* May 5, 2010, www.theguardian.com/business/2010/may/05/greece-debt-crisis-timeline.

6. "The Path to Prosperity: A Blueprint to American Renewal," House Budget Committee, archive.org/stream/408616-republican-2013-budget -proposal/408616-republican-2013-budget-proposal_djvu.txt.

7. Ibid.

8. Tim Fernholz, "How Influential Was the Rogoff-Reinhart Study Warning That High Debt Kills Growth?" *Quartz*, April 16, 2013. qz.com/75117/ how-influential-was-the-study-warning-high-debt-kills-growth/.

9. Tom A. Coburn, *The Debt Bomb* (Tennessee: Thomas Nelson, 2013), 29.

10. Annie Lowry, "A Study That Set the Tone for Austerity Is Challenged," *New York Times*, April 16, 2013, economix.blogs.nytimes.com/2013/04/ 16/flaws-are-cited-in-a-landmark-study-on-debt-and-growth/.

11. Matthew Yglesias, "Is The Reinhart-Rogoff Result Based on a Simple Spreadsheet Error?" *Slate*, Apri 16, 2013, www.slate.com/blogs/moneybox/ 2013/04/16/reinhart_rogoff_coding_error_austerity_policies_founded _on_bad_coding.html.

12. Mike Konczal, "Reinhart-Rogoff a Week Later: Why Does This Matter?" *Next New Deal* (blog), April 24, 2013.

13. Dean Baker, "How Much Unemployment Was Caused by Reinhart and Rogoff's Arithmetic Mistake?" CEPR.net, April 16, 2013, www.cepr.net/ blogs/beat-the-press/how-much-unemployment-was-caused-by-reinhart -and-rogoffs-arithmetic-mistake.

14. Ruth Alexander, "Reinhart, Rogoff . . . and Herndon: The Student Who Caught Out the Profs," BBC, April 20, 2013, www.bbc.com/news/ magazine-22223190.

15. Thomas Herndon, Michael Ash, Robert Pollin, "Does High Public Debt Consistently Stifle Economic Growth? A Critique of Reinhart and Rogoff," Political Economy Research Institute, April 15, 2013, www.peri.umass .edu/236/hash/31e2ff374b6377b2ddec04deaa6388b1/publication/566/.

16. Jared Bernstein, "Not to Pile On, But . . . Correcting Reinhart and Rogoff," JaredBernsteinBlog.com, April 16, 2013, jaredbernsteinblog.com/not -to-pile-on-but-correcting-reinhart-and-rogoff/.

17. Carmen Reinhart and Kenneth Rogoff, "Full Response from Reinhart and Rogoff," *New York Times*, April 17, 2013, www.nytimes.com/interactive/ 2013/04/17/business/17economix-response.html.

18. Kevin Robillard, "Krugman Called 'Spectacularly Uncivil,'" *Politico*, May 28, 2013, www.politico.com/story/2013/05/paul-krugman-attacked-as-uncivil -091904.

19. Paul Krugman, "How the Case for Austerity Has Crumbled," *New York Review of Books*, June 6, 2013, www.nybooks.com/articles/archives/2013/ jun/06/how-case-austerity-has-crumbled/.

20. Miles Kimball, Yichuan Wang, "After Crunching Reinhart and Rogoff's Data, We've Concluded That High Debt Does Not Slow Growth," *Quartz*, May 29, 2013, http://qz.com/88781/after-crunching-reinhart-and-rogoffs -data-weve-concluded-that-high-debt-does-not-cause-low-growth/. Also see: Mike Konczal, "Researchers Finally Replicated Reinhart-Rogoff, and There Are Serious Problems," The Roosevelt Institute, April 16, 2013.

rooseveltinstitute.org/researchers-finally-replicated-reinhart-rogoff-and
-there-are-serious-problems/.

21. Peter Coy, "FAQ: Reinhart, Rogoff, and the Excel Error That Changed History," *Bloomberg,* April 18, 2013, www.bloomberg.com/bw/articles/ 2013-04-18/faq-reinhart-rogoff-and-the-excel-error-that-changed-history.

22. "My Turn: Pete Peterson on Giving Away $1 Billion," *Newsweek,* May 29, 2009. www.newsweek.com/my-turn-pete-peterson-giving-away-1-billion -80225.

23. Alan Feuer, "Peter G. Peterson's Last Anti-debt Crusade," *New York Times,* April 8, 2011, www.nytimes.com/2011/04/10/nyregion/10peterson.html.

24. Peter Peterson, "Social Security: The Coming Crash," *New York Review of Books,* December 2, 1982, www.nybooks.com/articles/archives/1982/ dec/02/social-security-the-coming-crash/.

25. Daniel Marins, "The Reagan-O'Neill Myth of Bipartisan Social Security Reform," *Huffington Post,* November 20, 2012, www.huffingtonpost.com/ daniel-marans/the-reaganoneill-myth-of-_b_2162028.html.

26. "PGPF Mission," Peter G. Peterson Foundation, pgpf.org/about.

27. "Stacking the Deck: The Phony 'Fix the Debt' Campaign," *Nation,* February 20, 2013, www.thenation.com/article/stacking-deck-phony-fix-debt -campaign/.

28. "Washington Fiscal Summit Brings Together Key Administration and Congressional Leaders to Discuss America's Long-Term Fiscal Challenges," 2015 Fiscal Summit—Opportunity for America, www.fiscalsummit.com/ ?page_id=51.

29. "Peter G. Peterson Foundation," Conservative Transparency, conservativetransparency.org/donor/peter-g-peterson-foundation/.

30. "About Us," Committee for a Responsible Federal Budget, crfb.org/ about-us.

31. Concord Coalition, ConcordCoalition.org.

32. "Understanding Fiscal Responsibility," Columbia Teachers College, teachufr .org/about/.

33. Ibid.

34. Christopher Epps, "InDebtEd Campaign Encourages Young People to Address the Fiscal Crisis," America's Promise Alliance, December 19, 2008.

35. "Peter G. Peterson Foundation," Conservative Transparency, conservativetransparency.org/donor/peter-g-peterson-foundation/.

36. Suzy Khimm, "Pete Peterson Predicts Markets Will Panic over Our Debt Crisis. Sometime," *Washington Post,* January 18, 2013, www.washingtonpost .com/news/wonkblog/wp/2013/01/18/pete-peterson-predicts-markets -will-panic-over-our-debt-crisis-sometime/.

37. "Peter G. Peterson," Source Watch, www.sourcewatch.org/index.php/ Peter_Peterson.

38. Mary Bottari, "Pete Peterson Linked Economists Caught in Austerity Error," Center for Media and Democracy's PR Watch, April 18, 2013, www .prwatch.org/news/2013/04/12065/pete-peterson-linked-economists -caught-austerity-error.

39. Ibid.

40. Erik Wasson, "Bowles Dismisses 'Flaws' in Favorite Debt Study," *Hill,* April 19, 2013, thehill.com/policy/finance/295017-bowles-dismisses-flaws -in-favorite-debt-study.

41. Scott Keyes and Adam Peck, "Mark Sanford Cites Debunked Reinhart-Rogoff Study to Argue for Spending Cuts," ThinkProgress.org, May 1, 2013, thinkprogress.org/economy/2013/05/01/1945771/sanford-debunked -reinhart-rogoff/.

Chapter 5: On the Border of Truth: *Immigration Reform*

1. Solange Uwimana, "Right-Wing Media Seize on Muñoz Appointment to Renew Attacks on NCLR," MediaMatters.org, January 13, 2012, mediamatters.org/research/2012/01/13/right-wing-media-seize-on -muntildeoz-appointmen/186147.

2. "Frequently Asked Questions: The Obama Administration's Deferred Action for Childhood Arrivals (DACA)," National Immigration Law Center, www.nilc.org/FAQdeferredactionyouth.html.

3. Jeffery Passel and D'Vera Cohn, "Unauthorized Immigrant Population Stable for Half a Decade," Pew Research Center Fact Tank, July 22, 2015, www.pewresearch.org/fact-tank/2015/07/22/unauthorized-immigrant -population-stable-for-half-a-decade/.

4. Philip E. Wolgin, "What Would It Cost to Deport 11.3 Million Unauthorized Immigrants?" Center for American Progress, August 18, 2015, www .americanprogress.org/issues/immigration/news/2015/08/18/119474/ what-would-it-cost-to-deport-11-3-million-unauthorized-immigrants/.

5. Holly Bailey, "Bush's Spanish Lessons," *Newsweek,* May 28, 2005, www .newsweek.com/bushs-spanish-lessons-110249.

6. Rachel Weiner, "Reince Priebus Gives GOP Prescription for Future," *Washington Post,* March 18, 2013, www.washingtonpost.com/news/post-politics/ wp/2013/03/18/reince-priebus-gives-gop-prescription-for-future/.

7. Elise Foley, "Senate Immigration Reform Bill Passes with Strong Majority," *Huffington Post,* June 27, 2013, www.huffingtonpost.com/2013/06/27/ senate-immigration-reform-bill_n_3511664.html.

8. Ibid.

9. Jennifer Steinhauer and Jonathan Weisman, "In the DeMint Era at Heritage, a Shift from Policy to Politics," *New York Times,* February 23, 2014, www.nytimes.com/2014/02/24/us/politics/in-the-demint-era-at-heritage -a-shift-from-policy-to-politics.html?_r=0.

10. Molly Ball, "The Fall of the Heritage Foundation and the Death of Republican Ideas," *Atlantic,* September 25, 2013, www.theatlantic.com/politics/ archive/2013/09/the-fall-of-the-heritage-foundation-and-the-death-of -republican-ideas/279955/.

11. Robert Rector and Jason Richwine, "The Fiscal Cost of Unlawful Immigrants and Amnesty to the U.S. Taxpayer," Heritage Foundation, May 6, 2013, www.heritage.org/research/reports/2013/05/the-fiscal-cost-of-unlawful -immigrants-and-amnesty%20to-the-us-taxpayer.

12. Justin Berrier, "Right-Wing Media Push Heritage's Latest 'Fatally Flawed'

Immigration Study," MediaMatters.org, May 6, 2013, mediamatters.org/research/2013/05/06/right-wing-media-push-heritages-latest-fatally/193922.

13. Ibid.

14. "Robert Rector," The Heritage Foundation, www.heritage.org/about/staff/r/robert-rector.

15. "The Immigration Bill's '$6.3 Trillion Price Tag,'" FactCheck.org, July 3, 2013, www.factcheck.org/2013/06/the-immigration-bills-6-3-trillion-price -tag-2/.

16. Robert Rector and Jason Richwine, "The Fiscal Cost of Unlawful Immi- grants and Amnesty to the U.S. Taxpayer."

17. FactCheck.org, 2013.

18. Ibid.

19. "Douglas Holtz-Eakin," American Action Forum, americanactionforum .org/experts/douglas-holtz-eakin.

20. Douglas Holtz-Eakin, "Study: Immigration Reform, Economic Growth, and the Fiscal Challenge," American Action Forum, April 9, 2013, americanactionforum.org/research/study-immigration-reform-economic -growth-and-the-fiscal-challenge.

21. Pema Levy, "AEI Steers Clear of Dissertation Richwine Wrote While at AEI," *Talking Points Memo,* May 9, 2013, talkingpointsmemo.com/livewire/ aei-steers-clear-of-dissertation-richwine-wrote-while-at-aei.

22. Dylan Matthews, "Heritage Study Co-author Opposed Letting in Immi- grants with Low IQs," *Washington Post,* May 8, 2013, www.washingtonpost .com/news/wonkblog/wp/2013/05/08/heritage-study-co-author -opposed-letting-in-immigrants-with-low-iqs/.

23. Ibid.

24. Charles Murray, Southern Poverty Law Center, www.splcenter.org/fighting -hate/extremist-files/individual/charles-murray.

25. Daniel Strauss, "Can't Unring That Bell: Jeb Bush Says He's a Fan of Charles Murray's Books," *Talking Points Memo,* April 30, 2015, talkingpointsmemo .com/livewire/jeb-bush-charles-murray-the-bell-curve.

26. Levy, "AEI Steers Clear of Dissertation Richwine Wrote While at AEI."

27. Matthews, "Heritage Study Co-author Opposed Letting in Immigrants with Low IQs."

28. Benjy Sarlin, "Heritage: 'Race and Ethnicity' Not Part of Our Immigration Recommendations," *Talking Points Memo,* May 8, 2013, talkingpointsmemo .com/livewire/heritage-race-and-ethnicity-not-part-of-our-immigration -recommendations.

29. "Jason Richwine," The Heritage Foundation, www.heritage.org/about/staff/r/jason-richwine.

30. Hilary Tone, "UPDATED: Heritage Report Author: Hispanic Immigrants May Never Reach IQ Parity with Whites," MediaMatters.org, May 8, 2013, mediamatters.org/blog/2013/05/08/heritage-report-author-hispanic -immigrants-may/193962.

31. Jason Parle, "The Anti-immigration Crusader," *New York Times,* April 17, 2011, www.nytimes.com/2011/04/17/us/17immig.html.

32. Ibid.

33. "John Tanton's Network," Southern Poverty Law Center, www.splcenter .org/fighting-hate/intelligence-report/2015/john-tantons-network.

34. "Senator Jeff Sessions Recognizes NumbersUSA in the Congressional Record," NumbersUSA.com, May 11, 2012, www.numbersusa.com/ content/news/may-8-2012/sen-jeff-sessions-recognizes-numbersusa -congressional-record.html.

35. "Arizona's SB 1070," American Civil Liberties Union, www.aclu.org/ feature/arizonas-sb-1070.

36. Anh Phan, "The Top 5 Things You Need to Know About Kris Kobach," Center for American Progress, June 26, 2012, www.americanprogress.org/ issues/immigration/news/2012/06/26/11661/the-top-5-things-you -need-to-know-about-kris-kobach/. Also see: Van Lee, "Kansas City Star on the Ever-Controversial Kris Kobach." *America's Voice* (blog), April 9, 2012, americasvoice.org/blog/kansas-city-star-on-the-ever-controversial -kris-kobach/.

37. "Immigration Issue Spotlights Capitol Hill Media Marathon April 15th and 16th," PR Newswire, April 13, 2015, www.prnewswire.com/news -releases/immigration-issue-spotlights-capitol-hill-media-marathon-april -15th-and-16th-300065090.html.

38. Benjamin Franklin, "Letter to Peter Collinson," May 9, 1753, teachingamericanhistory.org/library/document/letter-to-peter-collinson/.

39. "Extremism in America: Jared Taylor/American Renaissance," Anti-Defamation League, January 11, 2011, www.adl.org/combating-hate/ domestic-extremism-terrorism/c/extremism-in-america-jared.html.

40. Heidi Beirich, "John Tanton's Private Papers Expose More than 20 Years of Hate," Southern Poverty Law Center, November 30, 2008, www.splcenter .org/fighting-hate/intelligence-report/2008/john-tanton's-private-papers -expose-more-20-years-hate.

41. "William Shockley," The Southern Poverty Law Center, www.splcenter .org/fighting-hate/extremist-files/individual/william-shockley.

42. John Tanton, "The Puppeteer Replies," The Social Contract Press, January 22, 2003, www.thesocialcontract.com/answering_our_critics/ puppeteer.html.

43. "John Tanton Is the Mastermind Behind the Organized Anti-immigration Movement," Southern Poverty Law Center, June 18, 2002, www.splcenter .org/fighting-hate/intelligence-report/2002/john-tanton-mastermind -behind-organized-anti-immigration-movement.

44. Josh Sanburn, "Inside the White Supremacist Group that Influenced Charleston Shooting Suspect," *Time,* June 22, 2015, time.com/3930993/ dylann-roof-council-of-conservative-citizens-charleston/.

45. For the definition of WITAN, see *Encyclopaedia Britannica:* "Witan, also called Witenagemot, the council of the Anglo-Saxon kings in and of England; its essential duty was to advise the king on all matters on which he chose to ask its opinion. It attested his grants of land to churches or laymen, consented to his issue of new laws or new statements of ancient custom,

and helped him deal with rebels and persons suspected of disaffection. Its composition and time of meeting were determined by the king's pleasure." www.britannica.com/topic/witan.

46. 'WITAN MEMO' III, October 10, 1986, www.splcenter.org/fighting -hate/intelligence-report/2015/witan-memo-iii.

47. Ibid.

48. "John Tanton," Southern Poverty Law Center, www.splcenter.org/fighting -hate/extremist-files/individual/john-tanton.

49. Ibid.

50. Ibid.

51. Salvatore Colleluori, "Washington Examiner Cites Misleading Chart to Claim Undocumented Immigrants Will Avoid Criminal Consequences," MediaMatters.org, June 25, 2013, mediamatters.org/blog/2013/06/25/ washington-examiner-cites-misleading-chart-to-c/194601.

52. Dan Stein, "Gang of Eight's Plan Would Give Illegal Immigrants Tax Amnesty, Too," FoxNews.com, April 30, 2013, www.foxnews.com/ opinion/2013/04/30/gang-eight-plan-would-give-illegal-immigrants-tax -amnesty-too.html?intcmp=trending.

53. Salvatore Colleluori, "Another False Immigration Amnesty Claim: Tax Edition," MediaMatters.org, May 1, 2013, mediamatters.org/blog/2013/05/ 01/another-false-immigration-amnesty-claim-tax-edi/193858.

54. Dan Stein, "GOP Should Reject Immigration Plan," *Politico,* April 10, 2013, www.politico.com/story/2013/04/5-reasons-gop-should-say-no-to -immigration-plan-089896.

55. Carrie Dawn, "Leahy: Hearing on Comprehensive Immigration Reform Set for April 17," NBC News, April 10, 2013, firstread.nbcnews.com/_news/ 2013/04/10/17689511-leahy-hearing-on-comprehensive-immigration -reform-set-for-april-17?lite.

56. Stein, 2013, www.politico.com/story/2013/04/5-reasons-gop-should-say -no-to-immigration-plan-089896.

57. "Senate Immigration Plan Would Stiffen Border Security, Increase Surveillance," Associated Press, April 10, 2013, www.foxnews.com/politics/ 2013/04/10/senate-immigration-plan-would-stiffen-border-security -increase-surveillance/.

58. Salvatore Colleluori and Solange Uwiman, "What the Media Should Know About the Anti-immigrant DC March for Jobs," MediaMatters.org, July 15, 2013, mediamatters.org/research/2013/07/15/what-the-media-should -know-about-the-anti-immig/194875. Also see: Testimony of Daniel Griswold, Senate Judiciary Committee, judiciary.house.gov/hearings/pdf/ Griswold01262011.pdf.

59. Ibid.

Chapter 6: Two Dangerous Weapons: *Guns and Lies*

1. "Sandy Hook Shooting: What Happened?," CNN, www.cnn.com/ interactive/2012/12/us/sandy-hook-timeline/.

2. Ibid.

3. Ibid.

4. Ibid.

5. Ibid.

6. Paul Harris and Matt Williams, "Colorado Massacre: Obama Visits Aurora Victims' Families and Survivors," *Guardian,* July 23, 2012, www.theguardian .com/world/2012/jul/23/obama-vists-aurora-survivors-victims.

7. Jesse Lee, "The President Speaks on the Shootings in Tucson," WhiteHouse .gov, January 8, 2011, www.whitehouse.gov/blog/2011/01/08/president -speaks-shootings-tucson-we-are-going-get-bottom-and-we-re-going-get -throug.

8. Erin Fuchs, "Obama's Gun Record Basically Consists of Expanding Gun Owners' Rights," *Business Insider,* December 23, 2012, www.businessinsider .com/gun-laws-obama-has-signed-2012-12.

9. Jason Howerton, "Gun Sales Soar During Obama's First Term: 'He Is the Best Thing That Ever Happened to the Firearm Industry,'" *The Blaze,* October 19, 2012, www.theblaze.com/stories/2012/10/19/gun-sales-soar -during-obamas-first-term-he-is-the-best-thing-that-ever-happened-to-the -firearm-industry/.

10. Eric Licthblau, "Irking N.R.A., Bush Supports the Ban on Assault Weapons," *New York Times,* May 8, 2003, www.nytimes.com/2003/05/08/us/ irking-nra-bush-supports-the-ban-on-assault-weapons.html?pagewanted= all.

11. Seth Cline, "Strong Majority of Americans, NRA Members Back Gun Control," *U.S. News & World Report,* January 28, 2013, www.usnews.com/ news/articles/2013/01/28/strong-majority-of-americans-nra-members -back-gun-control.

12. Molly Moorhead, "A Summary of the Manchin-Toomey Gun Proposal," PolitiFact, April 30, 2013, www.politifact.com/truth-o-meter/article/ 2013/apr/30/summary-manchin-toomey-gun-proposal/.

13. Ibid.

14. Molly Moorhead, "NRA Says Manchin-Toomey Would Have Criminalized Some Gun Transfers Between Family, Friends," PolitiFact, April 18, 2013, www.politifact.com/truth-o-meter/statements/2013/apr/18/national -rifle-association/nra-says-manchin-toomey-would-have-criminalized-so/.

15. Michael E. Hammond, "The Capitol Hill Report," Gun Owners of America, April 11, 2013, www.gunowners.org/congress04112013.htm.

16. "Text of Amendments," Congressional Record, April 11, 2013, www .congress.gov/congressional-record/2013/04/11/senate-section/article/ S2598-3.

17. Alan Korwin, "Manchin-Toomey Amendment Orchestrates Gun Registration, Read It Yourself," *Daily Caller,* April 16, 2014, dailycaller.com/2013/ 04/16/manchin-toomey-amendment-orchestrates-gun-registration-read-it -yourself/#ixzz3kyCF2Wka.

18. Jonathan Weisman, "Senate Blocks Drive for Gun Control," *New York Times,* April 17, 2013, www.nytimes.com/2013/04/18/us/politics/senate -obama-gun-control.html.

19. Statement by the President, White House, April 17, 2013, www.whitehouse .gov/the-press-office/2013/04/17/statement-president.

20. "Important Statement from the National Rifle Association," December 18, 2012, www.nraila.org/articles/20121218/important-statement-from-the -national-rifle-association.

21. "Remarks from the NRA Press Conference on Sandy Hook School Shooting, Delivered on Dec. 21, 2012 (transcript)," December 21, 2012, www .washingtonpost.com/politics/remarks-from-the-nra-press-conference -on-sandy-hook-school-shooting-delivered-on-dec-21-2012-transcript/ 2012/12/21/bd1841fe-4b88-11e2-a6a6-aabac85e8036_story.html.

22. Chris Mooney, "Double Barreled Double Standards," *Mother Jones,* October 13, 2003, www.motherjones.com/politics/2003/10/double-barreled -double-standards.

23. *Piers Morgan Tonight,* CNN, July 23, 2012. Accessed via Nexis.

24. Timothy Johnson, "STUDY: Gun-Related Murders Cost Nation up to $114 Billion Each Year," MediaMatters.org, June 19, 2012, mediamatters .org/blog/2012/06/19/study-gun-related-murders-cost-nation-up-to -114/184145. Also see: journals.lww.com/jtrauma/Abstract/2011/01000/ Homicide,_Suicide,_and_Unintentional_Firearm.35.aspx.

25. Julie Lurie, "When the Gun Lobby Tries to Justify Firearms Everywhere, It Turns to This Guy," *Mother Jones,* July 28, 2015, www.motherjones.com/ politics/2015/07/john-lott-guns-crime-data.

26. *Piers Morgan Tonight,* CNN, December 14, 2012, www.cnn.com/ TRANSCRIPTS/1212/14/pmt.01.html.

27. Dylan Matthews, "Did Gun Control Work in Australia?" *Washington Post,* August 2, 2012, www.washingtonpost.com/news/wonkblog/wp/2012/ 08/02/did-gun-control-work-in-australia/.

28. *Piers Morgan Tonight,* December 14, 2012.

29. Ibid.

30. Talkback Live, CNN, April 28, 1999. Accessed via Nexis.

31. Emily Arrowood, Hannah Groch-Begley, Melody Johnson, and Timothy Johnson, "Who Is Gun Advocate John Lott?," MediaMatters.org, December 17, 2012, mediamatters.org/research/2012/12/17/who-is-gun -advocate-john-lott/191885.

32. Julia Lurie, "When the Gun Lobby Tries to Justify Firearms Everywhere, It Turns to This Guy." *Mother Jones,* July 28, 2015, www.motherjones.com/ politics/2015/07/john-lott-guns-crime-data.

33. Ibid.

34. Ibid.

35. Arrowood et al., 2012.

36. Ibid.

37. Ibid.

38. Lurie, 2015.

39. Michelle Malkin, "The Other Lott Controversy," Townhall.com, February 5, 2003, townhall.com/columnists/michellemalkin/2003/02/05/the _other_lott_controversy/page/full.

40. John R. Lott Tripod website, johnrlott.tripod.com/malkinsoped.html.
41. Ibid.
42. Mooney, 2003.
43. Chris Brown, "John Lott Keeps on Digging." MediaMatters.org, April 5, 2011, mediamatters.org/blog/2011/04/05/john-lott-keeps-on-digging/178346.
44. Ibid.
45. Tim Lambert, "Mary Rosh's Blog," ScienceBlogs.com, January 21, 2003, scienceblogs.com/deltoid/2003/01/21/maryrosh/. Also see: Arrowood, Groch-Begley, Johnson, Johnson, 2012, mediamatters.org/research/2012/12/17/who-is-gun-advocate-john-lott/191885.
46. Ibid.
47. Tim Lambert, "The Other Sock Drops," ScienceBlogs.com, December 9, 2003, scienceblogs.com/deltoid/2003/12/09/othersock/.
48. Julian Sanchez, "The Mystery of Mary Rosh," *Reason Magazine,* May 2003, reason.com/archives/2003/05/01/the-mystery-of-mary-rosh.
49. Michelle Malkin, "The Other Lott Controversy," TownHall.com, February 5, 2003. townhall.com/columnists/michellemalkin/2003/02/05/the_other_lott_controversy/page/full.
50. John R. Lott Tripod website, johnrlott.tripod.com/malkinsoped.html.
51. CNN Live Event/Special, CNN, December 16, 2012, www.cnn.com/TRANSCRIPTS/1212/16/se.03.html.
52. "Connecticut School Shooting Reignites Gun Control Debate," Fox News, December 16, 2012, www.foxnews.com/transcript/2012/12/16/connecticut-school-shooting-reignites-gun-control-debate/.
53. "Starting Point with Soledad O'Brien," CNN, December 17, 2012, transcripts.cnn.com/TRANSCRIPTS/1212/17/sp.02.html.
54. "Mass Shootings since January 20, 2009," Mayors Against Illegal Guns, February 2013, www.washingtonpost.com/blogs/wonkblog/files/2013/02/mass_shootings_2009-13_-_jan_29_12pm1.pdf.
55. Daniel Webster, Jon Vernick, Katherine Vittes, Emma McGinty, Stephen Teret, and Shannon Frattaroli, "The Case for Gun Policy Reforms in America," Johns Hopkins Bloomberg School of Public Health, October 2012, www.jhsph.edu/research/centers-and-institutes/johns-hopkins-center-for-gun-policy-and-research/publications/WhitePaper020514_CaseforGunPolicyReforms.pdf#page=9.
56. Jeffrey Goldberg, "The Case for More Guns (and More Gun Control)," *Atlantic,* December 2012, www.theatlantic.com/magazine/archive/2012/12/the-case-for-more-guns-and-more-gun-control/309161/.
57. Timothy Johnson, "John Lott Continues Media Tour in Defense of 'Kill at Will,'" MediaMatters.org, May 1, 2012, mediamatters.org/blog/2012/05/01/john-lott-continues-media-tour-in-defense-of-ki/184794.
58. Jennifer Bendery, "Sybrina Fulton, Trayvon Martin's Mom, to Testify at Senate Hearing on 'Stand Your Ground' Laws," *Huffington Post,* September 13, 2013, www.huffingtonpost.com/2013/09/13/sybrina-fulton-trayvon-martin-stand-your-ground_n_3920820.html.
59. Timothy Johnson, "Gun Advocate John Lott: Trayvon Martin's Mother

Used as a Prop to Make Stand Your Ground Seem Racist," MediaMatters .org, November 1, 2013, mediamatters.org/print/blog/2013/11/01/gun -advocate-john-lott-travyon-martins-mother-u/196708.

60. John R. Lott, "Testimony Before the U.S. Senate Judiciary Committee's Subcommittee on the Constitution, Civil Rights, and Human Rights," Senate Judiciary Committee, October 29, 2013, www.judiciary.senate.gov/ imo/media/doc/10-29-13LottTestimony.pdf.

61. Tim Murphy, "GOP to Moms of Slain Black Sons: Stand Your Ground Laws Help Black People," *Mother Jones,* October 29, 2013, www.motherjones .com/politics/2013/10/gop-trayvon-martin-stand-your-ground-good -black-people.

62. Timothy Johnson, "Gun Advocate John Lott: Trayvon Martin's Mother Used as a Prop to Make Stand Your Ground Seem Racist."

63. "About," Crime Prevention Research Center, crimeresearch.org/about-us/.

64. Ibid.

65. CPRC Original Research, Crime Prevention Research Center, http:// crimeresearch.org/cprc-research/.

66. Steve Almasy, "In Notebook Read to Jury, James Holmes Wrote of 'Obsession,'" CNN, May 27, 2015, www.cnn.com/2015/05/26/us/james-holmes -trial-notebook/.

Chapter 7: One Lie, One Vote: *Voter I.D. Laws*

1. Robert Barnes and Mary Pat Flaherty, "'60s Radical Ayers Among Subjects of McCain 'Robo-Calls,'" *Washington Post,* October 18, 2008, www.washingtonpost.com/wp-dyn/content/article/2008/10/17/ AR2008101702878_pf.html.

2. Patrick Marley and Lee Bergquist, "RNC Chairman Priebus Alleges Rampant Vote Fraud," *Milwaukee Journal-Sentinel,* May 30, 2012, www.jsonline .com/news/statepolitics/rnc-chairman-priebus-alleges-rampant-vote -fraud-2f5jud3-155817075.html.

3. Richard Hansen, *The Voting Wars* (New Haven: Yale University Press, 2013), 43–44.

4. Joshua Green, "Karl Rove's Voter Fraud Fetish," *Atlantic,* April 2007, www.theatlantic.com/magazine/archive/2007/04/karl-roves-voter-fraud -fetish/305861/.

5. Eric Lipton and Ian Urbina, "In 5-Year Effort, Scant Evidence of Voter Fraud," *New York Times,* April 12, 2007, www.nytimes.com/2007/04/12/ washington/12fraud.html?pagewanted=2&_r=0.

6. Ibid.

7. Ibid.

8. Ibid.

9. Ibid.

10. Ibid.

11. Art Levine, "The Republican War on Voting," *American Prospect,* March 19, 2008, prospect.org/article/republican-war-voting.

12. Lipton and Urbina, 2007.

13. "An Investigation into the Removal of Nine U.S. Attorneys in 2006,"

Office of the Inspector General, September 2008, oig.justice.gov/special/
s0809a/chapter6.htm.

14. Ibid.

15. Ibid.

16. Ibid.

17. Amy Goldstein, "Justice Dept. Recognized Prosecutor's Work on Election Fraud Before His Firing," *Washington Post,* March 19, 2007, www.washingtonpost.com/wp-dyn/content/article/2007/03/18/ AR2007031801077.html.

18. Levine, 2008.

19. Justin Levit, "The Truth About Voter Fraud," Brennan Center for Justice, 2007, www.brennancenter.org/sites/default/files/legacy/The%20Truth %20About%20Voter%20Fraud.pdf.

20. Jason Noble, "Final Report: 117 Fraudulent Votes Found in Investigation," *Des Moines Register,* May 8, 2014, www.desmoinesregister.com/story/news/ politics/iowa-politics/2014/05/08/iowa-secretary-of-state-voter-fraud -report-matt-schultz/8858595/.

21. Jason Noble, "Guilty Pleas Resolve All Five Voter Fraud Convictions in Iowa," *Des Moines Register,* December 16, 2013, www.desmoinesregister .com/story/news/politics/2013/12/16/guilty-pleas-resolve-all-five-voter -fraud-convictions-in-iowa/4037125/.

22. Christian Belanger, "Lightning Strikes More Common in Texas than In-Person Voter Fraud, Says Cory Booker," PolitiFact, September 7, 2015, www.politifact.com/truth-o-meter/statements/2015/aug/18/cory -booker/lightning-strikes-more-common-person-voter-fraud-s/.

23. Ian Millhiser, "BREAKING: Federal Appeals Court Strikes Down Texas's Voter ID Law," ThinkProgress.org, August 15, 2015, thinkprogress.org/ justice/2015/08/05/3688384/breaking-federal-appeals-court-strikes -down-texass-voter-id-law/.

24. Marley and Bergquist, 2012.

25. Glenn Kessler, "The Case of 'Zombie' Voters in South Carolina," *Washington Post,* July 25, 2013, www.washingtonpost.com/blogs/fact-checker/post/ the-case-of-zombie-voters-in-south-carolina/2013/07/24/86de3c64-f403 -11e2-aa2e-4088616498b4_blog.html.

26. Ibid.

27. Corey Hutchins, "18 Months Later, S.C. Law Enforcement Closes Case on 'Zombie Voters,' Finds No Fraud," *Free Times,* July 3, 2013, www.free-times .com/blogs/18-months-later-sc-law-enforcement-closes-case-on-zombie -voters-finds-no.

28. Ibid.

29. Marilyn Smith, "Ohio Investigation Finds Minuscule Amount of Possible Voter Fraud," WOSU, May 23, 2013, wosu.org/2012/news-archive/2013/ 05/23/ohio-investigation-finds-minuscule-amount-of-possible-voter -fraud/.

30. "Republican Operative Paul Weyrich—I Do Not Want Everybody to Vote," YouTube, www.youtube.com/watch?v=QFIYS8xb-QY.

31. Hansen, 2013; Jane Mayer, "The Voter Fraud Myth," *New Yorker,* Octo-

ber 29, 2012, www.newyorker.com/magazine/2012/10/29/the-voter
-fraud-myth.

32. Ibid.

33. Ibid.

34. "Justice Fight Lingers at FEC," CBS News, November 5, 2007, www
.cbsnews.com/news/justice-fight-lingers-at-fec/.

35. Ibid.

36. Jeffrey Toobin, "Drawing the Line," *New Yorker,* March 6, 2006, www
.newyorker.com/magazine/2006/03/06/drawing-the-line-3.

37. CBS News, 2007.

38. Dan Eggen, "Politics Alleged in Voting Cases," *Washington Post,* January 23,
2006, www.washingtonpost.com/wp-dyn/content/article/2006/01/22/
AR2006012200984.html.

39. Greg Gordon, "Efforts to Stop 'Voter Fraud' May Have Curbed Legitimate Voting," *McClatchy Newspapers,* May 20, 2007, www.mcclatchydc.com/
news/article24463966.html.

40. Rick Hasen, "Hebert Finds Troubling von Spakovsky Emails in EAC
Released Documents," *Election Law Blog,* July 4, 2007, electionlawblog.org/
?p=8013.

41. Matt Corley, "Hans Von Spakovsky 101: How to Suppress the Vote Like a
Pro," ThinkProgress.org, September 26, 2007, thinkprogress.org/politics/
2007/09/26/13861/spakovsky-primer/.

42. Georgia Delegation Letter, Brennan Center for Justice, www.brennancenter
.org/sites/default/files/analysis/06-12-07%20Georgia%20Delegation
%20Letter.pdf.

43. Joseph D. Rich, Robert A. Kengle, David J. Becker, Bruce Adelson, and
Toby Moore, "Career DOJ Professionals Urge Rejection of von Spakovsky's FEC Nomination," Vote Trust USA, www.votetrustusa.org/index
.php?option=com_content&task=view&id=2489&Itemid=26.

44. Ibid.

45. Paul Kane, "Contested Nominee to FEC Drops Out," *Washington Post,*
May 17, 2008, www.washingtonpost.com/wp-dyn/content/article/2008/
05/16/AR2008051604040.html.

46. David C. Wilson and Paul R. Brewer, "The Foundations of Public Opinion on Voter ID Laws," *Public Opinion Quarterly,* December 24, 2013, poq
.oxfordjournals.org/content/early/2013/10/03/poq.nft026. Via Brian
Powell, "A 'Counting' Fraud: New Book by John Fund & Hans von Spakovsky Parrots Tired Voter Fraud Falsehoods," MediaMatters.org, August 16,
2012, mediamatters.org/research/2012/08/16/a-counting-fraud-new-book
-by-john-fund-amp-hans/189395.

47. Wendy Underhill, "Voter Identification Requirments/Voter ID Laws,"
National Conference of State Legislatures, August 10, 2015, www.ncsl.org/
research/elections-and-campaigns/voter-id.aspx.

48. "Voter ID History," National Conference of State Legislatures, August 6,
2015, http://www.ncsl.org/research/elections-and-campaigns/voter-id
-history.aspx.

49. Ryan Reilly, "Ahead of Voter ID Trial, Pennsylvania Admits There's No In-

Person Voter Fraud," *Talking Points Memo,* July 24, 2012, talkingpointsmemo
.com/muckraker/ahead-of-voter-id-trial-pennsylvania-admits-there-s-no
-in-person-voter-fraud.

50. Ryan J. Reilly, "PA Voter ID Law Would Keep 93-Year-Old Who Marched
with Martin Luther King from Voting," *Talking Points Memo,* May 2, 2012,
talkingpointsmemo.com/muckraker/pa-voter-id-law-would-keep-93-year
-old-who-marched-with-martin-luther-king-from-voting.

51. Bob Warner, "Voter ID Law May Hit More in Pa. than Originally Estimated," *Philadelphia Inquirer,* July 4 2012, articles.philly.com/2012-07-04/
news/32524446_1_voter-id-new-voter-id-cards.

52. Annie Rose-Strasser, "Pennsylvania Republican: Voter ID Laws Are
'Gonna Allow Governor Romney to Win,'" ThinkProgress.org, June 25,
2012, thinkprogress.org/election/2012/06/25/505953/pennsylvania
-republican-voter-id-laws-are-gonna-allow-governor-romney-to-win/.

53. John Fund and Hans von Spakovsky, *Who's Counting?: How Fraudsters and
Bureaucrats Put Your Vote at Risk* (New York: Encounter Books, 2012), 13.

54. Ibid, 14.

55. Steven Rosenfeld, "GOP Voter Fraud Hucksters Latest Lie: Felons Made
Franken U.S. Senator," Alternet, August 8, 2012, www.alternet.org/gop
-voter-fraud-hucksters-latest-lie-felons-made-franken-us-senator.

56. Ibid.

57. Brian Powell, "A 'COUNTING' FRAUD: New Book by John Fund & Hans
von Spakovsky Parrots Tired Voter Fraud Falsehoods," MediaMatters.org,
August 16, 2012, mediamatters.org/research/2012/08/16/a-counting
-fraud-new-book-by-john-fund-amp-hans/189395.

58. Ibid.

59. Lorraine Minnite, "An Analysis of Voter Fraud in The United States,"
Demos, 2003, www.demos.org/sites/default/files/publications/Analysis
.pdf.

60. Powell, 2012.

61. Minnite, 2003.

62. "'Voting Wars' Conference Will Look at Election Law Conflict and Politics," University of Virginia School of Law, March 18 2013, www.law
.virginia.edu/html/news/2013_spr/voting_wars.htm. Also see: Mayer,
2012.

63. Hans von Spakovsky, "Smoke of Registration Fraud Leads to Election
Fires," FoxNews.com, October 31, 2008, www.foxnews.com/story/2008/
10/31/smoke-registration-fraud-leads-to-election-fires.html.

64. "Keynote Address of Prof. Richard L. Hasen Given to the Voting Wars
Symposium," March 23, 2013, files.www.lawandpolitics.org/content/vol
-xxvii-no-4/Hasen_Final.pdf.

65. Ryan J. Reilly, "Election Expert Can't Find Report on 1984 Voter Impersonation Case Cited by von Spakovsky," *Talking Points Memo,* June 20, 2011,
talkingpointsmemo.com/muckraker/election-expert-can-t-find-report-on
-1984-voter-impersonation-case-cited-by-von-spakovsky.

66. Rick Hansen, "1984 New York Grand Jury Report on Voter Fraud Now
Available," *Election Law Blog,* June 23, 2011, electionlawblog.org/?p=19560.

67. "Keynote Address of Prof. Richard L. Hasen Given to the Voting Wars Symposium."

68. Mayer, 2012.

69. Ibid.

70. Ibid.

71. Dan Harris and Malia Patria, "Is True the Vote Intimidating Minority Voters from Going to the Polls?" ABC News, November 2, 2012, abcnews .go.com/Politics/true-vote-intimidating-minority-voters-polls/story?id= 17618823.

72. Stephanie Saul, "Looking, Very Closely, for Voter Fraud," *New York Times,* September 16, 2012, www.nytimes.com/2012/09/17/us/politics/groups -like-true-the-vote-are-looking-very-closely-for-voter-fraud.html.

73. Mayer, 2012.

74. Ibid.

75. Andrew Ross, "Corporations' Ties to Voter ID Laws," *San Francisco Chronicle,* August 26, 2012, www.sfgate.com/business/bottomline/article/ Corporations-ties-to-voter-ID-laws-3815349.php.

76. Von Spakovsky, 2011.

77. Shah, 2011.

78. "*Texas NAACP v. Steen* (consolidated with *Veasey v. Perry*)," Brennan Center for Justice, August 5, 2015, www.brennancenter.org/legal-work/naacp-v -steen.

79. "Texas Photo ID Trial Update: Wrapping Up the First Day of Trial," Brennan Center for Justice, September 2, 2014, www.brennancenter.org/blog/ texas-photo-id-trial-update-wrapping-first-day-trial.

80. "Exclusive: Lee Atwater's Infamous 1981 Interview on the Southern Strategy," *The Nation* YouTube Channel, November 13, 2012, www.youtube .com/watch?v=X_8E3ENrKrQ.

Chapter 8: Shut That Whole Lie Down: *Abortion*

1. "Akin on 'Legitimate Rape,'" YouTube, August 19, 2012, www.youtube .com/watch?v=4fSWnqn6VgU.

2. John Eligon and Michael Schwirtz, "Senate Candidate Provokes Ire with 'Legitimate Rape' Comment," *New York Times,* August 19, 2012, www .nytimes.com/2012/08/20/us/politics/todd-akin-provokes-ire-with -legitimate-rape-comment.html?_r=0.

3. Melisa M. Holmes, Heidi S. Resnick, Dean G. Kilpatrick, and Connie L. Best, "Rape-Related Pregnancy: Estimates and Descriptive Characteristics From a National Sample of Women," *American Journal of Obstetrics & Gynecology,* August, 1996, www.ajog.org/article/S0002-9378(96)70141-2/ abstract.

4. Glenn Kessler, "The Claim That the Incidence of Rape Resulting in Pregnancy is 'Very Low,'" *Washington Post,* June 13, 2013, www.washingtonpost .com/blogs/fact-checker/post/the-claim-that-the-incidence-of-rape -resulting-in-pregnancy-is-very-low/2013/06/12/936bc45e-d3ad-11e2 -8cbe-1bcbee06f8f8_blog.html.

5. Jonathan A. Gottschall and Tiffani A. Gottschall, "Are Per-Incident Rape-

Pregnancy Rates Higher than Per-Incident Consensual Pregnancy Rates?" *Human Nature* 14, no. 1 (March 2003): 1-20, http://link.springer.com/ article/10.1007%2Fs12110-003-1014-0; Kessler, 2013.

6. Amanda Terkle, "John Cornyn, Top Republicans Call on Todd Akin to Rethink Candidacy," *Huffington Post,* August 20, 2012, www.huffingtonpost .com/2012/08/20/john-cornyn-todd-akin-rape_n_1812169.html.

7. Alexander Burns, "Crossroads Pulls Out of Missouri After Akin Comments," *Politico,* August 20, 2012, www.politico.com/blogs/burns-haberman/ 2012/08/crossroads-pulls-out-of-missouri-after-akin-comments-132572.

8. Kate Sheppard, "Rep. Todd Akin: Wrong, but Not Alone," *MotherJones,* August 19, 2012, http://www.motherjones.com/mojo/2012/08/rep-todd -akin-wrong-not-alone.

9. *Starting Point with Soledad O'Brien,* CNN, August 21, 2012, www.cnn.com/ TRANSCRIPTS/1208/21/sp.02.html.

10. Brian Tashman, "Bryan Fischer: Todd Akin is 'Absolutely Right,'" Right -wingWatch.org, August 20, 2012, www.right-wingwatch.org/content/ bryan-fischer-todd-akin-absolutely-right.

11. Ibid. Also see: "FRC Action PAC Calls Attacks on Todd Akin 'Gotcha Politics,'" PR Newswire, August 20, 2012, www.prnewswire.com/ news-releases/frc-action-pac-calls-attacks-on-todd-akin-gotcha-politics -166779466.html.

12. Matt Lewis, "'Legitimate Rape'?: What Was Todd Akin Getting At?" *Daily Caller,* August 20, 2012, dailycaller.com/2012/08/20/legitimate-rape-what -was-todd-akin-getting-at/#ixzz3l5Lf0fgX.

13. Garance Franke-Ruta, "A Canard That Will Not Die: 'Legitimate Rape' Doesn't Cause Pregnancy," *Atlantic,* August 19, 2012, www.theatlantic .com/politics/archive/2012/08/a-canard-that-will-not-die-legitimate -rape-doesnt-cause-pregnancy/261303/.

14. Ibid.

15. Ibid.

16. Thomas W. Hilgers, *Abortion and Social Justice* (New York: Sheed & Ward, 1972); Tim Townsend, "The Roots of Akin's 'Legitimate' Rape Remarks," *USA Today,* August 23, 2012.

17. Ibid.

18. Ibid.

19. Ibid.

20. Ibid.

21. "Law Reform Efforts: Rape and Sexual Assault in United States of America," International Models Project on Women's Rights, October 18, 2013, www.impowr.org/content/law-reform-efforts-rape-and-sexual-assault -united-states-america.

22. "Faculty," Virginia Commonwealth University School of Medicine, www .medschool.vcu.edu/inova/faculty/mecklenburg.html.

23. "Best Hospitals for Adult Gynecology," *U.S. News and World Report,* http:// health.usnews.com/best-hospitals/rankings/gynecology?page=3.

24. Emily Bazelon, "Myth That Rape Rarely Causes Pregnancy Based on a Nazi

Experiment That Never Happened," *Slate,* July 26, 2013. www.slate.com/blogs/xx_factor/2013/07/26/myth_that_rape_rarely_causes_pregnancy_based_on_a_nazi_experiment_that_never.html.

25. Emily Bazelon, "The Nazi Anatomists," *Slate,* November 6, 2013, www.slate.com/articles/life/history/2013/11/nazi_anatomy_history_the_origins_of_conservatives_anti_abortion_claims_that.html.

26. Anna Palmer and Tarini Parti, "Akin Un-apologizes," *Politico,* July 10, 2014, http://www.politico.com/story/2014/07/todd-akin-new-book-108745.

27. Caitlin Macneal, "GOP Also Training Senate Candidates on How to Talk to Women," *Talking Points Memo,* December 11, 2013, talkingpointsmemo.com/livewire/gop-also-training-senators-on-how-to-talk-to-women.

28. Steven Harmon, "California GOP Leader Steps into Rape Pregnancy Controversy," Bay Area News Group, March 1, 2013, http://www.dailydemocrat.com/general-news/20130301/california-gop-leader-steps-into-rape-pregnancy-controversy.

29. Sofia Resnick, "Antiabortion Scholar: Restrictions Should Be Designed to Raise Costs for Women," *Mother Jones/American Independent,* September 21, 2012, http://www.motherjones.com/politics/2012/09/antiabortion-restrictions-raise-costs-women.

30. Janet Reitman, "The Stealth War on Abortion," *Rolling Stone,* January 14, 2014, www.rollingstone.com/politics/news/the-stealth-war-on-abortion-20140115.

31. Karen Tumulty and Morgan Smith, "Texas State Senator Wendy Davis Filibusters Her Way to Democratic Stardom," *Washington Post,* June 26, 2013, www.washingtonpost.com/politics/texas-state-senator-wendy-davis-filibusters-her-way-to-democratic-stardom/2013/06/26/aace267c-de85-11e2-b2d4-ea6d8f477a01_story.html.

32. "Fact #11: Abortion Is More Dangerous Than Childbirth," www.abortionfacts.com/facts/11.

33. Ibid.

34. "Donate," AbortionFacts.com, www.abortionfacts.com/donate.

35. Bonnie Rochman, "Why Abortion Is Less Risky than Childbirth," *Time,* January 25, 2012, healthland.time.com/2012/01/25/why-abortion-is-less-risky-than-childbirth/. Also see: Genevra Pittman, "Abortion Safer than Giving Birth: Study," *Reuters,* January 23, 2012, http://www.reuters.com/article/2012/01/23/us-abortion-idUSTRE80M2BS20120123.

36. Tara Culp-Ressler, "The Most Creative Ways That Anti-Choice Activists Try to Shut Down Abortion Clinics," ThinkProgress.org, April 14, 2015, thinkprogress.org/health/2015/04/14/3646230/abortion-clinic-targeting/.

37. Sandhya Somashekhar, "Admitting-Privileges Laws Have Created High Hurdle for Abortion Providers to Clear," *Washington Post,* August 10, 2014, www.washingtonpost.com/national/2014/08/10/62554324-1d88-11e4-82f9-2cd6fa8da5c4_story.html.

38. Ian Millhiser, "A Federal Judge Just Called Out the Big Lie Behind Texas's Latest Abortion Restriction," ThinkProgress.org, August 29, 2014,

thinkprogress.org/justice/2014/08/29/3477589/a-federal-judge-just
-called-out-the-big-lie-behind-texass-latest-abortion-restriction/.

39. Annie Murphy Paul, "The First Ache," *New York Times Magazine,* February 10, 2008, www.nytimes.com/2008/02/10/magazine/10Fetal-t.html
?pagewanted=all&_r=0.

40. Susan J. Lee, Henry J. Peter Ralston, Eleanor A. Drey, John Colin Partridge, and Mark A. Rosen, "Fetal Pain: A Systematic Multidisciplinary Review of the Evidence," *Journal of the American Medical Association,* August 24/31, 2005. http://jama.jamanetwork.com/article.aspx?articleid=201429.

41. "24-Week Fetuses Cannot Feel Pain," *New Scientist,* June 25, 2010, www
.newscientist.com/article/dn19089-24-week-fetuses-cannot-feel-pain/.

42. Stephanie Simon, "Hobby Lobby Aims for Obamacare Win," *Politico,* June 16, 2014, www.politico.com/story/2014/06/hobby-lobby-supreme
-court-case-107877.

43. Laura Basset and Ryan J. Reilly, "Supreme Court Rules in Hobby Lobby Case, Dealing Blow to Birth Control Coverage," *Huffington Post,* June 30, 2014, www.huffingtonpost.com/2014/06/30/supreme-court-hobby-lobby_n
_5521444.html.

44. "Brief of Amici Curiae Physicians for Reproductive Health, American College of Obstetricians and Gynecologists, American Society of Emergency Contraception, Association of Reproductive Health Professionals, American Society for Reproductive Medicine, Society for Adolescent Health and Medicine, American Medical Women's Association, National Association of Nurse Practitioners in Women's Health, Society of Family Planning, International Association of Forensic Nurses, American College of Nurse-Midwives, James Trussell, Susan F. Wood, Don Downing and Kathleen Besinque in Support of Petitioners," United States Supreme Court, www
.acog.org/-/media/Departments/Government-Relations-and-Outreach/
20131021AmicusHobby.pdf.

45. Binyamin Applebaum, "What the Hobby Lobby Ruling Means for America," *New York Times,* July 22, 2014, www.nytimes.com/2014/07/27/
magazine/what-the-hobby-lobby-ruling-means-for-america.html.

46. Sofia Resnick, "Taxpayer-Funded Crisis Pregnancy Centers Using Religion to Oppose Abortion," *American Independent,* April 24, 2012, www
.huffingtonpost.com/2012/04/24/abortion-religion-pregnancy-centers_n
_1446506.html.

47. Irin Carmon, "Caught on Tape: Antiabortion Center Resorts to Scary, Dangerous Lies," Salon.com, June 25, 2013, www.salon.com/2013/06/25/
caught_on_tape_crisis_pregnancy_centers_false_dangerous_advice/.

48. Resnick, 2012.

49. "Is Abortion Linked to Breast Cancer?," American Cancer Society, www
.cancer.org/cancer/breastcancer/moreinformation/is-abortion-linked-to
-breast-cancer.

50. "Table 25: Abortion and Breast Cancer Risk," Susan G. Koman, ww5
.komen.org/BreastCancer/Table25Abortionandbreastcancerrisk.html.

51. Chloe Angyal, "The GOP's Antiabortion Tactic: Order Teachers and Doc-

tors to Lie," MSNBC, July 8, 2013, www.msnbc.com/msnbc/the-gops
-antiabortion-tactic-order-teacher.

52. Zita Lazzarini, "South Dakota's Abortion Script—Threatening the
Physician–Patient Relationship," *New England Journal of Medicine,* November 20, 2008, www.nejm.org/doi/full/10.1056/NEJMp0806742.

53. Alexandra Sifferlin, "Study Linking Abortion to Mental Health Problems Is
Flawed," *Time Magazine,* March 8, 2012, healthland.time.com/2012/03/08/
study-linking-abortion-to-mental-health-problems-is-flawed/.

54. Ibid.

55. Stephanie Pappas, "Abortion-Mental Illness Link Doesn't Hold Up,
Researchers Find," *Live Science,* March 5, 2012, www.livescience.com/18846
-abortion-mental-illness.html.

56. Sifferlin, 2012.

57. Maria Cheng, "Abortion Not a Mental Health Risk but Unwanted Pregnancies Are, Studies Find," Associated Press, December 9, 2011, www
.huffingtonpost.com/2011/12/09/abortion-mental-health_n_1138545
.html.

Chapter 9: A Lie's Last Gasp: *Gay Marriage*

1. "California Proposition 8, the 'Eliminates Right of Same-Sex Couples to
Marry' Initiative (2008)," ballotpedia.org/California_Proposition_8,_the_
%22Eliminates_Right_of_Same-Sex_Couples_to_Marry%22_Initiative_
(2008).

2. Lionel Barber, "David Boies and Theodore Olson," *Vanity Fair,* July, 2014.
www.vanityfair.com/news/politics/2014/07/david-boies-theodore-olson
-marriage-equality.

3. *United States v. Windsor,* October 2012, www.law.cornell.edu/supct/pdf/12
-307.pdf.

4. *Obergefell vs. Hodges,* June 26, 2015, www.supremecourt.gov/opinions/
14pdf/14-556_3204.pdf.

5. Chuck Colson, "The Coming Persecution: How Same-Sex 'Marriage'
Will Harm Christians," *Christian Examiner,* September 11, 2008, www
.christianexaminer.com/article/the.coming.persecution.how.same.sex
.marriage.will.harm.christians/42641.htm.

6. Sarah Parnass, "Republicans Predict Fraud, Bestiality if Gay Marriage
Is Legalized," ABC News, April 4, 2013, abcnews.go.com/blogs/politics/
2013/04/republicans-predict-fraud-bestiality-if-gay-marriage-is-legalized/.

7. Sandhya Somashekhar, "How Kids Became the Strongest Argument for
Same-Sex Marriage," *Washington Post,* June 24, 2015, www.washingtonpost
.com/politics/how-kids-became-the-strongest-argument-for-same-sex
-marriage/2015/06/24/98955632-18fe-11e5-ab92-c75ae6ab94b5_story
.html.

8. American Sociological Association Amicus Brief, www.aclu.org/files/
assets/amicus_one-pager_for_american_sociological_association.pdf.

9. Robert P. George, National Organization for Marriage, nationformarriage
.org/about/bio/robert-p-george.

10. "About Robert P. George," The Public Discourse, www.thepublicdiscourse .com/author/rgeorge/.

11. Patrick Lee and Robert George, *Body-Self Dualism in Contemporary Ethics and Politics* (New York: Cambridge University Press, 2009), 193, www.amazon .com/Body-Self-Dualism-Contemporary-Ethics-Politics/dp/0521124190.

12. "Commissioners," United States Commission on Civil Rights, www.uscirf .gov/about-uscirf/commissioners.

13. Anne Morse, "Conservative Heavyweight: The Remarkable Mind of Robert P. George," *Crisis,* September 2003, 36–42, www.catholiceducation.org/ en/faith-and-character/faith-and-character/conservative-heavyweight-the -remarkable-mind-of-robert-p-george.html.

14. Letter to the President from U.S. Civil Rights Commissioners, Carl A. Anderson, Commissioner, and Robert P. George, Commissioner, August 4, 1993. Via Congressional Record: 139 Cong Rec S 10981.

15. David Kirkpatrick, "The Conservative-Christian Big Thinker," *New York Times,* December 16, 2009, www.nytimes.com/2009/12/20/magazine/ 20george-t.html.

16. Seth Lewis, "Proposed Constitutional Amendment Seeks to Define Traditional Marriage," *Baptist Press,* July 13, 2001, www.bpnews.net/11317/ proposed-constitutional-amendment-seeks-to-define-traditional-marriage.

17. Kirkpatrick, 2009.

18. Ibid.

19. Ibid.

20. "Itinerary for Pope's U.S. Visit Combines Official, Informal," *Washington Times,* March 30, 2008. www.washingtontimes.com/news/2008/mar/30/ itinerary-for-popes-us-visit-combines-official-inf/.

21. Kirkpatrick, 2009.

22. Ibid.

23. Ibid.

24. Ibid.

25. Robert P. George, "Just War in Iraq," *Wall Street Journal,* December 6, 2002, web.archive.org/web/20030317075927/http://www.ird-renew.org/ news/NewsPrint.cfm?ID=548&c=4.

26. Kirkpatrick, 2009.

27. "Robert P. George," The Hoover Institution, www.hoover.org/profiles/ robert-p-george.

28. "Robert P. George," Program in Law and Public Affairs, Princeton University, lapa.princeton.edu/people/robert-p-george.

29. "Board of Directors," Becket Fund for Religious Liberty, www.becketfund .org/bod/.

30. Executive and Advisory Boards, Catholic Education Resource Center, www .catholiceducation.org/en/center/executive-and-advisory-boards.html.

31. Advisory Board, Love and Fidelity Network, www.loveandfidelity.org/ advisory-board/.

32. "Lynde and Harry Bradley Foundation," Conservative Transparency, conservativetransparency.org/basic-search/?q=lynde+and+harry +bradley+foundation&sf%5B%5D=candidate&sf%5B%5D=donor&sf

%5B%5D=recipient&sf%5B%5D=transaction&sf%5B%5D=finances #finances.

33. Amelia Thomson-DeVeaux, "The Spirit and the Law," *American Prospect,* July/August, 2015, prospect.org/article/little-known-force-behind-hobby -lobby-contraception-case.

34. "List of Religious Organizations and Signatories," ManhattanDeclaration .org, manhattandeclaration.org/man_dec_resources/list_of_religious _leaders.pdf.

35. "Manhattan Declaration: A Call of Christian Conscience," ManahattanDeclaration.org, www.manhattandeclaration.org/man_dec _resources/Manhattan_Declaration_full_text.pdf.

36. National Organization for Marriage, 2009 IRS Form 990, Filed November 14, 2010. web.archive.org/web/20110112103909/http://nomexposed .org/wp-content/uploads/2011/01/NOM-2009-990.pdf.

37. "National Strategy for Winning the Marriage Battle," United States District Court for the District of Maine, samuel-warde.com/wp-content/uploads/ 2012/06/NOM-Deposition-Exhibit-3.pdf.

38. Ibid.

39. Ibid, 20.

40. Deborah Yoffe, "A Conservative Think Tank with Many Princeton Ties," *Paw,* July 16, 2008. www.princeton.edu/paw/web_exclusives/plus/plus _071608witherspoon.html.

41. Sofia Resnick, "New Family Structures Study Intended to Sway Supreme Court on Gay Marriage, Documents Show," *American Independent; Huffington Post,* March 10, 2013, www.huffingtonpost.com/2013/03/10/supreme -court-gay-marriage_n_2850302.html.

42. Mark Regnerus, "How Different Are the Adult Children of Parents Who Have Same-Sex Relationships? Findings from the New Family Structures Study," *Social Science Research,* 41 (2012) 752–770. Page 755. www .markregnerus.com/uploads/4/0/6/5/4065759/regnerus_july_2012_ssr .pdf.

43. Resnick, 2013.

44. Ibid.

45. Ibid.

46. Brandon Watson, "New Documents Contradict Regnerus' Claims on Gay Parenting Study," *Austin Chronicle,* March 29, 2013, www.austinchronicle .com/news/2013-03-29/new-documents-contradict-regnerus-claims-on -gay-parenting-study/.

47. Ibid.

48. Sofia Resnick, "Witherspoon Scholar Was 'Paid Consultant' on Parenting Study," *American Independent News Network,* americanindependent.com/ 217646/witherspoon-scholar-was-paid-consultant-on-parenting-study.

49. Ibid.

50. "Mark Regnerus and Witherspoon Institute Collaboration Report," www .scribd.com/doc/129660276/Mark-Regners-and-Witherspoon-Institute -Collaboration-Report.

51. Watson, 2013.

52. Mark Regnerus, "Queers as Folk," Slate.com, June 11, 2012, www.slate .com/articles/double_x/doublex/2012/06/gay_parents_are_they_really _no_different_.html.

53. Regnerus, 2012.

54. John Corvino, "Are Gay Parents Really Worse for Children? How a New Study Gets Everything Wrong," *New Republic,* June 11, 2012, www .newrepublic.com/article/104001/john-corvino-are-gay-parents-really -worse-children-how-new-study-gets-everything.

55. Nathaniel Frank, "Dad and Dad vs. Mom and Dad," *Los Angeles Times,* June 13, 2012, articles.latimes.com/2012/jun/13/opinion/la-oe-frank -same-sex-regnerus-family-20120613.

56. Jason Richwine, "The Left Continues to Harass Mark Regnerus and His Publisher," *National Review,* November 18, 2013, www.nationalreview.com/ corner/364202/left-continues-harass-mark-regnerus-and-his-publisher -jason-richwine.

57. Tom Bartlett, "Controversial Gay-Parenting Study Is Severely Flawed, Journal's Audit Finds," *Chronicle of Higher Education,* July 26, 2012, chronicle .com/blogs/percolator/controversial-gay-parenting-study-is-severely -flawed-journals-audit-finds/30255.

58. Ibid.

59. "Statement from the Chair Regarding Professor Regnerus," University of Texas at Austin, Department of Sociology, April 12, 2014, www.utexas .edu/cola/sociology/news/article.php?id=7572.

60. Ibid.

61. Sofia Resnick, "Mark Regnerus, University of Texas Professor, Wades Further into Gay Marriage Debate," *American Independent; The Huffington Post,* April 10, 2013. www.huffingtonpost.com/2013/04/10/mark-regnerus -university-of-texas_n_3049309.html.

62. Ibid.

63. *Hollingsworth vs. Perry,* United States Supreme Court, www.americanbar .org/content/dam/aba/publications/supreme_court_preview/briefs-v2/ 12-144-12-307_merits_reversal_ssp-ish.authcheckdam.pdf. Via Resnick, 2013.

64. Sofia Resnick, "Goal of UT Parenting Study Was to Influence SCOTUS Decisions on Gay Marriage, Docs Show," *American Independent,* March 10, 2013, americanindependent.com/218834/goal-of-ut-parenting-study-was -to-influence-scotus-decisions-on-gay-marriage-docs-show. Also see: Sofia Resnick, "New Family Structures Study Intended to Sway Supreme Court on Gay Marriage, Documents Show," *American Independent,* March 11, 2013, www.huffingtonpost.com/2013/03/10/supreme-court-gay-marriage_n _2850302.html.

65. Sofia Resnick, "House Legal Team Cites Parenting Study," *American Independent;* Advocate, July 20, 2012, www.advocate.com/politics/marriage -equality/2012/07/20/house-legal-team-cites-misleading-parenting-study.

66. "Brief of Amicus Curiae American Sociological Association in Support of Respondent Kristin M. Pery and Respondent Edith Schlain Windsor,"

United States Supreme Court, www.asanet.org/documents/ASA/pdfs/12 -144_307_Amicus_%20(C_%20Gottlieb)_ASA_Same-Sex_Marriage.pdf. Via Resnick, 2013.

67. "Transcripts and Audio: Supreme Court Arguments on California Gay Marriage Ban," NPR, March 26 2013, www.npr.org/2013/03/26/175351429/ audio-supreme-court-arguments-on-california-gay-marriage-ban.

68. Ibid.

69. "Defendant Attorney General Luther Strange's Sur-reply in Support of His Motion for Summary Judgment and in Opposition to the Plaintiffs' Motion for Summary Judgment," United States District Court for the Southern District of Alabama, November 13, 2014, www.scribd.com/doc/ 246520177/1-14-cv-00208-52#download.

70. Laura Zuckerman, "Idaho's Governor Appeals to Supreme Court to Reinstate Ban on Gay Marriage," Reuters, January 2, 2015, www.reuters.com/ article/2015/01/03/usa-gaymarriage-idaho-idUSL1N0UI05320150103.

71. *Deboer vs. Snyder,* United States District Court for the Eastern District of Michigan, March 21, 2014, www.documentcloud.org/documents/1094703 -friedman-ruling.html.

72. Ibid.

Chapter 10: Defeating Lies, Incorporated

1. "Kaiser Health Tracking Poll: December 2014," Kaiser Family Foundation, December 2014, Question 6g, files.kff.org/attachment/topline -methodology-kaiser-health-policy-news-index-december-2014.

2. Jenna Portnoy, "In Southwest Va., Health Needs, Poverty Collide with Antipathy to the Affordable Care Act," *Washington Post,* June 19, 2014, www.washingtonpost.com/local/virginia-politics/in-southwest-va-health -needs-poverty-collide-with-antipathy-to-the-affordable-care-act/2014 /06/19/4890bf8c-f4e7-11e3-9861-8dc65df15e56_story.html.

3. Jeffrey Jones, "In U.S., 55% of Uninsured Plan to Get Health Coverage," Gallup, November 13, 2014, www.gallup.com/poll/179393/uninsured -plan-health-coverage.aspx.

4. Interview with Naomi Oreskes by author, SiriusXM Satelite Radio, March 6, 2015.

5. "'Endless War' and Other Rallying Points," *New York Times,* www.nytimes .com/interactive/2014/10/31/us/politics/31lobbyist-docs.html. Via Lipton, 2014.

6. Chris Mooney, "The Republican Brain: Why Even Educated Conservatives Deny Science—and Reality," Alternet, February 22, 2012, www.alternet .org/story/154252/the_republican_brain%3A_why_even_educated _conservatives_deny_science_—_and_reality.

7. Ibid.

8. Ibid.

9. Ibid.

10. Dan M. Kahan, Maggie Wittlin, Ellen Peters, Paul Slovic, Lisa Larrimore Ouellette, Donald Braman, and Gregory N. Mandel, "The Tragedy of the

Risk-Perception Commons: Culture Conflict, Rationality Conflict, and Climate Change," Social Science Research Network, June 24, 2011, papers .ssrn.com/sol3/papers.cfm?abstract_id=1871503.

11. "Remarks by the President to a Joint Session of Congress on Health Care," WhiteHouse.gov, September 9, 2009, www.whitehouse.gov/the-press -office/remarks-president-a-joint-session-congress-health-care.

12. "Proof That 'You Lie!' Was a Lie," PoliticalCorrection.org, September 9, 2009, politicalcorrection.org/factcheck/200909090009.

13. Pam Belluck, "Medicare Proposes Paying Doctors for End of Life Counseling," *New York Times,* July 9, 2015, www.nytimes.com/2015/07/09/health/ medicare-proposes-paying-doctors-for-end-of-life-counseling.html?_r=0.

14. Laura Santhanam, "STUDY: Top Cable News Coverage of Federal Climate Change Report Cast Doubt on Science," MediaMatters.org, May 9, 2014, mediamatters.org/research/2014/05/09/study-top-cable-news-coverage -of-federal-climat/199247.

15. Kate Sheppard, "Controversial Daily Caller Editor Admitted to Posing as Radical Animal Rights Activist," *Mother Jones,* March 15, 2013, www .motherjones.com/environment/2013/03/david-martosko-daily-caller -humane-society-animal-rights-facebook.

16. "Richard Berman," *The Daily Caller,* dailycaller.com/author/rberman/.

Acknowledgments

Lies, Incorporated would not have been possible without the assistance of numerous individuals who gave their time and energy to this project.

I owe a debt of gratitude to Melinda Warner for doing a superb job fact-checking every sentence of the manuscript, making sure we were above all else accountable to the truth.

Edward Kastenmeier and his team at Vintage & Anchor were everything a writer could ask for in an editor, providing amazing feedback throughout the writing process. Jeff Alexander's advice on *Lies, Incorporated*'s first draft helped shape the final product.

Numerous current and former staff at Media Matters contributed to this book in a variety of ways. A special thank-you to Todd Gregory, Erik Hananoki, Ben Dimiero, Jeremy Holden, Doug Stauffer, Laura Keiter, Jess Levin, Matt Gertz, Hillary Tone, Julie Millican, Scott Derome, Pilar Martinez, John Whitehouse, and Angelo Carusone. I also would like to thank Matt Butler and Bradley Beychok for their leadership on this project, and Mary Pat Bonner for her unending support.

David Brock not only provided exceptional leadership but also taught me the skills necessary to author *Lies, Incorporated* during our work together on *The Fox Effect* and *The Benghazi Hoax.*

This book would not be possible without the shepherding of Will Lippincott. I am especially grateful for his time and friendship.

I also want to thank the team that put together my radio show,

The Agenda, every morning while I was in the midst of the writing process: Amber Hall, Jessica Lowther, Rachel Kurzius, Bridget Armstrong, and Tony Fowler. Thank you to Jeremy Coleman, Dave Gorab, and David Guggenheim for putting me on air, and to Rory Belfi and Frank Raphael for their support.

Finally, and above all else, I want to thank my wife, Julie, for providing love and support, along with dealing with the long days and nights I spent writing *Lies, Incorporated.*